Embrace the Fear of God

JOHN BEVERE

Books about Spirit-Led Living

The Inner Strength Series

LIVING WITH STRENGTH IN TODAY'S WORLD

EMBRACE THE FEAR OF GOD by John Bevere
Published by Charisma House
A part of Strang Communications Company
600 Rinehart Road
Lake Mary, Florida 32746
www.charismahouse.com

Unless otherwise noted, all Scripture quotations are from the New King James Version of the Bible. Copyright © 1979, 1980, 1982 by Thomas Nelson, Inc., publishers. Used by permission.

Scripture quotations marked NIV are from the Holy Bible, New International Version. Copyright © 1973, 1978, 1984, International Bible Society. Used by permission.

Scripture quotations marked NLT are from the Holy Bible, New Living Translation, copyright © 1996. Used by permission of Tyndale House Publishers, Inc., Wheaton, IL 60189. All rights reserved.

Cover design by Rachel Campbell

Library of Congress Catalog Card Number: 2001098130
International Standard Book Number: 0-88419-838-3

02 03 04 05 87654321
Printed in the United States of America

Contents

Introduction

I n the summer of 1994 I was invited to minister at a church in the southern part of the United States. It would end up being one of the most unpleasant ministry experiences I would ever have. Yet out of it, a passionate quest was birthed in my heart to know and embrace the fear of the Lord.

Two years prior, this was a church that had experienced a powerful move of God. An evangelist came for a period of four weeks, and the Lord revived this church with His presence. They were experiencing an abundance of what many call "holy laughter." It was so refreshing that the pastor and many of his people did what so often happens— they remained camped at the place of refreshment instead of continuing on to pursue God. They soon developed more interest in manifestations of refreshing than to know the Lord who refreshes.

The second night of our meetings, the Spirit of God led me to preach on the fear of the Lord. The next night I came into the service totally unprepared for what was about to happen. Without any previous discussion, the pastor stood up after praise and worship and spent a considerable amount of time correcting what I had preached the night before. I sat in the front row, almost in shock. The basis of his correction was that New Testament believers do not have to fear God. He backed this up with 1 John 4:18: "There is no fear in love; but perfect love casts out fear, because fear involves torment. But he who fears has not been made perfect in love." He had confused a *spirit of fear* with the *fear of the Lord*.

The following morning I found a deserted area outside my hotel where I spent a considerable amount of time praying. I came before the Lord with an open heart and submitted to any correction He desired to bring to me. I have learned that God's correction is always for my good. He corrects us, that we might be partakers of His holiness (Heb. 12:7–11). Almost immediately I sensed God's overwhelming love. I did not perceive His disappointment with what I had preached, but rather His pleasure. Tears ran down my face in His wonderful presence.

I continued in prayer and, after awhile, found myself crying out from deep within my spirit for the knowledge of the fear of the Lord. I raised my voice, drawing together all my strength from within, and cried, "Father, I want to know and walk in the fear of the Lord!"

> Holy fear is the key to God's sure foundation, unlocking the treasuries of salvation, wisdom and knowledge.

When I finished praying I didn't care what I might face in the future. All I wanted was to know His heart. I sensed that my request to learn this facet of His holy nature had deeply pleased Him. Since that day God has been faithful to reveal to me the importance of the fear of the Lord. He has revealed His desire for all believers to know the importance of it as well.

Although I always had known that the fear of the Lord was important, I did not comprehend just how integral it was until God opened my eyes in response to that prayer. I had always seen the *love* of God as the foundation for relationship with the Lord. I quickly discovered that the fear of the Lord was just as foundational. Isaiah says:

> The LORD is exalted, for he dwells on high; he will fill Zion with justice and righteousness. He will be the sure foundation for your times, a rich store of salvation and wisdom and knowledge; the fear of the LORD is the key to this treasure.
>
> —ISAIAH 33:5–6, NIV

Holy fear is the key to God's sure foundation, unlocking the treasuries of salvation, wisdom and knowledge. Along with the love of God, it composes the very foundation of life! We will soon learn that we cannot truly love God until we fear Him, nor can we properly fear Him until we love Him.

As you read this book, it is my sincere prayer that you too will be gripped from deep within your spirit with a desire to know and embrace the fear of the Lord for your own life.

Adapted from John Bevere, *The Fear of the Lord* (Lake Mary, FL: Charisma House, 1997), xiii–xvi.

ONE

Fear God— or Be Afraid of Him?

DEVELOPING
Inner Strength

When Israel left Egypt, Moses led the Israelites to Mount Sinai, where God would reveal His glory.

> *Then the LORD said to Moses, "Go to the people and consecrate them today and tomorrow, and let them wash their clothes. And let them be ready for the third day. For on the third day the LORD will come down upon Mount Sinai in the sight of all the people."*
> —EXODUS 19:10–11

This message was prophetic, for it speaks of our day as well. Before God manifested His glory, the people were to sanctify themselves. This included washing their clothes. Remember that a day with the Lord is as a thousand of our years. It is now almost two thousand years (two days) since the resurrection of the Lord Jesus Christ. God said that for those two thousand years (two days), His church was to consecrate, or set ourselves apart, from the world in preparation for His glory. Our garments were to be cleansed of the filth of the world (2 Cor. 6:16; 7:1). We were to become His bride without spot. After the two thousand years, He will again manifest His glory.

God manifested Himself not only by sight but also by voice and sound. When Moses spoke, God answered Him in the hearing of all. Often today God is referred to as our friend in a loose sense of His almost being a buddy. If we could but glimpse what Moses and the children of Israel saw, we might have a significant change of view. He is the Lord, and He has not changed!

We frequently hear messages derived from Paul's first letter to the church at Corinth. This book of the Bible is referenced often, especially in Spirit-filled circles. The Corinthian church was established approximately A.D. 51 (many years after the Day of Pentecost), and it was very open to—and therefore greatly benefited by—spiritual gifts. The anointing of the Holy Spirit was strong within its membership, not unlike several of our churches today.

Paul's second epistle to the church body at Corinth is not referenced as frequently as the first. This letter contains a greater emphasis on divine order, the fear of the Lord and the subsequent restoration of His glory. If read in context, this letter holds a strong and exciting message for today's believers. As we examine a portion of it, keep in mind that 2 Corinthians was written to people who were no strangers to the anointing and frequently operated in spiritual gifts.

The Glory of the Old Covenant vs. the New

In both of his letters to the Corinthians, Paul

referred often to the flight of the children of Israel from Egypt and to the revelation of God's glory to them in the desert. Their experience pertains to us as well, for all that happened to the Israelites in a natural sense were types and shadows of what we would experience in the realm of the Spirit. Paul emphasizes this:

> All these events happened to them as examples for us. They were written down to warn us, who live at the time when this age is drawing to a close.
>
> —1 Corinthians 10:11, nlt

Paul's first letter dealt with many fundamental elements of divine order of the heart for God's people. His second letter went deeper still. He moved on to discuss God's desire to reveal His glory and dwell in the hearts of His people. Paul began by comparing God's glory in the wilderness with His glory as revealed under the New Covenant.

In contrast, he writes:

> That old system of law etched in stone led to death, yet it began with such glory that the people of Israel could not bear to look

> at Moses' face. For his face shone with the glory of God, even though the brightness was already fading away. Shouldn't we expect far greater glory when the Holy Spirit is giving life?
>
> —2 Corinthians 3:7–8, nlt

On the mountain Moses beheld the form of the Lord and talked with Him as a man does with his friend. When he came down from the mountain, Moses covered his face because the brilliance of it frightened the people. Moses' countenance reflected that he had been in the presence of—the glory of—God.

In the New Covenant, God's plan is not for us to *reflect* His glory, but for His glory *to be seen in us!* It is one thing to reflect something, but quite another to abide in and emit it! That is God's ultimate goal! This is why Paul could say:

> In fact, that first glory was not glorious at all compared with the overwhelming glory of the new covenant.
>
> —2 Corinthians 3:10, nlt

Even though the glory of the Old Covenant did not compare with the glory of the New, the

Old was still so awesome that Paul reiterates, "Israel could not look steadily at the end of what was passing away" (v. 13). But then Paul is quick to lament:

> But their minds were blinded.
> —2 Corinthians 3:14

How tragic that they could not see the very thing they needed so desperately. Paul warns us so that we might not find ourselves blind and in the same dilemma.

> ## God's plan is not for us to reflect His glory, but for His glory to be seen in us!

So we must ask, "How were their minds blinded?" The answer holds knowledge and wisdom we lack desperately. That which we lack is necessary in order for us to walk in God's glory!

To obtain our answer, we must return to the time frame Paul discussed.

The Fear of God vs.
Being Afraid of God

In the biblical account with which we opened this chapter, the Israelites were stunned and fearful of the awesome manifestations of God that they witnessed. But Moses quickly warned them, "Do not fear…," encouraging them back into God's presence as he explained that God had come to test them.

Why does God test us? To find out what is in our hearts? Absolutely not. He already knows what is hidden in our hearts. He tests us so that *we* might know what is in our own hearts. What was the purpose of the test presented to the Israelites? It was so that they would know whether or not they feared God. If they feared Him they would not sin. Sin results whenever we draw away from Him.

Moses said, "Do not fear." Then he said that God had come "…that His fear may be before you." This verse makes a distinction between *being afraid of God* and *fearing Him*. Moses feared God, but the people did not. It is an infallible truth that if we do not fear God, we will be afraid of Him at the revelation of His glory, for every knee shall bow to Him, if not out of godly fear then out of terror (2 Cor. 5:10–11).

> So the people stood afar off, but Moses drew near the thick darkness where God was.
>
> —Exodus 20:21

Look at the difference in the responses to God's manifested glory: Israel drew back, but Moses drew near. This illustrates the different responses of believers today.

Similar in Many Ways

It is important that we realize the Israelites were not so very different from our modern church.

- *They all came out of Egypt,* which typifies salvation.
- *They all experienced and benefited from the miracles of God,* as have many in the church.
- *They all experienced deliverance from their oppressors,* which many have experienced today in the church.
- *They still desired their old lifestyle*—if they could have it without the

bondage they experienced previously. How often we see this in the church today. People are saved and delivered, yet their hearts never leave the lifestyle of the world, although that lifestyle led them to bondage.

- *They experienced the wealth of the sinner that God had laid up for the just.* The Bible records, "He also brought them out with silver and gold" (Ps. 105:37). Yet they used this blessing of God to build an idol! Have we done the same today? We hear of financial miracles, yet often those who are most blessed end up bestowing their affection and strength on material and financial blessings rather than upon the Lord who blessed them.

- *They experienced the healing power of God,* for when they left Egypt the Bible records, "There was none feeble among His tribes" (Ps. 105:37). That's even better than today's greatest miracle crusades. Moses left Egypt with three million strong, healthy people. Can you imagine a city of three million with no one sick or in the hospital? The Israelites had served under hardship for four hundred years. Imagine the healings and miracles that took place as they ate the Passover lamb!

The Israelites were no strangers to God's saving, healing, miracle-working and delivering power. In fact, they celebrated passionately whenever God moved miraculously on their behalf. It is interesting to note that the Israelites were drawn to His miraculous manifestations because they benefited from them, but they were scared and drew back when His glory was revealed!

How different are we today? We are still drawn to miracles. People will travel miles and give big offerings, hoping to receive double portions from God in miracle services. But what will happen when God's glory is revealed? Then hearts will be exposed in His glorious presence. We can live with sin undetected around the miraculous, but sin cannot hide in the light of His revealed glory.

What Blinded the People

Forty years later, the older generation had died in the desert, and Moses reviewed for a new generation what had happened at the mountain where God revealed His glory.

> So it was, when you heard the voice from the midst of the darkness, while the mountain was burning with fire, that you came near to me, all the heads of your tribes and your elders. And you said: "Surely the LORD our God has shown us His glory and His greatness, and we have heard His voice from the midst of the fire. We have seen this day that God speaks with man; yet he still lives. Now therefore, why should we die? For this great fire will consume us; if we hear the voice of the LORD our God anymore, then we shall die…You go near and hear all that the LORD our God may say, and tell us all that the LORD our God says to you, and we will hear and do it."
>
> —DEUTERONOMY 5:23–27

They cried out, "We cannot approach His glorious presence nor stand in the midst of Him and live." They wanted Moses to hear for them, and they promised to hear him and do whatever God said to do! They attempted to live by this pattern for thousands of years, but they could not obey His words. How different are we today? Do we get God's Word from our pastor and other preachers, but withdraw from the mountain of God? Are we afraid to hear His voice that lays bare the condition of our hearts? This heart condition is no different from that of the children of Israel.

Moses was very disappointed with Israel's response. He couldn't understand their lack of hunger for God's presence. How could they be so foolish? How could they be so blind? Moses brought his concerns before God in hope of a remedy to this condition. But see what happened:

> Then the LORD heard the voice of your words when you spoke to me, and the LORD said to me: "I have heard the voice of the words of this people which they have spoken to you. They are right in all that they have spoken."
> —DEUTERONOMY 5:28

I'm sure Moses was shocked at God's response. He must have thought, *What…the people are right? For once they are actually right! They really cannot come into the presence of God. Why?* God interrupted with the answer:

> Oh, that they had such a heart in them that they would fear Me and always keep all My commandments, that it might be well with them and with their children forever!
> —Deuteronomy 5:29

God lamented, "Oh, that they had such a heart in them that they would fear me." They all could have been like Moses, reflecting God's glory and knowing His ways, if they had but possessed hearts that feared God as Moses did! But their hearts remained darkened and their minds blind to the very thing they so desperately needed.

What blinded them? The answer is clear: They did not have hearts that feared the Lord. This was evidenced by their disobedience to the commandments and Word of God. If we compare Moses with the children of Israel, we find the difference between the one who fears God and one who does not.

Trembling at God's Word

A person who fears God trembles at His Word and

in His presence (Isa. 66:2; Jer. 5:22). What does it mean to tremble at His Word? It can all be summed up in one statement:

> To willingly obey God even when it appears more advantageous to compromise or not obey His Word.

Our hearts must be firmly established in the fact that God is good. He is not a child-abuser. A person who fears God knows this, for he knows God's character. That is why he or she will draw near to God even when others would draw back in terror.

That person realizes that any immediate or impending difficulty encountered at God's hand will ultimately bring forth good. Most would mentally agree with this, yet in times of hardship what we *truly believe* is clearly revealed. Only then will we see our faith for what it is by the light of the fire of trials.

The hardships that Israel faced exposed the contents of their hearts. Let's examine their different responses to God's Word. The children of Israel would obey God's Word as long as they saw the immediate benefit for them. But the moment they suffered or could no longer see the benefits, they lost sight of God and complained bitterly.

For centuries Israel had prayed and cried for deliverance from their Egyptian oppressors. They longed to return to the land of promise. God sent their deliverer, Moses. The Lord told Moses, "I have come down to deliver them out of the hand of the Egyptians, and to bring them up from that land to a good and large land, to a land flowing with milk and honey" (Exod. 3:8).

Moses went before Pharaoh and proclaimed God's words to "let His people go." But Pharaoh responded by increasing their hardship. No longer would straw be provided for the overwhelming tally of bricks the Israelite slaves were to produce. They would have to glean by night and labor by day. The total number of bricks could not diminish although their straw had been removed. God's word of freedom had increased their suffering. They complained under this oppression and told Moses to "leave us alone and quit preaching to Pharaoh—you are making life worse for us."

When God finally did deliver them from Egypt, Pharaoh's heart was hardened again, and he pursued the Israelites into the wilderness with his

EMBRACE THE FEAR OF GOD

finest chariots and warriors. When the Hebrews saw that Egypt had rallied against them and they were backed up to the Red Sea, they again complained. "Is this not the word that we told you in Egypt, saying, 'Let us alone that we may serve the Egyptians?' For *it would have been better for us* to serve the Egyptians than that we should die in the wilderness" (Exod. 14:12, emphasis added).

> We want soft and pleasant
> words when the bitter
> is what's necessary for
> cleansing us from impurities.

Notice the words, "It would have been better for us." In essence, they were saying, "Why should we obey God when it is only making our lives miserable? We are worse off—not better." They were quick to compare their former lifestyle with their present condition. Whenever the two did not balance, the Israelites wanted to go back. They desired comfort over obedience to God's will. Oh, how they lacked the fear of God! They did not tremble at His Word.

God split the sea, and the children of Israel crossed on dry land and saw their oppressors buried. They celebrated God's goodness and danced and praised before Him. They were certain they would never again doubt His goodness! But they did not know their own hearts. Another test would arise and again expose their unfaithfulness. Just three days later they complained again that they did not want bitter water, but sweet. (See Exodus 15:22–25.)

How often do we do the same? We want soft and pleasant words when the bitter is what's necessary for cleansing us from impurities. That is why Solomon said, "But to a hungry soul every bitter thing is sweet" (Prov. 27:7).

A few days passed, and the children of Israel again complained about the lack of food. They said, "Oh, that we had died by the hand of the LORD in the land of Egypt" (Exod. 16:1–4). Can you see how religiously they were behaving?

Again the Israelites complained of a lack of water (Exod. 17:1–4). Over and over, they complained whenever they encountered a new hardship. As long as it looked good for them, they kept God's Word.

But if obedience meant hardship, the Israelites quickly complained.

A Different Heart

Moses was quite different. His heart had been tested long before. We are told:

> By faith Moses, when he became of age, refused to be called the son of Pharaoh's daughter, choosing rather to suffer affliction with the people of God than to enjoy the passing pleasures of sin, esteeming the reproach of Christ greater riches than the treasures in Egypt; for he looked to the reward.
>
> —HEBREWS 11:24–26

The children of Israel did not choose their bondage. Moses had been presented with the finest of everything the world could offer, but he refused it all to suffer affliction with God's people. His was quite a different attitude from that of the children of Israel. They wanted to return to Egypt (the world), having quickly forgotten its oppression. They only remembered that they had feasted on the things they now lacked in the wilderness of

God's testing. Moses chose hardship, "…for he looked to the reward." What reward was he looking for? We find the answer in Exodus, chapter 33.

> Then the Lord said to Moses, "Depart and go up from here, you and the people whom you have brought out of the land of Egypt, to the land of which I swore to Abraham, Isaac, and Jacob, saying, 'To your descendants I will give it.' And I will send My Angel before you, and I will drive out the Canaanite and the Amorite and the Hittite and the Perizzite and the Hivite and the Jebusite. Go up to a land flowing with milk and honey; for I will not go up in your midst, lest I consume you on the way, for you are a stiff-necked people."
>
> —Exodus 33:1–3

God told Moses to go down and take the people to the land He had promised them, the very land they had waited hundreds of years to inherit. God even promised Moses the escort of a choice angel, although He would not accompany them.

But Moses quickly responded, "If Your Presence does not go with us, do not bring us up from here" (Exod. 33:15).

I am glad that the option of entering the Promised Land without God was not placed before the children of Israel. If they would have chosen a comfortable life in Egypt over God, they surely would have chosen the Promised Land without Him. They probably would have had a party and left without a second thought! But Moses had not set his sights on the Promised Land, so his response was different.

Moses said, "The promise is nothing without Your presence!" He refused God's offer because his reward was the presence of the Lord. Think of the position Moses was in when he responded, "Do not bring us up from here." Where was "here"? The desert!

Moses lived under the same conditions as the rest of Israel. He wasn't endowed with superhuman ability that exempted him from the hardships the rest of Israel experienced. He thirsted and hungered the same as they, yet we never see him complaining with the others. He was offered an "out" from this suffering and the opportunity to go to the land of his dreams, but he refused.

One method God will use to test us is making us

an offer He expects us to refuse. The offer may initially promise greater success, but at what price? It may even look as though our ministry will expand and go further. But in the depths of our hearts we know that to choose it would be against God's ultimate desire. Only those who tremble at His Word would choose that which appears less beneficial.

In 2 Kings, chapter 2, Elijah told Elisha three times to stay put. Each order was yet another test. It would have been easier for Elisha to stay, but Elisha insisted, "As the LORD lives, and as your soul lives, I will not leave you!" (2 Kings 2:2). He knew the heavenly reward was far more important than his temporary comfort!

Alike Outwardly, Different Inwardly

Outwardly, or physically, you could not tell the difference between Moses and the children of Israel. They were all descendants of Abraham. They had all left Egypt under intervention of God's miraculous power. They were all positioned to inherit God's promises. All professed to know and serve Jehovah. The difference was hidden in the inner recesses of their hearts. Moses feared God; therefore, he perceived God's heart and ways. But because the children of Israel did not fear God, they were blinded, and their understanding was darkened.

It is no different today. Christianity has become almost a club. You remember what a club is all about from when you were a child. You'd join clubs because you wanted to belong. In the safety of a club, you were unified with the other members because of a common interest or cause. It felt good to be a part of something bigger than yourself. The club was behind you and gave you a sense of security.

There are many professing Christians who no more fear God than those who have never set foot in the church. As secure members of the Christianity club, why should they be afraid? As a matter of fact, demons tremble more than some in the church. James warned those who professed salvation but who lacked the fear of God, "You believe that there is one God. You do well. Even the demons believe—and tremble!" (James 2:19).

In Matthew 7:21–23, Jesus said there would be those who would cast out devils, and do other wonders in His name, calling Him Lord and Savior, yet neglecting to live in obedience to the will of God. Jesus described this condition as "tares growing among wheat." You would not easily be able to tell the difference between the wheat and the tares. Just as it did with Israel, the fire of God's glorious presence will ultimately expose the contents of every heart. This will be the church's condition upon entering the season of harvest (Matt. 13:26).

> ## The fire of God's glorious presence will ultimately expose the contents of every heart.

Malachi prophesied that in these last days God would send a prophetic voice—as He did with Samuel, Moses and John the Baptist—to prepare His people for His glory. It would not be one, however, but many prophetic messengers. These messengers would arise with such a unity of purpose that they would speak as one man, calling for those who are deceived to return with all their hearts to the Lord.

Thus, divine order will be restored in the hearts of God's people. These prophets are not messengers of judgment, but of mercy. Through them, the Lord calls to His own to escape judgment. Malachi records:

> Behold, I send My messenger, and he will prepare the way before Me. And the Lord, whom you seek, will suddenly come to His temple…But who can endure the day of His coming? And who can stand when He appears? For He is like a refiner's fire and like launderers' soap.
>
> —Malachi 3:1–2

Malachi is not describing the catching away of the church. He says that the Lord will come to—not for His temple. Hosea said that after two thousand years the Lord would come to us, His temple, as the latter rain. That speaks of His manifested glory. Malachi then asks, "But who can endure His glorious coming to His temple?" Both prophets confirm that this event is not the same as the catching away of the church.

Malachi answers his own question, presenting two outcomes of God's glorious presence. First it is to refine and purify those who fear Him (vv. 3, 16–17). Second, it will judge the hearts of those who *say* they serve Him but in reality *do not fear Him* (Mal. 3:5; 4:1). Once this purification occurs, he tells us:

> Then you shall again discern between the righteous and the wicked, between one who serves God and one who does not serve Him.
> —MALACHI 3:18

Before the glory was manifested, you could not tell the one who serves God from the one who merely provides lip service to the Lord. Hypocrisy cannot hide from the light of God's glory. The club mentality will finally be gone. This lends a better understanding of Jesus' stern warning for the New Testament believer:

> And I say to you, My friends, do not be afraid of those who kill the body, and after that have no more that they can do. But I will show you whom you should fear: Fear Him who, after He has killed, has power to

cast into hell; yes, I say to you, fear Him!

—Luke 12:4–5

The fear of God keeps us from the destructive path of the deceived. Moses said that the fear of God in the hearts of His people is the strength to walk free from sin (Exod. 20:20). Solomon wrote, "By the fear of the Lord one departs from evil" (Prov. 16:6). Jesus warned the believers for a specific purpose, and He preceded His exhortation to fear God with a warning about the deceptive trap of hypocrisy: "For there is nothing covered that will not be revealed, nor hidden that will not be known" (Luke 12:2).

> The fear of God keeps us from the destructive path of the deceived.

When we cover or hide sin to protect our reputations, we place a veil over our hearts. We mistakenly think this veil causes us to appear pure, when actually we are not. This ultimately leads to hypocrisy. So now we not only deceive others but ourselves. (See 2 Timothy 3:13.) As with the children of Israel, we are blinded and cannot see.

The fear of God is our only protection from hypocrisy. Then we will not hide sin in our hearts, because we will fear God more than the opinions of mortal men. We will become more concerned with what God thinks of us than what man thinks. We will be more concerned with God's desires than with our temporary comfort. We will esteem His Word more valuable than man's. We will turn our hearts to the Lord! And Paul says:

> Nevertheless when one turns to the Lord, the veil is taken away.
>
> —2 CORINTHIANS 3:16

Adapted from *The Fear of the Lord*, 133–148.

TWO

Fear God, Not Man

DEVELOPING
Inner Strength

In Acts 2 the disciples were filled with the Holy Spirit and spoke with tongues and prophesied. They were so filled that they acted like drunken men. Laughter and joy overflowed in these new believers. God was strengthening and refreshing them. God delights in doing this. He is not a vindictive God who delights in gloom, but rather He delights in love, mercy, righteousness, peace and joy.

The disciples saw many people saved over the next few days. But some of these new converts had come to the Lord for blessings rather than for who He is. This caused them not to give God the reverence He deserved. They gradually grew too "familiar" with the Lord. This familiarity caused them to treat the things of God as if they were common. They did not tremble at His presence or word. We see evidence of this in Acts chapter 5.

I believe the presence of God was more powerful at the time of the Book of Acts than it is today. For example, Acts records that Peter walked the streets of Jerusalem and the sick were healed as his shadow touched them (Acts 5:15). We don't see those kinds of miracles today.

I believe that as His presence and glory increases, there will be similar accounts to the one in Acts chapter 5. Notice what happened after Ananias and Sapphira fell over dead.

> So great fear came upon all the church and upon all who heard these things.
> —ACTS 5:11

The deep awe and reverence for the Lord were restored. They realized they needed to rethink their treatment of God's presence and anointing. Remember, God has said, "By those who come near Me I must be regarded as holy; and before all the people I must be glorified" (Lev. 10:3).

To fully embrace the fear of the Lord, we must understand the difference between the fear of the Lord and the fear of man. The fear of God includes, but is more than, respecting Him. Fearing Him means to give Him the place of glory, honor, reverence, thanksgiving, praise and preeminence He deserves. (Notice it is what *He* deserves, not what we *think* He deserves). He holds this position in our lives when we esteem Him and His desires over and above our own. We will hate what He hates and love what He loves, trembling in His presence and at His Word.

You will serve and obey whom you fear!

To fear man is to stand in alarm, anxiety, awe, dread and suspicion, cowering before mortal men. When entrapped by this fear we will live on the run, hiding from harm or reproach and constantly avoiding rejection and confrontation. We become so busy safeguarding ourselves and serving men we are ineffective in our service for God.

Afraid of what man can do to us, we will not give God what He deserves.

The Bible tells us, "The fear of man brings a snare" (Prov. 29:25). A snare is a trap. Fearing man steals your God-given authority. His gift then lies dormant in you. You feel powerless to do what is right because the empowering of God is inactive.

Isaiah 51:7–13 admonishes:

> Listen to Me, you who know righteousness, you people in whose heart is My law: Do not fear the reproach of men, nor be afraid of their insults…Who are you that you should be afraid of a man who will die, and the son of a man who will be made like grass? And you forget the Lord your Maker.

When we please men to escape reproach, we forget the Lord. We depart from His service. "For if I still pleased men, I would not be a bondservant of Christ" (Gal. 1:10).

You will serve and obey whom you fear! If you fear man, you will serve him. If you fear God, you will serve Him. You cannot fear God if you fear man because you cannot serve two masters (Matt.

6:24)! On the other hand, you will not be afraid of man if you fear God!

When God Is Quiet, Our Hearts Are Revealed

God has withheld His glory to test and prepare us. Will we be reverent even when His presence is not manifest? In so many ways the modern church has behaved like the children of Israel. In fact, Paul said their experiences were written down as examples for us (1 Cor. 10:6).

The Israelites were excited when God blessed them and performed miracles for them. When God parted the Red Sea, brought them across on dry ground and then buried their enemies, they sang, danced and shouted for victory (Exod. 15:1–21). However, a few days later, when His mighty power was not apparent and food and drink were scarce, they complained against God (Exod. 15:22).

Later Moses brought the people to Mount Sinai to consecrate them to God. God came down on the mountain in the sight of all His people. It was quite awesome, with thunder and lightning and a thick cloud on the mountain. Moses then brought the people out of the camp to meet God, but "when the people saw it, they trembled and stood afar off" (Exod. 20:10–18). They pulled back in terror—not in the fear of God, but in the fear for their own lives. When God came down they realized they loved their own lives more than they loved God.

They told Moses, "'You speak with us, and we will hear; but let not God speak with us, lest we die.' And Moses said to the people, 'Do not fear; for God has come to test you, and that His fear may be before you, so that you may not sin.'" (Exod. 20:19–20).

The fear of God draws you toward God's presence, not away from it.

Exodus 20:21 continues the account, "So the people stood afar off, but Moses drew near the thick darkness where God was." Moses told God what they had said and how they were afraid. God answered, "They are right in all that they have spoken. Oh, that they had such a heart in them that they would fear Me and always keep all My commandments, that it might be well with them and with their children forever!" (Deut. 5:28–29).

Notice the people drew back while Moses drew near. This reveals the difference between Moses and Israel. Moses feared God; therefore, he was unafraid. The people did not fear God; therefore, they were afraid. The fear of God draws you toward God's presence, not away from it. However, the fear of man causes you to withdraw from God and His glory.

When we are bound by the fear of man we will feel more comfortable in the presence of men than in the presence of God, even in church! The reason: The presence of God lays open our hearts and brings conviction.

Not Sinai but Zion

To prove that the fear of God is a New Testament reality we go to this account in the Book of Hebrews:

> For you have not come to the mountain that may be touched and that burned with fire, and to blackness and darkness and

tempest, and the sound of a trumpet and the voice of words, so that those who heard it begged that the word should not be spoken to them anymore...But you have come to Mount Zion.

—Hebrews 12:18–22

First we are reminded of what happened on Sinai. Then we are told about the mountain we have come to called *Zion*. God spoke on the earth from that mountain at Sinai. Now the same God speaks from heaven on this new mountain, Zion.

See that you do not refuse Him who speaks. For if they did not escape who refused Him who spoke on earth, much more shall we not escape if we turn away from Him who speaks from heaven.

—Hebrews 12:25

Notice the words "much more"! Our judgment is much more severe when we don't listen to and obey the voice of God. The grace we are given under the New Testament is not for us to use to live as we please. Why didn't the Israelites heed His voice? They did not fear God. Keep this in mind as you continue to read, and you will see clearly that the reason people do not listen under the New Covenant is the same:

> Therefore, since we are receiving a kingdom which cannot be shaken, let us have grace, by which we may serve God acceptably with reverence and godly fear. For our God is a consuming fire.
>
> —HEBREWS 12:28–29

Notice it says "reverence and godly fear." If the fear of God were limited to just reverence, the writer would not have separated the concept of godly fear from it. Also notice that the writer did not conclude with, "For our God is a God of love," but rather, "Our God is a consuming fire." This statement about God corresponds with the reason the children of Israel backed away from His presence. "For this great fire will consume us; if we hear the voice of the Lord our God anymore, then we shall die" (Deut. 5:25). God has not changed! He is still holy, still the consuming fire!

Yes, He is love, but He is also a consuming fire. In our churches we have emphasized God's love and heard very little on the fear of God. Because we have not preached the whole counsel of God, our view of love is warped.

The love we've preached is a weak love. It does not have the power to lead us into consecrated living. It has dampened our fire and left us lukewarm. We have become like spoiled children who do not reverence their father! If we do not grow in the fear of the Lord, we risk the danger of becoming familiar with God and treating as common the things He considers holy.

Note this verse also: "Let us have grace, by which we may serve God acceptably with reverence and godly fear" (Heb. 12:28). Grace is not given merely to cover up our irreverence and sin—it is given to empower us to serve God acceptably. And the acceptable way of serving Him is out of love with reverence and godly fear.

Along these lines Paul also wrote, "Work out your own salvation with fear and trembling" (Phil. 2:12). Where is our fear and trembling? Have we forgotten He is the just *Judge?* Have we forgotten His judgment? Read the following exhortation carefully.

> Do not be haughty, but fear. For if God did not spare the natural branches [Israel], He

may not spare you either. Therefore consider the goodness and severity of God: on those who fell, severity; but toward you, goodness, if you continue in His goodness. Otherwise you also will be cut off.

—Romans 11:20–22

We have become experts in His goodness; however, it is not just His goodness we are to consider. We must understand the severity of God as well. His goodness draws us to His heart, and His severity keeps us from pride and all manner of sin. A person who only considers the goodness forsakes the fear that will keep him from pride and worldliness. Likewise, the person who only considers the severity of God is easily ensnared in legalism. It is both the love and the fear of God that keep us on the narrow path to life.

A person is seduced into sin when he counts as common or familiar what God esteems as holy. Too often we take lightly the things God takes seriously, and we treat seriously the things God treats lightly. We are very serious about appearing respectable to other people, but that's not as important to God as the motives of our hearts.

I've known men who were entrapped in sin, all the while saying, "I love Jesus." They measured their spiritual condition by what they felt for Jesus. But did they love Him enough to die to the sin that bound them? No. They had no fear of God!

His goodness draws us to His heart, and His severity keeps us from pride and all manner of sin.

As I visited one minister in prison who had fallen into sexual immorality and financial corruption, he told me, "John, I always loved Jesus, even when I was deceived. He was my Savior but not my Master." He had made decisions motivated by the fear of man. He wanted to please people. He desired the accolades that come from men. This led him into corruption. In that prison God showed him His love and mercy, and He taught him the fear of the Lord. This minister now fears the Lord and has been restored.

Refusing God's Invitation

Returning to the illustration of Mount Sinai, I want to point out something most people miss. God instructed both Moses and Aaron to come up to the mountain (Exod. 19:24). Moses went up, but for some reason we find Aaron back in the camp (Exod. 32:1)! I believe Aaron returned to camp because he was more comfortable in the presence of the other "believers" than in the presence of God. Are we not like this in our churches today? We are more comfortable going to church, fellowshiping with other Christians and keeping busy with ministry duties than with the Lord. We avoid being alone in His presence, instead surrounding ourselves with people and activity, hoping this will hide our emptiness.

Joshua, on the other hand, had a heart after God. He wanted to be as close to the presence of God as possible. He stayed at the foot of the mountain for forty days while Moses was with God (Exod. 32:17). He got as close as he could without going where only Moses and Aaron had been invited. Joshua feared God enough not to be presumptuous.

As Joshua waited at the mountain, the people in

the camp grew restless. They were in a strange land; their leader had been gone for more than a month; and God still had not revealed Himself. They started questioning God and Moses.

> The people gathered together to Aaron, and said to him, "Come, make us gods that shall go before us; for as for this Moses, the man who brought us up out of the land of Egypt, we do not know what has become of him."
> —Exodus 32:1

In appearance, they respected and feared God. "Oh, Moses," they had pleaded, "He is too awesome for us. You go talk to Him and tell us what He says. We'll listen and obey." They had just seen how terrible and powerful God was, yet they did not fear Him as they built idols for themselves. Now that God was quiet, their true nature was revealed.

We can easily fear God while He is doing miracles and demonstrating His power. But God is looking for those who will also reverence and fear Him when they do not perceive His presence or power, like children who obey even when their father is not watching. The truly obedient are so when no one is around to monitor them!

God said to Israel, "Is it not because I have held My peace from of old that you do not fear Me?" (Isa. 57:11). He essentially asked, "Why don't My people fear Me?" Then He answered His own question by observing that the people did not fear Him because He had not manifested Himself in terrifying power for some time. In other words, when the people didn't see Him displayed awesomely, they acted as if He weren't there. God's silence exposed the people's true heart motive.

> ## The truly obedient are so when no one is around to monitor them!

It is in the midst of the desert while facing trials, not in an anointed, powerful service, that a true believer is revealed. What a person is like in the "press" is what he is really like. Watch what Aaron did under pressure:

> And Aaron said to them, "Break off the golden earrings which are in the ears of

your wives, your sons, and your daughters, and bring them to me." So all the people broke off the golden earrings which were in their ears, and brought them to Aaron. And he received the gold from their hand, and he fashioned it with an engraving tool, and made a molded calf. Then they said, "This is your god, O Israel, that brought you out of the land of Egypt!"

—Exodus 32:2–4

They made an idol out of God's blessing, the spoils of Egypt. But even more alarming is that Aaron, the one who would not come up the mountain, made the idol. He had been Moses' spokesman. He had stood at his side and watched every great miracle and plague. But now he feared the people and gave them what they wanted. He feared man more than God, so the people easily intimidated him. There was no boldness in him; the gift of God was dormant. This made him a weak leader. When confronted by Moses, he blamed the people who had intimidated him. Aaron said:

Do not let the anger of my lord become hot. You know the people, that they are set on evil. For they said to me, "Make us gods that shall go before us; as for this Moses, the man who brought us out of the land of Egypt, we do not know what has become of him." And I said to them, "Whoever has any gold, let them break it off." So they gave it to me, and I cast it into the fire, and this calf came out.

—Exodus 32:22–24

Aaron did not take responsibility for what he had done. Yes, his assessment of the people was correct. It was their idea, not Aaron's. But because he feared them, he was not strong enough to break the intimidation of the crowd and lead them correctly. He was entrapped by the fear of man.

> # The man who fears God is only concerned with what God says about him.

Leaders who fear men will back down and give the people what they want rather than what they need! They become easy prey for intimidation. It doesn't matter how much the leader says he loves God and His people, as long as he fears man he will never see true progress in himself or the people he leads!

The man who fears God is only concerned with what God says about him. The man who fears men is more concerned with what men think about him than what God thinks. He offends God in order not to offend man.

What Happens When We Don't Fear God?

God said to Moses, "Oh, that they had such a heart in them that they would fear Me" (Deut. 5:29). But the people did not, and look what happened.

After a year of living in the wilderness, it was time to go and take the Promised Land. The Lord told Moses, "Send men to spy out the land of Canaan, which I am giving to the children of Israel" (Num. 13:1). Notice He said, "I am *giving…*" He did not say, "Spy out the land and see if they can take it."

So Moses sent them. They spied for forty days, and they discovered the inhabitants were well established in the land and the cities very large and well guarded.

All twelve spies saw the same people, the same

armies, the same large, fortified cities and the same giants. Joshua and Caleb were ready to go in at once and take what God had promised. However, the other ten spies were intimidated by what they saw. They saw only big armies and giants, whereas Joshua and Caleb saw how good and faithful God was!

The ten spies told the people it would be impossible to take the land. They had been slaves for more than four hundred years and were not skilled in war as the armies they saw were. The people immediately became afraid and started complaining.

> Why has the Lord brought us to this land to fall by the sword, that our wives and children should become victims? Would it not be better for us to return to Egypt?
> —Numbers 14:3

In this verse we find the root of man's fear: Would it not be better for us? These people were intimidated because they thought only of themselves. They did not say, "What God says is best." Instead they asked, "What is best for us?"

How clear can it be? The root of the fear of man is the love of self. When you love your life, you seek to save it. You will be intimidated by anything that threatens it.

God brought these people to the place where they had no choice but to trust Him. It appeared they would all be destroyed by the inhabitants of this new land. But instead of trusting God, they acted as if God had saved them from the Egyptians only to have the Canaanites kill them. Of course this sounds ridiculous, but we all may face times when we are required to follow the Lord into situations that appear dangerous or damaging to our lives.

The root of the fear of man is the love of self.

We can only follow Him in these circumstances when we have settled in our hearts that God is good. There is only good in Him. He would never do anything to us for only His benefit at our eternal expense or harm! We must remember, God judges everything by eternity, while man judges by seventy or eighty years!

God's Rejection or Man's?

Caleb and Joshua chose the difficult road. God said they had a different spirit in them and had followed Him fully. All the rest did not want their welfare jeopardized by obeying God. God was faithful to Caleb and Joshua. They were the only ones of that generation to enter the Promised Land. (See Numbers 14:24, 30.)

Those who sought to save their lives forfeited them. God pronounced their fate by saying, "But as for you, your carcasses shall fall in this wilderness…and you shall know My rejection" (Num. 14:32, 34). It is a sobering thought to know that many will be rejected by God because they feared rejection by man.

I pray that we all will learn to delight ourselves in the fear of the Lord. For "the fear of the LORD is a fountain of life, to turn one away from the snares of death" (Prov. 14:27).

Adapted from John Bevere, *Breaking Intimidation* (Lake Mary, FL: Charisma House, 1995), 141–156.

THREE

Friendship With God

DEVELOPING
Inner Strength

From the time of his birth, Isaac had a close, ever-growing relationship with his father, Abraham. The life of this boy meant more to Abraham than his own. His great wealth was nothing in comparison to the joy of this son. Nothing meant more to Abraham than this precious son given to him by God. The day came when God decided to test that relationship.

> *Now it came to pass after these things that God tested Abraham, and said to him, "Abraham!" And he said, "Here I am." And He said, "Take now your son, your only son Isaac, whom you love, and go to the land of Moriah, and offer him there as a burnt offering on one of the mountains of which I shall tell you."*
>
> —GENESIS 22:1–2

Can you imagine Abraham's shock at hearing these words? Never had he dreamed that God would ask such a hard thing of him. He was stunned. Father and son were so close. After all the years of waiting for this priceless young man, God had asked for more than even Abraham's own life—He had asked for his heart. It made no sense.

But Abraham knew that God did not make mistakes. There was no denying what God had already made clear. There were only two options for a covenant man—obey or break covenant. To break covenant was not even a consideration for this man of faith—he was so immersed in godly fear.

We know it was a test, but Abraham did not. We never know God is testing us until we are on the other side of it. It may be possible to cheat on a university test, but no one can cheat on the exams God gives. If we have not studied and done our homework by purifying our hearts and cleansing our hands, we will not be able to pass God's tests, no matter how clever we are!

I believe it is the heart's desire of every true believer to walk in the fear of God. It is the only thing that will ever bring lasting fulfillment. It is God's motive for creation and purpose in redemption, the very focus of His heart, and a treasure reserved for those who fear Him. By way of introduction, let's turn to Solomon's wisdom:

> The fear of the LORD is the beginning of knowledge.
>
> —PROVERBS 1:7

The knowledge of what? Is Solomon referring to scientific knowledge? No, for many scientists exalt man and have no fear of God. Does this verse refer to social or political accomplishment? No, for the world's ways are foolishness to God. Is it knowledge of the Scriptures? No, for although the Pharisees were experts in the law, they were displeasing to God. Our answer is found in Proverbs 2:5: Fear the Lord, and you will gain knowledge of God. Let me put it to you in simpler terms: You will come to know God intimately. The psalmist confirms this by saying, "The secret of the Lord is with those who fear Him" (Ps. 25:14).

The fear of the Lord is the beginning, or starting

place, of an intimate relationship with God. Intimacy is a two-way relationship. For example, I know *about* the president of the United States. I can list information about his accomplishments and his political stance, but I do not actually *know* him. I lack a personal relationship with him. Those in the president's immediate family and his close associates *know* him. If we were in the same room, I would quickly recognize the president, but he would not know me. Although I'm a citizen of the United States and know *about* him, I could not speak to him as though he were my friend. That would be inappropriate and even disrespectful. I would still be under his jurisdiction and authority as president and under his protection as commander in chief, but his authority over me would not automatically grant me intimacy with him.

Another example would be those of us who are so taken with the athletic and Hollywood celebrities of our day. Their names are common in the households of America. The media has laid bare their personal lives through numerous television interviews and newspaper and magazine articles. I hear fans talk as though these celebrities were close friends. I have even seen people caught up emotionally in the marriage problems of their favorite celebrities and have watched them grieve as if they were a part of the family when their sports or screen heroes died.

If these fans ever met their celebrity hero on the street, they would not even receive a nod of acknowledgment. If they were bold enough to stop this celebrity, they may find the real person to be quite different from the image he or she portrays. The relationship between celebrities and their fans is a one-way relationship.

> The fear of the Lord is the beginning, or starting place, of an intimate relationship with God.

I have grieved over this same behavior in the church. I listen to believers talk about God as though He were just a buddy, someone they hang out with. They casually tell how God has shown them this or that. They say how much they desire His presence and hunger for His anointing. Often those young or not yet stable in their relationship with the Lord will feel uncomfortable and spiritually deficient around these "close friends" of God.

Within minutes you will usually hear these individuals contradict themselves. They will say something that clearly reveals that their relationship with God is not unlike that between a fan and his favorite celebrity. They prove to be expounding about a relationship that is just not there.

The Lord said we cannot even begin to know Him on intimate terms until we fear Him. In other words, an intimate relationship and friendship with God will not even begin until the fear of God is firmly planted in our hearts.

We can attend services, come forward in answer to every altar call, read our Bibles daily and attend every prayer meeting. We can preach great and motivating sermons, work hard in the ministry for years and even receive the respect and admiration of our peers. But if we do not fear God, we are only climbing the rungs of the religious ladder. What's the difference between these religious rituals and suffering from the celebrity syndrome?

I know people who can tell me more about a celebrity's personal life than they can tell me about their own. They are full of insight, scoop, facts and details. Such knowledge of someone does not guarantee intimacy with them. These celebrity followers are like people who watch the lives of others through glass windows. They see the *what, where* and *when,* but they do not know the *why.*

God's Friend

God called two men His friends in Scripture. This is not to say there were not others—only that God specifically acknowledged these two, intentionally recording their friendships. I believe He did this so we could benefit and receive insight into what God looks for in a friend.

The first is Abraham. Abraham was called the "friend of God" (2 Chron. 20:7). When Abraham was seventy-five years old, God came to Abraham and cut a covenant with him. Within the parameters of this covenant, God promised Abraham his heart's desire—a son. Before the birth of this son, Abraham made several mistakes, some that were quite serious.

Yet through it all Abraham believed and obeyed God. He was fully persuaded that God would perform all that was promised.

When Abraham was ninety-nine years of age, his wife became pregnant, and their promised son, Isaac, was born! Can you imagine the joy Abraham and Sarah experienced after waiting so many years? Can you imagine the love they had for this promised child?

God once asked me to give up something I thought He had given me. It meant more to me than anything else. I had desired it for years. It was to work for a particularly well-known evangelist, one I dearly loved.

My wife and I had been offered positions on staff as assistants to this man and his wife. Not only did I love this man, but I also saw it as God's opportunity to bring to pass the dream He had implanted deep within me—that I might preach the gospel to the nations of the world.

I fully expected God to say *yes* to this wonderful offer, but He made it clear that I was to turn it down. I wept for days after refusing this offer. I knew I had obeyed God, yet I did not understand *why* He had asked such a hard thing of me. After weeks of bewilderment, I finally cried out, "God, why did You make me put this on the altar?"

He quickly answered my cry: "To see if you were serving Me or the dream."

> # An intimate relationship and friendship with God will not even begin until the fear of God is firmly planted in our hearts.

Only then did I understand that I had been tested. In the midst of it, I had not realized what He was doing. The only things that kept me from going my own way were my love for God and my fear of Him.

Abraham's Fear of God Was Confirmed

I love Abraham's response to God's most difficult command to him—the willingness to sacrifice

Isaac, the son he loved so much. In response to God's command, we read, "So Abraham rose early in the morning" (Gen. 22:3). He did not talk it over with Sarah. There was no hesitation. He had decided to obey God. There were just two things that meant more to Abraham than his promised Isaac—his love and fear of God. He loved and feared God above all else.

God told Abraham to take a three-day journey. This allowed him time to ponder what he had been told to do. If there had been any wavering within him, this time period would have exposed it. When he and Isaac arrived at the designated place of worship, Abraham built an altar, bound his son, laid him on the altar and reached for his knife. He raised the knife above Isaac's throat.

At this point, God spoke through an angel, stopping him in the midst of his obedient act. "Do not lay your hand on the lad, or do anything to him; for now I know that you fear God, since you have not withheld your son, your only son, from Me" (Gen. 22:12).

Abraham proved his fear by esteeming God's desires as even more important than his own.

God knew that if Abraham passed this test, he would pass them all.

> Then Abraham lifted his eyes and looked, and there behind him was a ram caught in a thicket by its horns. So Abraham went and took the ram, and offered it up for a burnt offering instead of his son. And Abraham called the name of the place, The-LORD-Will-Provide.
>
> —GENESIS 22:13–14

With the completion of this test, God revealed a new facet of Himself to Abraham. He revealed Himself as Jehovah-Jireh. This revelation of God's character means "Jehovah Sees." No one since Adam had known Him in this manner. God revealed His heart to this humble man who had become His friend. The Lord was revealing to Abraham the things that to other men were yet "secrets" of His heart and character.

But it is important to understand that God did not reveal Himself as "Jehovah Sees" until Abraham had passed His test of holy fear. Many claim to know the different characteristics and attributes of God's nature, yet they have never obeyed Him in the hard places. They can sing, "Jehovah-Jireh, my provider, His grace is sufficient for me…" But it is only a song until He is revealed through obedience as such. Until we pass God's test of obedience, such statements proceed from our heads and not our hearts. It is when we venture into the hard, arid wilderness of obedience that God reveals Himself as Jehovah-Jireh and friend. (See Isaiah 35:1–2.)

> Was not Abraham our father justified by works when he offered Isaac his son on the altar? Do you see that faith was working together with his works, and by works faith was made perfect? And the Scripture was fulfilled which says, "Abraham believed God, and it was accounted to him for righteousness." And he was called the friend of God.
>
> —JAMES 2:21–23

Notice that Abraham was justified by his corresponding works. The proof of his holy fear and faith was his obedience. To *fear* God is to *believe* God. To *believe* God is to *obey* Him. James pointed out that Abraham's obedience, fueled by his holy fear of God, resulted in friendship with God. God makes it clear:

> Friendship with the LORD is reserved for those who fear him. With them he shares the secrets of his covenant.
>
> —PSALM 25:14, NLT

It could not be any clearer! Read this verse from Psalm 25 again, and hide it within your heart. Why is there an abundance of shallow preaching from pulpits? Why do Christians lack the depth of our forefathers? It is the result of a growing disease in the church. It is a virus called "An Absence of the Fear of the Lord!"

God said He reveals His secrets to those who fear Him. With whom do you share the secrets of your heart—acquaintances or intimate friends? With intimate friends, of course. Secrets wouldn't be safe with mere acquaintances. Well, God does the same—He shares His heart only with those who fear Him.

The Man Who Knew God's Ways

There is another man whom God called His friend—Moses. He was a man who knew God's ways. Exodus 33:11 says, "So the LORD spoke to Moses face to face, as a man speaks to his friend." Moses' face was unveiled for he feared God. Therefore, he was able to talk with God on an intimate level. The result was:

> He made known His ways to Moses, His acts to the children of Israel.
>
> —PSALM 103:7

Because Israel did not fear God, they were denied intimacy with Him. His ways and the secrets of His covenant were not revealed to the Israelites. They knew Him in much the same way as I know the president of the United States. I know the president by his accomplishments, provisions and acts. The Israelites were not privy to the why of God's covenant. They did not understand God's motives, intentions and the desires of His heart.

The Israelites only perceived God's character as it was displayed in the natural world. They often mistook His methods for "taking" or "withholding" when they did not get precisely what they wanted. It is impossible to know God merely by observing what He does in the natural world. That would be like knowing a celebrity only from the media reports. God is Spirit, and His ways are hidden from the wisdom of this natural world (John 4:24; 1 Cor. 2:6–8). God will only reveal Himself to those who fear Him. The children of Israel did not see the wisdom or understanding behind all that He was doing. Therefore, they were constantly out of step with Him.

God Shares His Plans With His Friends

God shares the motives and intentions of His heart with His friends. He discusses His plans with them and even confides in them. The Lord asked, "Should I hide My plan from Abraham?" (Gen. 18:17, NLT).

The Lord spoke this to the angelic servants who were with Him in the presence of Abraham. God then turned to Abraham.

> So the LORD told Abraham, "I have heard that the people of Sodom and Gomorrah are extremely evil, and that everything they do is wicked. I am going down to see whether or not these reports are true. Then I will know."
> —GENESIS 18:20–21, NLT

The Lord then confided to Abraham that impending judgment hovered over the cities of Sodom and Gomorrah. Abraham interceded and pleaded for the lives of the righteous.

> Abraham approached him [God] and said, "Will you destroy both innocent and guilty alike? Suppose you find fifty innocent people there within the city—will you still destroy it, and not spare it for their sakes? Surely you wouldn't do such a thing, destroying the innocent with the guilty. Why, you wouldn't do that! Should not the Judge of all the earth do what is right?"
>
> And the Lord replied, "If I find fifty innocent people in Sodom, I will spare the entire city for their sake."
>
> —Genesis 18:23–26, nlt

Abraham had asked that the lives of others be spared from the hand of God's judgment. Only a friend talks that way to a king or judge who has the power to execute judgment. Coming from a servant or subject, such a petition would be disrespectful. But Abraham actually entered into a negotiation process with God. Abraham then talked God down from fifty to ten, and God went on His way to search out the ten righteous people in Sodom and Gomorrah. It became obvious that the report of wickedness was true, for not even ten righteous people could be found in either city. The Lord found only Lot, Abraham's nephew, and his family.

Lot represents fleshly, carnal Christians—those who lack the burning, holy fear of God.

God showed His friend Abraham what He planned to do. He confided in Abraham because Abraham feared God. His fear had raised him to the level of God's confidant.

Defiled by the World

Lot may have been considered righteous, but he was also worldly. He had no more insight of impending judgment than the residents of these wicked cities. Although he was righteous, Lot was caught unaware of what was about to occur. Lot represents fleshly, carnal Christians—those who lack the burning, holy fear of God. Their relationship with the Lord is not too different from that of star-struck fans and celebrities.

This is seen by where Lot chose to dwell (among the inhabitants of Sodom and Gomorrah), the type of wife he chose and the children he would later father through incest—the Moabites and Ammonites. Lot had chosen what had initially looked best for him, but in the end he was proven to have chosen unwisely.

In contrast, Abraham chose a separated life. He sought a city whose builder and maker was God. Lot chose fellowship with the ungodly over a separated life. Their ungodly ways whittled away at his righteousness. Eventually that exposure to ungodliness bore fruit in Lot's life and in the lives of his descendants. Lot's standards were not dictated by God—they were dictated by the society around him. Lot became "oppressed by the filthy conduct of the wicked (for that righteous man, dwelling among them, tormented his righteous soul from day to day by seeing and hearing their lawless deeds)" (2 Pet. 2:7–8).

The Day of Judgment would have come upon Lot as a thief in the night had it not been for God's mercy and His friendship with Abraham. God sent angelic messengers, just as He will send prophetic messengers with a warning to the carnal believers in the church who remain oblivious to impending judgment.

In the urgency and fury of impending judgment, Lot's wife chose to look back. She had been warned not to look back as the Lord sent destruction upon the cities that were so full of evil. But Lot's wife had been so influenced by the world that its pull was stronger on her than the fear of the Lord. This is why Jesus warns the New Testament believers to "remember Lot's wife" (Luke 17:32).

> You cannot love
> the world and be a
> friend of God as well.

Abraham feared God. He was God's friend. Lot lacked all but a small measure of this. He had just enough fear of the Lord to flee immediate judgment, but judgment overtook those who followed him.

Lot later proved to know neither God's heart nor His ways. James bluntly addresses believers with, "Adulterers and adulteresses! Do you not know that friendship with the world is enmity with God? Whoever therefore wants to be a friend of the world makes himself an enemy of God" (James 4:4).

You cannot love the world and be a friend of God as well. James describes the condition of a believer who still seeks a relationship with the world as an adulterer and an enemy of God. Solomon tells us, "He who loves purity of heart and has grace on his lips, the king will be his friend" (Prov. 22:11).

Only the pure in heart are friends with God. We must ask our selves, *What purifies my heart? My love for God?* The love for God awakens the desire to purify, but it alone does not purify the heart. We can say we love God with great affection, yet we may still love the world. This is the entrapment of millions in the church. What force keeps us pure before this awesome King? Paul answered in clear and concise terms:

> Therefore, having these promises, beloved, let us cleanse ourselves from all filthiness of

the flesh and spirit, perfecting holiness in
the fear of God.

—2 Corinthians 7:1

True holiness or purity of heart is perfected or
made mature in the fear of God! "By the fear of the
Lord one departs from evil" (Prov. 16:6).

But look again at the beginning of 2 Corinthians
7:1: "Therefore, having these promises…" What
promises? They are found in the previous verses.
Let's read them:

> For you are the temple of the living God. As
> God has said: "I will dwell in them and
> walk among them. I will be their God, and
> they shall be My people." Therefore "Come
> out from among them and be separate, says
> the Lord. Do not touch what is unclean,
> and I will receive you. I will be a Father to
> you, and you shall be My sons and daugh-
> ters, says the Lord Almighty."
>
> —2 Corinthians 6:16–18

This is exactly how God described His desire to
dwell with the children of Israel in His glory in the
wilderness. He said, "I am the Lord their God, who
brought them up out of the land of Egypt, that I

may dwell among them" (Exod. 29:46). And again, "I will walk among you and be your God, and you shall be My people" (Lev. 26:12). There is a parallel: He is the same holy God. He will not dwell in a defiled or unholy temple.

> True holiness or purity of heart is perfected or made mature in the fear of God!

Let's understand the full meaning of these truths for today. God outlines the conditions or requirements of our covenant with Him that we might dwell in the presence of His glory. We must come out from among the world's system and be separate. This is a cooperative work of the fear of God and His grace. That is why Paul begins this sixth chapter of 2 Corinthians by pleading with the Corinthian church "not to receive the grace of God in vain" (v. 1).

In Hebrews chapter 12, the writer further clarifies this point, strongly exhorting us to pursue holiness, for if we do not, we will not see God.

> Pursue…holiness, without which no one
> will see the Lord: looking carefully lest
> anyone fall short of the grace of God.
>
> —Hebrews 12:14–15

Notice again that this chapter talks about receiving the grace of God in vain! We can fall short of it! The writer goes on to describe what keeps grace active and productive in our lives: "Let us have grace, by which we may serve God acceptably with reverence and godly fear" (v. 28). The fear of God prevents us from receiving His grace in vain. It keeps us from the desire to have a relationship with the world. It is the grace of God, coupled with the fear of God, that produces holiness or purity of heart. God promises that if we cleanse ourselves from the filth of the world, He would dwell in us in His glory. Hallelujah!

Adapted from *The Fear of the Lord*, 171–184.

FOUR

The Blessings of Holy Fear

DEVELOPING
Inner Strength

If you fear God, you will serve Him. If you fear man, you will serve man. You must choose. Solomon, after an entire life of both success and hardship, could say:

> Let us hear the conclusion of the whole matter: Fear God and keep His commandments, for this is man's all.
>
> —ECCLESIASTES 12:13

Solomon pursued wisdom throughout his entire life. He obtained it, and it ushered in great success. However, he went through a period of torment and vexation in his latter years. The fear of God in his heart had waned. He no longer obeyed the commandments of God. He married foreign wives and served their gods.

At the close of his life, he looked back, and after much meditation he wrote the Book of Ecclesiastes. In this book, Solomon examines life apart from the fear of God.

His response to every probing question was, "Vanity!"

At the very end of the book, he concludes that the whole matter of life is summed up in fearing God and keeping His commandments!

> Let us hear the conclusion of the whole matter: fear God and keep His commandments, for this is man's all.
>
> —ECCLESIASTES 12:13

The fear of the Lord is a subject that cannot be fully disclosed, no matter how many books are written. It is a continuous revelation. The same is true with God's love. Proverbs 23:17 says, "Be zealous [passionate] for the fear of the LORD all the day." We cannot become too passionate with its fire.

Because it is impossible to fully detail the fear of the Lord in finite terms, it is likewise difficult to define. It encompasses a broad spectrum like the force of the love of God. The definition I offer will be partial and merely a beginning, for it is impossible to describe in words the inner transformation of the heart. We will grow in the revealed knowledge of God throughout eternity. Proportionately, the revelation of His love and our holy fear of Him will expand.

The fear of man opposes the fear of God. The fear of man ensnares (Prov. 29:25). To fear man is to stand in alarm, anxiety, awe, dread, suspicion or cowering before mortal men. Those entrapped by this type of fear will live on the run, hiding from harm or reproach, constantly avoiding rejection and confrontation. They become so busy safeguarding themselves that they are soon ineffective in their service for God. Afraid of what man can do, they deny God what He deserves.

> The fear of God should burn bright in our hearts no matter how long we've been saved.

The fear of God includes, but is not limited to, respecting and reverencing Him, for we are told to tremble at His presence. Holy fear gives God the place of glory, honor, reverence, thanksgiving, praise and preeminence He deserves. (Notice it is what He deserves, not what we think He deserves.)

God holds this preeminent position in our hearts and lives as we esteem His desires over and above our own, hating what He hates and loving what He loves, trembling in His presence and at His Word.

The Blessings of Fearing God

I encourage you to read through your Bible, and with the use of a concordance, locate each scripture that relates to the fear of God. Record them for future reference. In my search, I compiled over fifty typewritten pages. I found some very definite promises for those who fear the Lord. Allow me to share just a few.

The fear of God…

- Positions our hearts to receive answers (Heb. 5:7).
- Assures that God's great goodness abounds (Ps. 31:19).
- Promises angelic protection (Ps. 34:7).
- Secures God's continual attention (Ps. 33:18).
- Supplies His provision (Ps. 34:9).
- Contains great mercy (Ps. 103:11).
- Provides assurance of food (Ps. 111:5).
- Promises protection (Ps. 115:11).
- Fulfills our desires and delivers us from harm (Ps. 145:19).
- Provides wisdom, understanding, and time management (Prov. 9:10–11).
- Is our confidence and protection in the face of death (Prov. 14:26–27).

- Provides peace of mind (Prov. 15:16).
- Results in complete satisfaction (Prov. 19:23).
- Leads to riches, honor, and life (Prov. 22:4).
- Will keep us on the path (Jer. 32:40).
- Produces a secure household (Exod. 1:21).
- Provides clarity and direction (Ps. 25:12).
- Results in enjoyment of our labor, and full, rewarding lives (Ps. 128:1–4, NLT).
- Produces successful leadership (Exod. 18:21; 2 Sam. 23:3).

These are but a few of God's promises for those who fear Him. There are many more. I encourage you to find them in your time of reading and studying God's Word.

The fear of God should burn bright in our hearts no matter how long we've been saved. In fact, it is a key element to receiving salvation. Paul proclaims, "Those among you who fear God, to you the word of this salvation has been sent" (Acts 13:26).

Without this holy fear, we will not recognize our need for salvation.

Adapted from *The Fear of the Lord*, 187–193.

Conclusion

No matter where you are spiritually, I encourage you to pray with me. If you have not previously submitted yourself to the lordship of Jesus, now is the time to turn your life over to Him. You have heard the Word, and faith has risen in your heart. If the Holy Spirit has brought deep conviction and you are ready to turn from the world and sin and give yourself wholly to Him, now is the time. It's time to make the decision to completely submit your life to His lordship. It's time to confirm it through prayer.

> *Father in heaven, in the name of Jesus, I humble myself and come to You to seek Your mercy and grace. I have heard Your Word, and the desire to love, fear and know You now burns in my heart. I ask forgiveness for the life I have lived irreverently before coming to You. I repent of all disrespect and hypocrisy I have tolerated in my life.*

I turn to You, Jesus, as my Savior and Lord. You are my Master, and I give my life completely to You. Fill me with Your love and holy fear. I desire to know You intimately in a deeper dimension than I have ever known anyone or anything else. I acknowledge my need and dependency for and on Your Holy Spirit and ask that You would fill me now.

Lord, Your Word promises that as I turn to You with all my heart the Holy Spirit will reveal Your true image and character to me, and I will be changed from glory to glory. Like Moses, I ask to see Your face. In this secret place, I will be changed.

Lord Jesus, thank You for the abundant mercy and grace You've extended to me. For all You have already done and all You are about to do, I give You the glory, honor and praise, both now and forever. Amen.

Adapted from *The Fear of the Lord*, 195–197.

If you are enjoying the Inner Strength Series by
John Bevere, here are some other titles from
Charisma House that we think will minister to you...

Breaking Intimidation
**Break free from the fear
of man**
John Bevere
ISBN: 0-88419-387-X
Retail Price: $13.99

The Bait of Satan
**Don't let resentment
cripple you**
John Bevere
ISBN: 0-88419-374-8
Price: $13.99

Thus Saith the Lord?
**How prophetic excesses
have hurt the church**
John Bevere
ISBN: 0-88419-575-9
Retail Price: $12.99

The Devil's Door
**Recognize the trap of
rebellion**
John Bevere
ISBN: 0-88419-442-6
Price: $12.99

Pathway to His Presence
**A 40-day devotional
leading into His presence**
John and Lisa Bevere
ISBN: 0-88419-654-2
Price: $16.99

The Fear of the Lord
**Gain a holy fear and awe
of God**
John Bevere
ISBN: 0-88419-486-8
Price: $12.99

ISLANDS *of* FATE

FRED BRUEMMER

ISLANDS *of* FATE

FRED BRUEMMER

KEY PORTER BOOKS

THIS BOOK IS DEDICATED to the memory of the young man whose heart I carry. He died in a motorcycle accident more than twenty years ago. Because at that moment of utter shock and grief, a family had the greatness of spirit to think of others: two persons, then blind, received the wonderful gift of sight; two people suffering the torture of kidney failure, received each a kidney and were able to lead near-normal lives. And I, then near death from advanced cardiomyopathy, received his heart and lived to write this book and many others, to experience the joy and continuation of life in our grand-children, to see the world in gratitude and wonder. My profound gratitude goes also to the doctors and nurses of the organ transplant section of the Royal Victoria Hospital in Montreal. Their skill, devotion, and care made this miracle of a second life possible, for me and for many others.—F.B.

Library and Archives Canada Cataloguing in Publication

Bruemmer, Fred
    Islands of fate / Fred Bruemmer.

Includes bibliographical references.
ISBN 1-55263-824-3

    1. Islands. 2. Voyages and travels. I. Title.

G500.B77 2006   910'.914'2   C2006-902517-7

The Canada Council | Le Conseil des Arts
for the Arts | du Canada
since 1957 | depuis 1957

ONTARIO ARTS COUNCIL
CONSEIL DES ARTS DE L'ONTARIO

The publisher gratefully acknowledges the support of the Canada Council for the Arts and the Ontario Arts Council for its publishing program. We acknowledge the support of the Government of Ontario through the Ontario Media Development Corporation's Ontario Book Initiative.

We acknowledge the financial support of the Government of Canada through the Book Publishing Industry Development Program (BPIDP) for our publishing activities.

Key Porter Books Limited
Six Adelaide Street East, Tenth Floor
Toronto, Ontario
Canada M5C 1H6

www.keyporter.com

Text design: Ingrid Paulson and Martin Gould
Electronic formatting: Martin Gould
Maps: John Lightfoot
Photography: Fred Bruemmer

Printed and bound in China

06 07 08 09 10 11 6 5 4 3 2 1

TABLE OF CONTENTS

These 14 hectares (35 acres) of hell, part of France's notorious convict colonies in French Guiana, were reserved for its most feared political prisoners. Most famous was Captain Alfred Dreyfus, wrongfully convicted of treason and banished for life to Devil's Island. *L'affaire Dreyfus* became the greatest, most divisive scandal of nineteen-century France.

On remote, storm-haunted Attu Island, the only battle of World War II took place that was fought on American soil. Westernmost island of the Aleutian chain, closer to Asia than North America, Attu in 1942 was inhabited by thirty-nine Aleuts and two white teachers. On June 7, 1942, more than two thousand crack Japanese combat troops landed. The subsequent battle for Attu was long and terrible. The Japanese fought to the death: of 2,600 soldiers only twenty-eight surrendered.

There were four treasures in the Arctic that southern man desired: walrus tusks, polar bear skins, gyrfalcon, and the spiraled narwhal tusks that were sold in the south as the miracle-working horns of unicorns. To obtain them, Vikings sailed from their Greenland settlements far north and probably traded with Inuit on tiny Skraeling Island, where archaeologists have found the remains of many Inuit houses, Viking tools, and chain-mail armour.

On tiny Garden Key, one of the seven islands that make up the Dry Tortugas archipelago, 110 kilometres (68 miles) southwest of Key West, Florida, the young United States built Fort Jefferson, the largest all-masonry fortification of the U.S.A. Constructed by slaves with more than sixteen million bricks, the massive fortress near the southernmost point of the United States, was supposed to protect the southern flank of the young republic. It never served that purpose. Instead it became a feared military prison, its most famous and tragic inmate was Dr. Samuel Mudd who treated John Wilkes Booth's broken leg after Booth assassinated President Abraham Lincoln.

Their boats are sacred and, they believe, immortal. Their prey is gigantic and dangerous. They are the sea hunters of Lamalera, an isolated village on the tiny Indonesian island of Lembata, 1,900 kilometres (1,181 miles) due east of Jakarta. In boats of ancient design, with golden-yellow palm-leaf sails, they cruise the Savu Sea in search of whales, manta rays and giant sharks. Under the searing tropical sun, the lean, dark men of Lamalera pursue their huge and dangerous prey with simple weapons, as their ancestors have done for more than seven hundred years.

It is an island of stunning beauty, of emerald meadows and mist-wrapped tropical mountains, fringed by the world's southernmost coral reef. Captain Henry Lidgbird Ball discovered the small, scimitar-shaped island, 600 kilometres (373 miles) east of Australia, on February, 17, 1788, and named it after Richard, Lord Howe, First Lord of the Admiralty. The island, he reported "afforded plenty of fine turtles, fowls, fish, cocoanuts and cabbages." First settled by American whalers and their Maori wives, Lord Howe remains an island paradise. One third of its plants are endemic and some of its birds are unique in the world.

"Zanzibar," wrote the historian Alan Moorehead, was "the only center of overseas commerce...along the whole East African seaboard." Its fame was ancient. Two thousand years ago when Africa was only vaguely known, Greeks and Romans obtained from Zanzibar gold, ivory, and slaves. In the nineteenth century, that trade became immense. Between 1830 and 1873 about six hundred thousand humans were sold on the infamous slave markets of Zanzibar, and thousands of tons of ivory. Zanzibar was also the island of spices. In the nineteenth century, it produced 90 per cent of the world's supply of cloves.

Eleven kilometres (7 miles) from Cape Town, not far from the south tip of Africa, lies tiny Robben Island. Once it was the island of seals, called *robben* by the Dutch. During the apartheid era, it gained worldwide infamy as South Africa's maximum security prison for political prisoners. Nelson Mandela spent twenty-seven years in prison, eighteen of them on Robben Island. Today it is a UN World Heritage site, South Africa's national shrine visited by more than three hundred thousand people each year and by thousands of penguins that now breed on the former prison island.

A genius at war, Napoleon rose from lowly cadet in Corsica to emperor of France. By 1810, he was master of most of Europe. He led his troops into sixty-four battles, won most of them but lost the last one, at Waterloo. Still afraid of him, his enemies banished him to tiny and remote St. Helena Island in the South Atlantic. Upon this lonely island, heavily guarded, Napoleon lived in bitterness and pain, with an ever-dwindling retinue of courtiers, dictating his memoirs. He died on St. Helena on May 5, 1821. He was fifty-one years old. Some claim that he was poisoned.

INTRODUCTION

COUNTLESS ISLANDS dot our earth, but only a few are famous. Touched by history and fate, they figure largely in the lives of humans or are the vital refuge of unique animals.

The Republic of Indonesia consists of 17,110 islands. Six thousand have names; 922 are permanently inhabited; two have amazing histories: Komodo, the island home of the Komodo dragon, the largest lizard on earth, and remote Lembata, home to daring sea hunters whose boats have not changed in seven hundred years.

Islands can be enchanting, like Ireland, "the Emerald Isle." Or Sri Lanka, once called Ceylon or, long ago, Serendip, the "Island of Gems," by early Arab travellers. From this our word "serendipity" is derived, for Sri Lanka then was considered to be one of the "Islands of the Blest," where, according to ancient belief, Adam first set foot on earth and Buddha left Sri Pada (the Sacred Footprint) atop Adam's Peak before ascending to paradise.

Islands can determine destiny. Japan might have become a part of China, or at least its abject vassal, had this island fortress not been defended by waves, warriors, and wind. When Kublai Khan's armies tried to land and conquer Japan in 1281, the fleet was struck by Kamikaze (the Divine Wind). The typhoon destroyed four thousand ships and killed more than a hundred thousand Chinese soldiers. Kublai Khan, like other rulers, tended to be casual about casualties. But this was too much. Japan, the island empire, was never invaded.

Had England, Shakespeare's "sceptred isle...this fortress built by Nature for herself," not been an island, Napoleon might well have invaded and conquered it. The history of Europe would then probably have been dramatically different. But, defended by Nature and Nelson, England defied Napoleon's grandiose plans, a fact he could contemplate at leisure during the last years of his life spent on small and isolated St. Helena Island, far from France in the South Atlantic Ocean, chosen by fate and enemies as his place of banishment.

Of the many islands I have visited, I have chosen twenty-five for this book. Nearly all are small islands that have been singled out by fate. On tiny Attu Island in the Aleutians (population forty-one in 1942), for example, Americans and Japanese fought one of the most prolonged and bloody battles of World War II.

On some of these islands, I lived for weeks, on a few for many months. I was happy there, because I love islands. Islands are insular and special. Islanders are insular and special. These twenty-five islands are even more special than others, islands of fate and fame and, a few, of infamy.

Most books have many parents. I am grateful to Jordan Fenn, publisher of Key Porter Books for his help and constant encouragement. Michael Mouland, the senior editor, who guided some of my previous books from manuscript to finished work, has done it again with *Islands of Fate*. I thank him for his kindness and patience.

My wife, Maud, shared with me the joy of islands. It is appropriate, for she was born and grew up on an island: Sumatra, Indonesia, when it was still a part of the Dutch East Indies. We and our children and grandchildren now live on an island: Montreal Island in the St. Lawrence River.

Chapter 1

DEVIL'S ISLAND, FRENCH GUIANA
Island of the Damned

O N JUNE 9, 1899, the French navy cruiser *Sfax* arrived at the Îles du Salut (the Salvation Islands) off French Guiana to pick up a single prisoner. "I finally left this cursed island where I had suffered so much," the prisoner wrote in his diary.

The "cursed island" was Devil's Island, the most feared and most famous of France's convict islands. The prisoner was Captain Alfred Dreyfus. His arrest and conviction for treason, based, it was later learned, on forged evidence, became a cause célèbre, the greatest scandal of nineteenth-century France.

"*L'affaire Dreyfus*" divided France. It pitted right against left, liberals against conservatives, the army against its detractors, those who fought for the glory of France against those who fought for justice.

While the fight raged in France, Dreyfus, that "poor martyr" as Queen Victoria called him, the most famous prisoner of his time, lived on Devil's Island, the most infamous of islands, "removed from the world of the living," he wrote in his diary. He had been banished to Devil's Island *à perpétuité* (forever).

"Sad island!" wrote Dreyfus. "A few banana trees, a few coconut palms, an arid soil and everywhere basaltic rocks."

It had other names. "Fourteen hectares [35 acres] of hell," a journalist called it. Among convicts, "*la bagne*" (penal colony), Devil's Island and the other penal stations, were known as "*la guillotine sèche*," (the dry guillotine).

No one escaped from Devil's Island. It is surrounded by vicious currents and patrolled by numerous sharks. Day and night six armed guards "watched my every movement," wrote Dreyfus. The guards never spoke to

Heat, humidity, and the encroaching jungle destroy the ancient convict buildings on Île Royale. Dreyfus arrived on this island and was transported to neighbouring Devil's Island.

him. And he was not allowed to speak to the guards. He lived, Dreyfus said, "in the silence of the tomb."

Guiana, that immense region of South America between the Orinoco River and the Amazon facing the Atlantic Ocean, first loomed large into European consciousness as "the golden land of Manoa," the realm of the fabled El Dorado, the king whose body was coated with gold.

Several Spanish expeditions searched in vain for El Dorado. Then, in 1595, the English under Sir Walter Raleigh, took up the quest for Guiana gold. He returned with little gold but fabulous tales. "The empire of Guiana is the richest land in the world," Raleigh reported. It has "abundant gold and silver in its mines...[and is so rich] that even the peasants use gold and silver plates."

El Dorado remained elusive. But three European nations claimed and occupied sections of Guiana: British Guiana, now the Republic of Guyana; Dutch Guiana, now Surinam; and French Guiana, still French and, since 1947, an overseas department of the French republic.

Fifteen kilometres (9 miles) north of the French Guiana mainland in the Atlantic Ocean lay three uninhabited islands, initially called the Triangle Islands. They soon acquired an evil reputation and were named "the Devil's Islands" because, said a captain's account from 1678, "the currents near these islands are terrible."

The year 1763 was a bad one for France. It had just lost the Seven Years War.

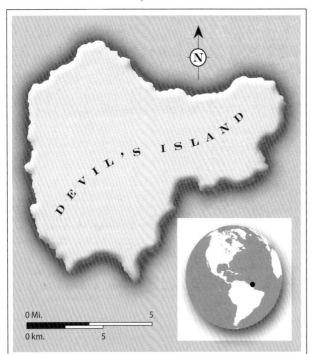

It was forced to cede Canada to Great Britain. It needed a new overseas base and Etienne François duc de Choiseul, minister of war and of the navy, picked on French Guiana.

France's new imperial bastion, the duke decreed, had to have settlers, soldiers, and slaves. To encourage immigration, the Devil's Islands, where some of the settlers' ships were to land, were given a more attractive name: Les Îles du Salut (the Salvation Islands). Only the smallest of the three islands was now called Devil's Island.

The colonization venture was a

disaster. Sixteen thousand settlers from France were sent to French Guiana. Ten thousand died, victims of malaria, yellow fever, typhoid, dysentery. Most of the six thousand survivors fled back to France. French Guiana became infamous as a foul and feverous land of disease and death.

An ideal place, thought the leaders of the French Revolution, to dump their opponents. In France the prisons were full, the guillotines busy. Beginning in 1792, surplus "enemies of the state," priests, royalists, aristocrats, rival revolutionaries, were sent by the shipload to rot in French Guiana. The survivors were freed in 1799 and repatriated to France.

The idea lingered: a place to get rid of "undesirables." Great Britain had Australia. Russia had Siberia. France picked French Guiana. In 1852, the deportation decree was signed. Between 1852 and 1938, seventy-four thousand convicts were sent to French Guiana. Most died within a few years, killed by heat, disease, brutality. Dry penal statistics note that the average annual mortality rate of prisoners lay between 20 and 25 per cent.

The men worked in chain gangs. They built the first roads of French Guiana. They felled the giant trees of the tropical forest. They lived in dark, moist, fetid barracks. The food was bad. The most powerful, most vicious prisoners formed gangs that raped and brutalized the weaker ones.

The Îles du Salut were better yet somehow worse. The climate was better, less hot and humid than the mainland, with a pleasant breeze from the sea. The work was easier. But the islands were the prisoners' nightmare.

"These islands are the terror of the convicts," wrote the journalist Albert Londres. "They are the ultimate pit, the deep end of the convict system." The islands meant isolation. They were oubliettes with palms.

On Île Royale, the largest island (28 hectares [69 acres]), were the administrative buildings, the wardens' houses, and about a thousand convicts living in crowded barracks.

Most prisoners worked in the laterite quarries, cutting the mottled, reddish clay that hardened on contact with air. Others built houses, planted trees, worked in the bakery, the piggery, the cowsheds. A few, the lucky ones, the most trusted, worked as houseboys for the guards, administrators and their families.

Neighbouring Île Saint-Joseph, 20 hectares (49 acres), was reserved for *les durs* (the toughs), for *les incos* (the incorrigibles), for those not yet broken in body and spirit.

The prisoners on Saint-Joseph worked chained together. At night they slept manacled to the bare boards that were their beds. They lived in limbo, utterly cut off from the outside world, shackled to their work, their beds, their island. Many died. Some went insane.

The smallest of these islands (14 hectares [35 acres]), the most feared, most notorious, was Île du Diable, (Devil's Island), known in convict lingo as "*le rocher noir*" (the Black Rock). It was the hell-on-earth reserved for political prisoners.

No one ever escaped from Devil's Island. Prisoner number 51,367, Henri Charrière, known as "Papillon" (a butterfly with spread wings was tattooed on his chest), claimed he had escaped from Devil's Island and told about that spectacular feat in his bestselling book *Papillon*, which, in 1973, was made into the eponymous movie with Steve McQueen and Dustin Hoffman.

A good story, but slightly flawed, for Charrière, a convicted murderer, had never been on or near Devil's Island. He escaped at 4:30 a.m. on September 5, 1934 from the hospital in the convict colony of Saint-Laurent-du-Maroni. That was a fact. The rest he invented.

There were several excellent reasons why no one escaped from Devil's Island. It is 15 kilometres (9 miles) from the mainland. Prisoners were watched day and night by armed guards. Swirling currents race past the island. Sharks were common near the island and may have been used to eating convicts.

Dead wardens, their wives, and many children were buried in cemeteries on Île Royale and Île Saint-Joseph. A dead convict was wrapped in a shroud, a boat took him off-shore, and he was dumped into the ocean. In the prison slang of the Salvation Islands, dead convicts were "shark food."

In the fall of 1894, a French spy in the German embassy in Paris discovered a hand-written bordereau received by Major Max von Schwartzkoppen, the German military attaché. It listed secret French documents.

Suspicion fell on Captain Alfred Dreyfus, a French general staff officer. His handwriting was similar to that on the bordereau. He had access to secret documents. And, most damning, he was a Jew.

On October 15, 1894, Dreyfus was arrested and charged with treason. The army, genuinely convinced of his guilt, expected a confession, a quick trial, conviction, banishment of the traitor to Devil's Island. End of Dreyfus. End of story.

But Dreyfus did not confess. "I am innocent!" He said it over and over and over. That worried the army. Their evidence was really quite meagre. So, to be sure, they added a bit, fabricated letters, forged a few documents. That became the "secret file."

Dreyfus was tried in camera by court martial. When the judges questioned the paltry evidence, the army produced its secret file. Assuming the papers to be genuine, the court found Dreyfus guilty. He was convicted of treason and sentenced to degradation and deportation for life. While he stood rigidly at attention, an officer of the *Garde Républicaine* ripped off his buttons and broke his sword.

The secret file with its faked but damning evidence was never shown to Dreyfus or his lawyer.

A convict ship took Dreyfus to Devil's Island. Less than a year ago, he wrote in his diary, *"Tout dans la vie semblait me sourire."* (All in life seemed to smile upon me).

Now, surrounded by mute and armed guards, he lived in a stone hut, its windows barred, alone on this "cursed island."

He felt forsaken, abandoned. "Alone!" "Alone!" That

Wrongfully convicted of treason, Captain Alfred Dreyfus was banished for life to the notorious convict colonies of French Guiana. For four years he was the lone prisoner of Devil's Island.

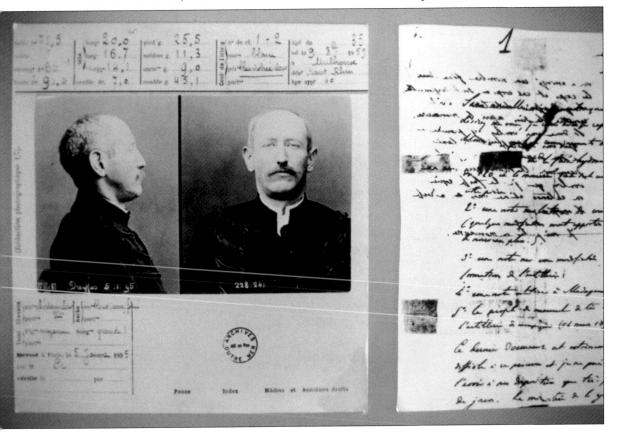

cri de coeur runs like a leitmotif through the pages of his diary.

He was not alone. His wife and brother demanded a revision. His trial and conviction, based on "secret" evidence and anti-Semitism, had been an evil, judicial farce. Prominent liberals joined the "Dreyfusards." Wild rumours swept through France and were gleefully printed by the press as fact.

One of the many extravagant stories, linking French phobias, claimed the *l'affaire Dreyfus* was a plot between the German kaiser and international Jewry to discredit the glorious army of France.

"*Vive l'armée!*" screamed the conservatives.

"*A mort les juifs!*" (Death to the Jews) howled the Parisian mob.

It became a battle between justice and glory. Either Dreyfus was guilty or the army was guilty. All Europe watched in fascination. France, at times, teetered on the brink of civil war.

In October 1896, Monsieur Lebon, minister of colonies, warned the chief of the penal system in French Guiana, "Should Dreyfus die...and you were to feed him, like the other convicts, to the sharks, everyone would say you let him escape. Embalm him and ship him back to France."

A giant joined the fray: Émile Zola, France's most famous author. Zola did not like Dreyfus nor did he care for Jews. But he believed passionately in honour and justice. Both, he felt, had been trampled by "*cette abominable affaire Dreyfus!*"

Zola wrote an open letter to Félix Faure, president of France. He summarized the entire case and then, like the thunderbolts of an enraged Zeus, he accused the guilty: "*J'accuse*" (I accuse) began each paragraph.

The letter was published on January 13, 1898 by the newspaper *L'Aurore* with a massive headline that became forever famous: "*J'accuse!*"

Right-wing violence reached such a fever pitch, Zola had to flee to England.

A court of appeals ordered a new court martial.

Dreyfus, slowly rotting on Devil's Island knew nothing of his fame or fate. Years passed in silence. The diary entries became increasingly despondent. A brilliant mathematician, he at first created clever problems and then worked out the solutions. Later, he still wrote out complex mathematical problems. But there were no more solutions. He filled pages with strange doodles.

On June 5, 1899, the commander of the islands came to Devil's Island and read to Dreyfus the order of the court. After four years of silence, a human spoke to him: "Captain Dreyfus is no longer a deported person....he resumes his rank and may put on again his uniform." Four days later the navy cruiser *Sfax* arrived to take Dreyfus back to France.

A military court, unable to admit error, found Dreyfus again guilty. He was pardoned by the president of France. Finally, in 1906, Dreyfus was exonerated by a civilian court, reinstated in the army as major and decorated with the Legion of Honour.

Others took his place on Devil's Island. The naval officer Benjamin Ullmo, found guilty in 1908 of treason, lived in the "Dreyfus House." He spent his time talking to the sharks. "I gave them names," he told the journalist Albert Londres. "They came when I called on days when I needed company." He spent fifteen years on Devil's Island.

In 1938, when deportations ended, 5,598 convicts remained in French Guiana. In 1953, the "*bagne*" was finally closed and the last surviving "*bagnards*" returned to France.

In 1971, the Îles du Salut became the property of the French National Space Agency. A cinetheodolite was installed on Île Royale to track the Ariane space rockets launched from the mainland by the European Space Agency.

On Île Royale the former main hall of the wardens has become a large restaurant with a view of nearby Devil's Island. It serves cocktails and fairly good bouillabaisse. Near it are pleasant bungalows. The convict islands of terror and suffering have become a tourist resort.

My wife, Maud, and I came to French Guiana to photograph leatherback turtles, the world's largest living reptiles and the rarest of all marine turtles. Some are 2 metres (8 feet) long. They weigh up to 907 kilograms (2,000 pounds).

Leatherback turtles are an ancient species. They have changed little in a hundred million years. Once they nested in hundreds of thousands on remote tropical beaches. In recent decades they have been slaughtered. Few remote beaches remain in our overcrowded world that are safe for 1-ton turtles. A 1998 survey showed that only 34,500 nesting female leatherback turtles were left.

One relatively safe area is a remote beach in northwest French Guiana. We spent fourteen nights there with the giant turtles.

We sat on the warm sand and waited in the humid, velvety dark of the tropical night. Crescents of foam rushed onto the beach and suddenly a turtle emerged; a massive shape, one of the last survivors of an ancient world.

Wheezing and gasping, the giant turtle struggled up the beach. We did not move. When they emerge, the turtles are skittish. One movement, a flicker of light, and they return to the sea.

Once the turtle began her ritual of reproduction, probably unchanged in millions of years, she went into trance. We could approach. She no longer noticed us.

Slowly, methodically, using her hind flippers, she dug into the sand, scooping out a nearly metre-deep, flask-shaped egg chamber. She laid about one hundred glossy-white, soft-shelled, billiard ball–sized eggs, covered the nest with sand, then did her best to hide her precious eggs by scattering sand with flailing front flippers in all directions to efface all signs of her presence. Exhausted, she returned to the sea.

Her ancestors went through the selfsame motions eons ago, when dinosaurs roamed the earth and ichthyosaurs swam in the sea. They all died out millions of years ago. Only these turtles still survive. We spent magical nights with them, filled with awe and wonder.

Powerful currents and deadly sharks isolate Devil's Island. Watched day and night by silent guards, Captain Alfred Dreyfus, innocent of any crime, spent four years on this island.

From the turtle beach we drove to Kourou, the "Space

City" of France and its European partners. About once a month a satellite is launched. The next one would be German and Kourou was full of German space scientists.

Two of the German scientists and a French colleague shared our table on the daily ship to Île Royale. They talked mostly about golf and fishing—in English.

"English is the language of space," said the Frenchman, a bit sour.

We stayed at the island *auberge*. For an extra five euro we got a room with a view over Devil's Island, separated from Île Royale by a narrow channel. Two fancy boats were anchored near Devil's Island. People were fishing. From afar, Devil's Island looked palmy and paradisiacal.

"How do I get to Devil's Island?" I asked one of the island gendarmes.

"You don't," he said.

"Why?"

"Too difficult. Too dangerous. You can photograph it from here."

"How about those boats near the island?"

"Those are rich guys from the Space Centre. Fishing. It's a great place for fishing. But they never go ashore on Devil's Island."

The next three days it rained. The Îles du Salut get more than 2 metres (7 feet) of rain per year. "*Pluie tropicale. Journée lugubre,*" (Tropical rain. Mournful day) Dreyfus often wrote in his diary.

When it cleared, I tackled the foreign legion. Soldiers of the famous French foreign legion guard the Space Centre. Some come to Île Royale to rest, relax, drink beer, fish. They had a boat.

"Can you take me to Devil's Island?" I asked.

"Naw," they said. "We're not supposed to land there. Anyway, it's too dangerous."

They joshed. "You can swim across," one suggested. "Make the sharks happy."

"Are there sharks?"

"Oh yes," they all agreed. "Lots of sharks."

Île Royale was pleasant, park-like, with palms and massive mango trees. Nervy, busy squirrel monkeys picked mangoes, took quick bites, and dropped them. Beneath the trees, agoutis—rust-coloured, hare-sized rodents—rushed to grab the falling fruit.

I photographed Guillotine Square. The stone foundations that once supported the machine of death still exist. Nearby are remnants of the tiny cells for those condemned to die. The guillotine was always set up at night. The men in the death cells could hear it being built.

It rained again. Maud and I sat on our balcony and drank wine. We were, after all, in France. I read the Dreyfus diaries and looked, from time to time, toward Devil's Island, hazy green in the pouring rain. Lovely, yet evil.

"The hours are leaden," wrote Dreyfus. "*Quelle île maudite!*" (What a cursed island!)

In 1995, sixty years after his death and a hundred years after his banishment to Devil's Island, the French army officially absolved Captain Alfred Dreyfus of treason charges.

Chapter 2

ATTU ISLAND, ALASKA, U.S.A.
Island of War: Japan versus U.S.A.

THE BATTLE OF ATTU WAS HEROIC. The Battle of Attu was horrible. The Battle of Attu was tragic and ludicrous. It was fought for possession of an island so remote, so barren, neither side really wanted it.

It was the only World War II battle fought on American soil. Japan invaded Attu. America mustered an immense invasion force to get its island back.

Attu is the westernmost of Alaska's 1,920-kilometre- (1,200-mile-) long Aleutian Islands' chain. Five time zones west of Juneau, the state's capital, it is much closer to Asia than to the American mainland, and only 400 kilometres (250 miles) from the Russian-owned Commander Islands off Siberia.

Attu is 59 kilometres (37 miles) long by 24 kilometres (15 miles) wide. In 1942, when elite Japanese troops invaded the island, only its coastline had been mapped. The mountainous, deep-valleyed interior was unknown. On the very first day of the invasion, some Japanese soldiers got lost.

Attu lies within a region that has the world's worst weather. Here the frigid air masses of the Siberian high engage the warm, humid ones of the near-permanent Aleutian low in titanic conflict. The result, according to the U.S. Coast Pilot, "is the most unpredictable [weather] in the world. Winds of up to 90 miles an hour [140 kilometres an hour] are commonplace...[and]

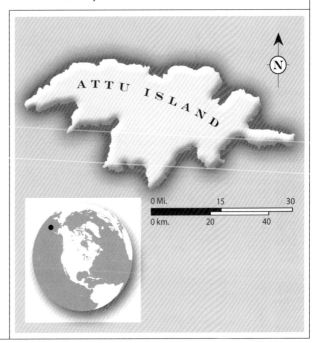

howling storms may be expected at any time during the year..."

Local winds, called williwaws, scream down valleys and mountain sides with gusts of more than 170 kilometres an hour (110 miles an hour). In spring, summer, and fall it rains. In winter it snows. Dense fog shrouds the island for days, sometimes for weeks. Attu has, on average, only eight clear days per year.

The Battle of Attu began on May 11, 1943 when the first of sixteen thousand American troops went ashore at the island's ominously named Massacre Bay. The island was defended by 2,650 Japanese soldiers. The Battle of Attu lasted nineteen days. Of the 2,650 Japanese soldiers, 2,622 died in battle or committed suicide. Only twenty-eight surrendered.

During those nineteen days of fighting, 549 American soldiers were killed and 1,148 were wounded. By some weird aberration of military logic, most of the troops sent to Attu had been trained and equipped for desert warfare. Sloshing ankle-deep through freezing, oozing, churned-up tundra muck in leaking leather boots, another 1,400 soldiers were crippled by frostbite and trench foot.

For the United States, the Battle of Attu ranked second only to the assault of Iwo Jima as the most costly for the nation. Yet it is a battle that has been nearly forgotten. Perhaps because so many died and suffered for nothing.

That cruel futility was summarized by the famous military historian Samuel Eliot Morison: "None of the operations accomplished anything of great importance or had any appreciable effect on the outcome of the war...."

A rare sunny day at usually rain-drenched Attu Island. On average, Attu has only eight clear days a year. Storms are frequent. Fog enshrouds the island for weeks. In winter, snow covers the island.

Both sides would have done well to have left the Aleutians to the Aleuts for the course of the war."

The Aleuts would certainly have agreed, for they were the first to suffer, had suffered, in fact, since they were "discovered" by Europeans.

Vitus Bering, the Danish-born explorer extraordinaire of Russia's tsars discovered the Alaskan mainland and the Aleutian Islands in 1741. On the return trip, his ship broke up on the bleak, uninhabited Commander Islands. Bering died, but survivors reached Siberia with wondrous tales of the region's sea mammal wealth and with nine hundred sea otter pelts.

When Siberia's *promyshlenniki* (fur traders), saw those pelts, their eyes glittered with greed. On the fur-hungry Chinese luxury market, each of these sea otter pelts, the densest, warmest, most luxurious fur in the world, was worth more than one hundred dollars, then the equivalent of a Russian worker's annual salary.

Using any conveyance that could reasonably be expected to float, including *shitiks* (boats made of green lumber, the planks sewn together with thong or osier withes, and caulked with moss), the fur traders rushed to the new land. One ship in three did not return.

The *promyshlenniki* robbed and enslaved the Aleuts, and sent cargo after cargo of sea otter pelts back to Siberia. In a few decades the once-free and proud Aleuts had been reduced from an estimated twenty thousand to a broken, subservient remnant of barely two thousand.

In September 1745, it was Attu's turn. The Tobolsk merchant Mikhail Nevodchikov landed with a crew of forty-five. The natives were amazed, but friendly. They sang. They danced. They welcomed the strangers with presents.

About a hundred people lived then on Attu Island, so isolated, they spoke Attuan, a distinct dialect of the Aleut language.

Peace was short-lived. The Russians demanded furs, demanded women. When the men resisted, the Russians shot them. They killed fifteen men near the southeast coast, at a place still called Murder Point. It overlooks Massacre Bay, a name that later filled U.S. troops with justified fear and foreboding.

After the killers came the missionaries. They baptized the remaining natives (twenty-seven men were left on Attu in 1774) and gave them Russian names.

In 1867, the United States bought Alaska from Russia for 7.2 million dollars. The sea otters were nearly extinct. Attu lapsed again into isolation, visited only by one ship a year.

The men fished, hunted birds, and trapped blue foxes. The women collected the abundant shellfish and dug up edible roots. Using dried, finely shredded ryegrass steeped in natural dyes, women wove baskets of such beauty, they are now worth a fortune.

In 1937, when the American biologist Victor B. Scheffer came to Attu, forty natives lived in the small village of Chichagof Harbor. "Frame houses, a school and Russian Orthodox church rested in the shadow of a great mountain. In the village we watched an old woman with a beautifully wrinkled face weaving one of the now priceless Attu baskets."

In early June of 1942, forty-one people lived on remote Attu in peaceful isolation, thirty-nine natives, an elderly white school teacher, and his wife. On June 7, a fleet of warships steamed into Massacre Bay and 1,200 crack Japanese combat troops landed on the beach.

The school teacher was shot. His wife and the terrified and bewildered natives, many of whom spoke only Attuan, were taken to an internment camp on Hokkaido. Only twenty-one survived, incidental victims of Japan's ambitious global strategy.

Admiral Isoroku Yamamoto, commander-in-chief of Japan's Imperial Fleet, had a daring plan to eliminate American naval power in the Pacific.

First, the destruction of much of the U.S. Pacific fleet by a surprise attack on Pearl Harbor.

Second, the occupation of Midway Island, to be made into a mighty Japanese air force base within easy flying distance of Hawaii.

Third, the occupation of Attu, 3,200 kilometres (2,000 miles) north of Midway. This, Yamamoto hoped, would lure the remaining American ships into the open sea. The then superior naval forces of Japan would then destroy all American ships.

With America's naval power vanquished, with Japan master of the Pacific, Yamamoto hoped to obtain a peace with the United States that would ensure the security of Japan's newly conquered Asian empire.

It might have worked. But it didn't. America won the vital Battle of Midway.

With that, Attu lost its military importance. But Japan wanted to keep it as a symbol of victory, to offset the debacle at Midway and to divert American forces. For political and propaganda reasons, the United States felt it had to reconquer Attu.

And so America and Japan sent twenty thousand men to Attu to kill and be killed in a needless battle.

The American build-up lasted months. "The hazards of surface and air navigation are greater [in the Aleutians] than in any other part of the world," wrote the historian Samuel Eliot Morison.

When American troops finally landed at Massacre Bay on May 11, 1943, top brass promised the War Department that Attu would be won in three days.

The American generals misjudged the terrible weather, the soggy terrain, and, above all, the determination of an enemy whose only choice was death with honour.

Colonel Yasuyo Yamasaki, commanding the 2,650 Japanese soldiers on Attu Island, knew there was no hope. There would be no relief, no succour, no evacuation. Imperial Command expected him and his men to do and die. To die was honourable, to surrender shameful.

The Japanese retreated to higher ground. Hidden in fog, they pinned down the advancing American soldiers with machine guns and mortar fire. Casualties mounted. American and Japanese suffered equally from cold, wind and icy rain.

"It sleeted and was extremely cold," medical Lieutenant Nebu Tatsuguchi wrote in his diary, found after the battle by American soldiers. "I am suffering from diarrhea and feel dizzy." He had studied medicine in California and had married there. He and his wife had returned to Japan in 1940.

The Battle of Attu dragged on. American troops were harnessed to the heavy guns and rope-hauled them through freezing mud up steep hillsides. Frostbite maimed the men.

The Japanese had little food left. Rations were severely cut. "Consciousness becomes vague," wrote Tatsuguchi. The Japanese killed four hundred of their wounded soldiers with lethal morphine injections.

On the night of May 29, Colonel Yamasaki, in a last desperate effort to seize U.S. supplies and guns, led his remaining one thousand soldiers in a fierce banzai attack up Engineer Hill. They nearly reached the American howitzers. Under deadly, concentrated fire, the attack slowed, and then stopped.

The Japanese retreated, regrouped. Colonel Yamasaki, sword in hand, led the final charge. A bullet killed him. The surviving five hundred Japanese soldiers held grenades to their bodies, pulled the pins, and blew themselves to pieces. Only twenty-eight Japanese soldiers surrendered.

Among those who died was medical Lieutenant Nebu Tatsuguchi. On May 29, he made a last entry in his diary: "Assembled in front of headquarters. The

Fields of lupines and the remnants of Navy Town, the great military base built on Attu Island after the defeat of the Japanese troops that occupied the island in World War II.

last assault is to be carried out. All patients in hospital were to commit suicide. Only thirty-three years of living and I am to die here. I have no regrets. Banzai to Emperor. I am grateful that I have kept the peace in my soul which Christ bestowed on me. At 6 p.m. took care of all patients with grenades. Goodbye to my beloved wife, who loved me to the last. Until we meet again, Miseka, who just became four years old. I feel sorry for you, Tokiki, born this year and never having seen your father."

After nineteen terrible days the battle ended and military crews buried the American and Japanese dead in common graves on Attu.

Nebu Tatsuguchi's wife and two children died on August 6, 1945. They lived in Hiroshima.

A short-lived city grew on Attu. For a while America's top military strategists toyed with the idea of making Attu a staging base for an invasion of Japan from the north.

Money, men, and *matériel* poured into Attu. Navy Town was built with hundreds of Quonset huts. Runways were constructed. A church was built. At one time, ten thousand servicemen were stationed on Attu.

Then the idea of invading Japan via Attu was abandoned and so was Navy Town.

The twenty-one Attu natives who survived the war never returned to their island. They were resettled on Adak, another Aleutian island.

When the biologist Victor B. Scheffer returned to Attu shortly after the war, nothing remained of the native village except "the rubble of burned and shattered homes...[and a monument] to a people who never came back."

"I will not be able to go to Attu," I told Bob Reeve, president of Reeve Aleutian Airways and an Alaska legend.

"Why not?" He had a rough voice, a weather-beaten face and wore a battered stetson in his office. He was seventy-five years old, the most famous of a special breed, the daring bush pilots of Alaska.

"I phoned the coast guard," I explained. "They say I need a permit. It may take a long time."

"Nonsense," he growled. He reached for the phone. In a minute he was past all the secretaries and was speaking to someone *very* important.

"I've got this Canadian here," he rasped. "The guy who did that big book on the Arctic. He's going to Attu tomorrow. There seems to be some problem with a permit."

Rusting remnants of war: an unexploded bomb on Attu Island. For the U.S. the Battle of Attu was, after Iwo Jima, the most costly of World War II.

He listened. "Well, yes. That's good. You'll call them, will you."

They talked a bit more. About friends, fishing, family. He hung up.

"You're on the plane to Attu tomorrow," said Bob. "You can stay at the coast guard station."

"Take Gravol," his secretary advised. "That flight can be bouncy."

It was a mail, cargo, passenger flight. I was the only passenger. After six hours in clouds, the plane banked sharply, passed over Murder Point and Massacre Bay with rusting hulks of landing craft and barges, and landed at Attu International Airport with its welcoming sign:

LAND OF THE BIRD
Attu Is., ALASKA
POP. Men: 36, Women: 0
POS. Long. 173 E, Lat. 52 N
MOST WESTERN POINT OF THE U.S.A.

In the middle of the sign squatted the colorful "Horny Bird," mascot of these isolated coast guard men.

While the men read their mail, I wandered through the public rooms of the long-range (aid to) navigation (loran) station to determine the exact position of ships or aircraft. The workrooms were off-limits to me. Apart from keeping track of U.S. ships and planes, the men presumably snooped a bit on their Soviet neighbours (this was the Cold War era).

Many rooms were decorated with explicitly erotic pinups. No wonder the poor guys were horny.

Attu, treeless like all the storm-haunted Aleutian islands, was lush, green, a deep, moist, saturated green, greener than Ireland in spring.

Now, in mid-July, the mountain tops were still snow-streaked, the slopes covered with flowers. Most days it drizzled. The light was grey, yet often luminous, a soft, even light that is ideal for flower photography.

I photographed orchids on Attu. Pure white bog orchids and rose-purple orchids were growing on the tundra. Many plants liked the shelter of moist bomb craters.

War had been good for lupines. They like disturbed ground. There had been plenty of disturbance on Attu.

The remnants of Navy Town mouldered away in a sea of lupines. It was oddly beautiful. All things metal were now a rich rust-red. Green, rust-red, the blue of lupines, the grey of weathered wood. Delicate primroses grew out of cracks of the wartime airstrip.

Snow buntings now lived in Navy Town. Its dying buildings gave them perfect shelters for their nests. A snowy owl sat on a rust-red hydrant.

Nature was slowly covering, reclaiming, dissolving the wastes of war. The dead soldiers, American and Japanese, had been exhumed and reinterred at a military cemetery near Anchorage.

I walked to Chichagof Harbor. Attu is rubber-boot country: spongy, soft, and wet. "Watch out for live shells and rusty nails," the loran station CO had told me. "And stick to roads and trails. When the fog rolls in, it's so thick you can't see your boots."

The Aleut village had vanished. A small brass plaque set into a cement pedestal read:

ATTU VILLAGE
"In this village the Aleuts made their home."

Now flowers grew on the site of homes and people that had been destroyed by war.

Engineer Hill, where thousands fought and died was still covered with shells, bomb craters, and with jagged bits of metal that had once torn young men apart.

Some of the men from the loran station collected and polished the brass shell casings and made from them beautiful ashtrays.

Near the top of Engineer Hill the U.S. navy erected a simple monument to Colonel Yamasaki who "was killed in action near this point."

In the lush, rank grass near Massacre Bay lay many barrels and bombs: debris of war, slowly rusting away. Eider ducks now nested in the shelter of some of the bombs.

Chapter 3

SKRAELING ISLAND, HIGH ARCTIC, CANADA
The Island of Inuit and Vikings

IN 1867, THE UNITED STATES bought Alaska from Russia for 7.2 million dollars. Most Americans know that.

In 1930, Canada acquired the rights to more than 259,000 square kilometres (100,000 square miles) of its present High Arctic from Norway. It paid sixty-seven thousand dollars. Very few Canadians know that.

The basic rule of exploration was "finders keepers." Vitus Bering discovered Alaska in 1741 and claimed it for Russia. Jacques Cartier discovered Canada in 1534 and claimed it for France. James Cook explored Australia in 1770 and claimed it for Great Britain. Natives came with the real estate.

Between 1898 and 1902 the Norwegian Otto Sverdrup explored and mapped southern Ellesmere Island and many adjacent islands that are now known collectively as the Sverdrup Islands. He took possession of this region, an area larger than Great Britain, in the name of the King of Norway.

Canada was upset. It did not want to have a Norwegian annex in its arctic attic. Fortunately for Canada, Norway was not really that keen on owning such an enormous chunk of remote, barren Arctic. It offered Canada a Solomonic solution: pay the cost of Sverdrup's expedition and the High Arctic is all yours.

Canada, very parsimonious in those days, hummed, hawed, and dickered for ten years. Finally, in 1930, it paid the sixty-seven thousand dollars and became sole owner of its High Arctic (and all the oil and natural gas it may contain).

Remnants of a Thule-culture house on Skraeling Island and the skull of a bowhead whale. More than twenty Norse artifacts, including parts of chain-mail armour, were discovered by archeologists in these ancient Inuit homes.

While exploring the east coast of Ellesmere, Sverdrup discovered a small island in Alexandra Fiord and gave it the odd name of Skraeling Island.

Skraeling is an Old Norse word, a contemptuous term meaning "dwarfish, troll-like people." That's what the Vikings called the Inuit. What the Inuit called the Vikings has not been recorded.

The name intrigued one of Canada's foremost archaeologists, Peter Schledermann, and, in 1977, he visited Skraeling Island "to ascertain Sverdrup's reason for choosing this name."

"Almost immediately the answer lay before us: clusters of ruins of ancient Thule-culture winter houses built of sod, stone and whalebone," wrote Schledermann.

A thousand years ago many Thule-culture Inuit had lived on this remote High Arctic island, less than 1,280 kilometres (800 miles) from the North Pole.

It was, said Schledermann, "one of the most interesting archaeological sites in North America...with the northernmost major prehistoric settlement so far discovered."

That was a surprise. But a much greater surprise awaited Schledermann. In the summer of 1978, while excavating with meticulous care one of the forty ancient Inuit house sites on Skraeling Island, his trowel struck metal: two slightly rusted, interlocking rings.

"In more than 15 years of archeological exploration I can recall no greater prize," wrote Schledermann. "The rings had obviously come from a suit of chain mail, the typical armor of medieval Europe."

Soon more Norse artifacts were discovered in the ancient Inuit houses: knife blades, Viking boat rivets, a woodworker's plane from about 1200 CE and pieces of woollen cloth dated at about 1250 CE. Schledermann believes the Vikings may have reached Skraeling Island nine hundred years ago and traded there with Inuit.

The Vikings probably made that risky trip through immense pack ice fields to the High Arctic to obtain from the Inuit there something of immense value: unicorn horns.

In China, India, the Middle East, North Africa and, above all, in medieval and Renaissance Europe genuine unicorn horn was much more

SKRAELING ISLAND

0 ft   2000 ft

0m   500m

precious than gold. It had a marvellous, magic property: it could detect and neutralize poison.

To be poisoned was a major professional hazard for princes, prelates, and potentates. Poison was a favourite means employed by restive subjects to get rid of unpopular rulers. Princes poisoned rivals and poison smoothed the road to power for ambitious and greedy relatives.

Marie de Medici (1573–1642), queen of France, employed a personal poisoner, an unctuous Florentine with blotched hands and a cold serpent's smile. The Medicis were a brilliant but lethal family. It was said that Marie's father, Francis I, Grand-duke of Tuscany, was poisoned by his brother, the Cardinal Ferdinand, and her mother died fifteen hours later.

To evade death by poison, rulers craved the one perfect antidote, the *alexipharmic sans pareil*: the horn of the unicorn. "Genuine unicorn [horn] is good against all poison," declared the Swiss scientist and physician Konrad von Gesner in 1551. "Experience proves that anyone having taken poison...recovered good health on immediately taking a little unicorn horn." These horns were among the most prized possessions of poison-prone princes and they paid fortunes for them.

The eating utensils of the kings of France were made of unicorn horn. A German prince, the margrave of Bayreuth, paid "six hundred thousand rix-dollars" for his unicorn horn. The unicorn horn owned by Queen Elizabeth I was valued at ten thousand pounds sterling, a sum that, in sixteenth-century Britain, would buy an estate complete with castle. The world's wealthiest ruler, the sultan of Turkey, sent twelve unicorn horns as a munificent gift to His Most Catholic Majesty King Philip II of Spain (1527-1598).

Unicorn horn sold for up to ten times its weight in gold and many rulers bought them as a sort of super-expensive life insurance.

Artists loved the unicorn and often painted it, usually as a gallant white steed from whose forehead sprouts a single spiraled horn. There are unicorns in the paintings of Raphael, Rubens, and Hans Holbein, and Leonordo da Vinci made a lovely sketch of the animal. Da Vinci also wrote a treatise on how to capture unicorns. His main advice: use a virgin as bait.

There was one problem. While the belief in the unicorn was ancient and universal and it was often depicted in art, its existence had to be taken largely on faith. The horns were sold by famous physicians. But the animal was more mythic than real. However, the scientist Konrad von Gesner argued in 1551, that the unicorn "must be on earth or else its horn would not exist."

Unicorn horns certainly existed. Hundreds, perhaps thousands, can still be seen in the treasuries, palaces and museums of the world. A unicorn horn is quite distinctive: an ivory horn, straight, torqued and tapered, and up to ten feet long. It is the only spiraled horn in all creation.

Nearly all "genuine" unicorn horns have one thing in common: they are, in fact, the sinisterly spiraled tusks of male narwhals, small whales of the High Arctic. The unicorn-narwhal connection was one of the best-kept trade secrets of all time. Most narwhal tusks (unicorn horns) came from Greenland. Vikings hunted narwhals. Most tusks, though, they obtained from the kayak-equipped Inuit, the expert narwhal hunters. It was to acquire these precious "unicorn" tusks that Vikings made the long and risky trip to the High Arctic to trade with the natives on Skraeling Island.

The Vikings were raiders, traders, explorers, settlers. In 862 CE, they discovered Iceland and soon settled it. In 986 CE, Erik the Red left Iceland with fourteen ships and four hundred settlers, their cattle and their chattel, and founded two settlements in the relatively mild southwesternmost part of Greenland.

Ivory, the "white gold," lured Vikings north to the High Arctic: the tusks of walrus and the spiraled ivory tusks of male narwhal, sold in Europe as the wonder-working unicorn horn.

The colonists were subsistence farmers and hunters. In about 1100 CE, when the colony was at its peak, it had three hundred farms, sixteen churches, a cathedral at Gardar, the bishop's seat, a nunnery, a monastery, and altogether about three thousand people.

The Greenland Vikings imported wood, grain, iron, clothes, malt, wine, church vestments, and such trinkets and adornments as they could afford.

They exported fox furs, sealskins and seal oil, dried fish, butter, cheese, and a heavy woollen cloth called *wadmal*, all goods of low value. The real treasures of their land and sea, coveted and paid for in gold and silver by European nobles and Arab princes, were live polar bears and polar bear skins; walrus tusks and walrus hides (the best material for ship's cables); live gyrfalcon, the magnificent white falcon of the Arctic (for which, even now, oil-rich Middle Eastern sheiks and princes pay up to a hundred thousand dollars); and, most precious and rare, the narwhal tusks from the High Arctic that were sold as unicorn horns.

To obtain these costly vital goods, Vikings rowed and sailed far north to lands they called Nordrsetur, a region shrouded in secrecy and mystery. While the Vikings were usually volubly boastful about their travels and exploits, they were mute about their trips to Nordrsetur. It would have been disastrous had the truth leaked out that the marvellous unicorn horns were, in fact, merely the teeth of an arctic whale.

The Icelandic writer Bjørn Jonsson (1574–1656) in his *Annals of Greenland*, based on old sources, wrote, "All the landowners in Greenland had great ships built for voyages to Nordrsetur...furnished with all manner of hunting gear." In 1266, they reached a region "with many glaciers and seals and white bears. They returned with a valuable cargo of live polar bears, sealskins and walrus ivory."

Narwhal tusks were never mentioned. But it is known that two *knorrir*, the large (15–18-metre [50–60-foot]) Viking trading ships carrying cargoes of "unicorn horns" from Greenland were wrecked upon Iceland's coast, one in 1126, the other in 1242. Some of the "very precious dentes balenarum [whale teeth]" were recovered. All were "inscribed in runic letters with an indelible red gum so that each sailor might know his own at the end of the voyage."

The Vikings were perfectly able to catch or kill polar bears and slow-moving walruses. But their boats were not suitable for hunting the shy, fast-swimming narwhals. They were also pressed for time. To reach the narwhals' summering grounds in northernmost Baffin Bay and in Kane Basin between Ellesmere Island and Greenland, the Vikings had to sail and row 1,920 kilometres (1,200 miles) or more from their south-Greenland settlements.

The Vikings' sailing ships or six-oared wooden boats were too slow and noisy for successful narwhal hunting. The Inuit hunted narwhals with fast, sleek, silent kayaks. They ate the whales and traded the tusks to the Vikings for the things their land lacked and that consequently were very precious to them: wood and metal.

On Skraeling Island the remains of long-ago whale hunts are everywhere: the scattered, often moss-covered bones of bowhead whales and narwhal. On this remote High Arctic island the tall, blond, bearded Scandinavian Vikings met the people they called "Skraelings" and described as "swarthy...men with wiry hair. They had large eyes and broad cheeks." They probably traded on Skraeling Island: European metal for High Arctic "unicorn horns."

In one of the ancient Inuit ruins on Skraeling Island, the archaeologist Peter Schledermann found "a small carved wooden head" dated from about 1100 CE. "Although plainly Inuit in style," wrote Schledermann, "the face to me seems strongly Nordic. It is as if the carver had seen a Norseman with his own eyes and sought to capture that startling vision forever in wood."

I spent part of three summers camped on a raised beach at Alexandra Fiord looking out toward Skraeling Island. Jim Allan, director of British Columbia–based Ecosummer Expeditions, had asked me to accompany his small groups of High Arctic tourists as arctic naturalist–historian-photographer.

For me, the timing was perfect. I was doing research for my book on narwhals (published in 1993 as *The Narwhal: Unicorn of the Arctic Sea*). I had spent months studying the history and provenance of "unicorn horns" (narwhal tusks) in the treasuries of Europe. And I had lived for six months with the Polar Inuit of northwest Greenland, now the northernmost people on earth and, quite possibly, descendants of the Inuit who, ten centuries ago, had lived on Skraeling Island. Like the Skraeling Islanders, the Polar Inuit were expert sea mammal hunters, their main prey seals, walruses, and whales, especially narwhals.

Alexandra Fiord is as far north of Montreal, where I live, as Paris, France is to the east of it. We flew six hours by jet from Montreal to Resolute on Cornwallis Island, hub of air traffic in the Far North. From there we continued north for another three hours by Twin Otter, a powerful, dual-engine aircraft, the workhorse of the Arctic.

We crossed Devon Island, which long ago I had traversed by dog team, and Jones Sound where I had once spent weeks with Inuit who hunted polar bears. Beneath us was an empty land, Ellesmere Island; austere and majestic, its ice caps and glaciers glittering in the sun. Toward the east, in the distance, we saw the mighty ice cap of Greenland.

We came to an abrupt stop on the bumpy tundra airstrip. Below us, near the beach, stood the white-painted houses of what had long been the northernmost police station in the world. The buildings, now unoccupied, are still owned and maintained by the Royal Canadian Mounted Police.

In 1926, to emphasize Canada's authority over the High Arctic, the RCMP built two posts on the east coast of Ellesmere Island, one on the Bache Peninsula (closed in 1933), the other at Alexandra Fiord. For the Mounties and their Inuit assistants, standing guard for Canada in the farthest north was a lonely life, broken only by the brief annual visit of a supply ship.

The region, we quickly found, is still rich in the animals that were once the ultimate luxury and status symbol of medieval Europe and the Middle East and were sold there by Vikings. Polar bears, fortunately for us since we lived in tents, did not come near us. But just south of us, at Cape Faraday, Peter Schledermann "had 29 visits from polar bears during our final two weeks" of archaeological work.

Gyrfalcon, the largest of all falcons, nested on a cliff ledge of a sphinx-shaped island in Alexandra Fiord. These were the nearly pure white birds that were once so precious and prestigious only emperors, kings, and princes of the church were allowed to have them.

Herds of massive, madder-brown walruses lolled and lazed in dense groups upon the ice floes. As our Zodiac boats passed them, they stared at us with puzzled hauteur, their ivory tusks shining in the soft light of the midnight sun. The Vikings paid their tithes to the Holy See in walrus ivory and sold tons of it in Europe and the Middle East to be carved into chess sets and madonnas, crozier handles for Christian bishops, and sword hilts for Muslim princes.

We often visited Skraeling Island, made famous when Dr. Peter Schledermann wrote a long article about the "Eskimo and Viking Finds in the High Arctic" published in the May 1981 issue of *National Geographic*. Ten years later, Dr. Schledermann and Dr. Karen McCullough, both of the Arctic Institute of North America, were still excavating the winter houses that had been part of the northernmost village on earth.

"Why Skraeling Island?" I asked Dr. Schledermann.

"Sod," he said. "Lots of sod to build their houses. And they were close to the Flagler polynya, an arctic oasis of open water, very rich in sea mammals."

They had eaten well. Bones were everywhere on Skraeling Island. Most numerous, said Schledermann, were seal and walrus bones. Then narwhals, and finally the big bones of bowhead whales.

Narwhals were important to the Inuit. Dried narwhal sinew was the thread they used to sew fur clothing and the seal-skin covers of their kayaks. They and their sled dogs ate the dark narwhal meat and the energy-rich, pinkish blubber. Narwhal skin, called *muktuk*, was a special treat: crunchy, nut-flavoured and richer in vitamin C per unit of weight than lemons or oranges.

"We find few things made of narwhal ivory," said Schledermann. "Narwhal ivory is brittle. The Inuit preferred the fine-grained, dense, strong, walrus ivory. We've found a staggering amount of things made of walrus ivory: tools and hunting weapons, toys for their children, and carvings of animals and humans."

The narwhal tusks that were of little value to them, the Inuit may have traded to those strange blond, bearded men who came from the south in large wooden boats. They brought wood and metal that were as treasure to the Inuit. And they acquired those spiraled ivory narwhal tusks that they sold for gold as the magic horns of unicorns.

Narwhals are still common near Skraeling Island. I sat on a hill on Skraeling Island in mid-August. The brief summer was nearly over. The night was gloomy, silent, the light, a soft bluish-grey. Soft snow fell on the ancient Thule-culture houses. Walruses, squabbling on packed ice floes, bellowed in the distance.

Suddenly I heard the distinctive, plosive *pooff, pooff, pooff,* of breathing narwhals: sixteen whales were swimming past Skraeling Island, their heart-shaped flukes rising and falling in smooth cadence, the males' ivory tusks flashing in the dark water.

The whales were safe. The cold climate of the Little Ice Age that destroyed the Greenland Vikings also forced the Inuit to leave the highest Arctic. By about 1600, no Inuit were left on Ellesmere Island. Their stone-, sod-, and whale-bone-house ruins are still on Skraeling Island along with Viking wood, wool, and metal objects from a long-ago era when Vikings and Inuit met and traded in Canada's High Arctic.

Chapter 4

KOMODO ISLAND, INDONESIA
The Island of Dragons

THERE ARE DRAGONS on Komodo Island, Chinese fishermen claimed centuries ago. They were afraid of Komodo, a small volcanic island east of Java in Indonesia, and rarely landed on it.

The Chinese have a thing about dragons, people said, and paid no attention. Still, rumours persisted and finally, in 1910, a Dutch colonial officer visited Komodo, one of a chain of islands known as the Lesser Sundas, surrounded by powerful and dangerous ocean currents.

The Chinese had been right. Giant, prehistoric-looking lizards lived on Komodo. The Dutchman shot one of the "dragons" and sent its skin and skeleton to Java, where Major P.A. Ouwens, director of the zoological museum in Buitenzorg (now Bogor) published a description of the animal and gave it its scientific name: *Varanus komodoensis*.

It is, in fact, the world's largest lizard: a giant, ancient, and primitive monitor lizard. It really should be called Komodo monitor, but soon after its discovery it was dubbed the "Komodo dragon" and the apt and catchy name has stuck.

Fortunately, shortly after their discovery in 1910, the dragons received total protection from native rulers and Dutch colonial authorities. In 1980, Indonesia created Komodo National Park and the great lizards, regarded as national treasures, are protected by park rangers.

Perhaps more importantly, the dragons have no commercial value. The skins of adults are scarred, gravelly-coarse, lacklustre, and full of osteoderms, speckles of bone calcium in the skin that make the scaly hides valueless for handbags or shoes.

Today, about five thousand dragons live on the mountainous hammer-shaped 252-square-kilometre (98-square-mile) Komodo Island, on the neighbouring and much smaller Rinca and Gili Montang islands, and on the southwest coast of the island of Flores.

Adult dragons are powerful, deadly predators, and fast, active hunters; not the passive, lazy carrion-eaters of early stories. The maximum length is about 3 metres (10 feet). They weigh up to 136 kilograms (300 pounds), and much more after a meal, for Komodo dragons are mighty eaters. Given the chance, a 91-kilogram (200-pound) dragon can devour 68 kilograms (150 pounds) of meat and bone at a single meal.

They eat fast. "I once saw...a 2.5-metre [8-foot] female [dragon] weighing 59 kilograms [110 pounds] at the time, swallow a 31-kilogram [68-pound] wild boar in 17 minutes," wrote University of Florida zoologist Walter Auffenberg, the foremost expert on Komodo dragons.

Their main prey are stocky, coarse-haired Sunda sambar deer and wild boar. They can kill 680-kilogram (1,500-pound) feral water buffalos and, on Rinca Island, they kill feral horses.

On rare occasions, Komodo dragons kill and eat humans. While my wife, Maud, and I lived on Komodo Island, a schoolteacher on neighbouring Rinca, gathering wood in the forest, was attacked by a dragon with its typical lightning lunge from ambush.

The first bite ripped out much of the teacher's thigh. He slashed at the giant lizard with his parang, the heavy machete-like Malayan knife, and the lizard fled. Prompt medical attention and massive doses of antibiotics saved his life, but he is forever crippled.

Komodo dragons are opportunistic feeders. Humans are not normally on their menu, but if they are hungry, and the chance presents itself, humans become prey. Over the years, several Komodo men, women, and, above all, children have been killed and eaten by the dragons. And they have killed at least one tourist.

In 1974, the Swiss baron Rudolf von Reding-Biberegg went to see the dragons with a group of tourists. The seventy-eight-year-old stopped to rest. The others walked on. They never saw him again. Only his camera was found and a slashed leather strap.

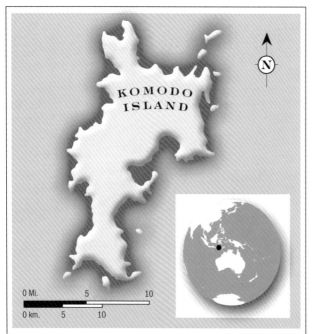

There is a village on the island, Kampong Komodo, with about five hundred worried inhabitants. They are descendants of convicts banished in the sixteenth century to the dragon island from the large island of Flores.

The colonists, terrified of the giant, man-eating lizards, built their village on high posts and as near to the sea as possible. Ladders, too narrow and steep for adult dragons to climb, lead up to the houses.

Attracted by food smells and fish remains, the dragons frequently come to the village. Mothers snatch small children away and sometimes bang pots and pans to chase away the wandering dragons. Generally, though, the villagers are very casual about their reptilian visitors. Walking dragons, they say, rarely attack. It's the hidden ones in the forest, waiting in ambush near deer trails and human paths that are potentially deadly. They lunge, snap, and rip. They usually maim. Their septic saliva kills.

One gruesome spectacle has been abolished. For some years, whenever tourist groups arrived, usually from cruise ships, they were taken by park rangers to see the dragons. Led and followed by guards with stout forked sticks, and accompanied by a bleating sacrificial goat, the tourists walked for half an hour to a steep-banked dry riverbed.

Below, the dragons waited. Above, guards cut the goat's throat and then threw it down to the dragons. It was, and was meant to be, a thrilling spectacle for well-tipping, camera-clicking visitors. It thrilled some, but horrified others, especially tourist children who had been petting the goat, and that grisly show has now been scrapped.

To keep the dragons interested and in the open where tourists can see and photograph them, guards do feed the animals from time to time with fish offal from the village, the odd dead dog, or a shot deer. Since a dragon only needs one good meal a month, they don't mind waiting at places where they are fed.

A long time ago, Komodo dragons also killed and ate elephants. Dwarf elephants! During the Pleistocene, two species of miniature elephants lived on Komodo and the neighbouring islands and, scientists believe, were then a main prey for the dragons. Even dwarf elephants are large and heavy. These two species were about 1.5 metres (5 feet) high at the shoulder and weighed about 680 kilograms (1,500 pounds)—as much as a water buffalo. Both species of island dwarf elephants are extinct. Now, the dragons eat anything they can catch and kill, from grasshoppers to buffalo. Their main prey is deer and boar.

Komodo dragons are survivors from the age when giant reptiles roamed and ruled the earth. Nearly all became extinct, except a few, like turtles, tortoises, crocodiles, and Komodo dragons. Now mammals rule the earth. But no mammalian predator powerful enough to kill or compete with the dragons ever settled on Komodo Island. There, the dragons continue to rule supreme.

We found the dead deer at dawn. It lay in a thicket where it had died during the night. The right hind leg was deeply gashed.

"Ora," said our guide, Emanuel Jeranu, "the dragon did that," using the local Mangarrai-dialect name for the Komodo dragon. In the early morning heat of the tropics, the carcass was beginning to bloat. We dragged it into a grassy clearing in the forest and waited. The air was still, the heat oppressive,

About four thousand dragons live on remote Komodo Island, Indonesia. Discovered by Dutch explorers in 1910, they are the largest lizards on earth.

full of the monotonous susurration of cicadas. High in the treetops screamed a gang of yellow-crested cockatoos.

Minutes later, guided by its phenomenal sense of smell, a Komodo dragon lumbered out of the dense underbrush near the clearing; great power in slow motion, its massive, triangular, armour-plated head held low, its rough, pebbly skin clay-grey, the powerfully muscled legs armed with long, black, sharp sickle-shaped claws, its long, forked, pink tongue sliding in and out of its mouth like a pale flame, testing the air. The monitor was a vision from ages long past, or straight out of Jurassic Park.

The great dragon advanced slowly, cautiously. It disregarded us completely. Its whole interest was focused on the dead deer. It flickered its tongue over the carcass, walked around it, tested it, then finally bit into the hindquarters of the deer, and spread its front legs for added power. The dragon jerked violently and at the same time sliced skin and meat with short, slightly curved, scalpel-sharp teeth with serrated cutting edges, teeth that, according to dragon expert Walter Auffenberg, "bear greater resemblance to those of...carnosaurian dinosaurs than to the teeth of living reptiles and mammals." The great lizard ripped, cut, and gulped huge chunks of meat and skin. It was in a hurry, for already other dragons were approaching.

It had taken weeks of walking before we found a just-killed deer and watched a gathering of dragons.

We had flown from Bali to the island of Flores and travelled from there on a cheap but crowded inter-island ferry to Komodo. The island looked rugged, its high coast pleated into sharp ridges and deep valleys, the valleys green, the ridges dry and sienna-brown.

We rented a room from the parks department. The head warden, a heavyset, dark-haired man was gruff at first. He'd had it with visitors, their endless questions and demands. Later, he was charming and helpful.

Steep, dragon-proof stairs led up to our thatched bungalow. The room was basic: a thin mattress on the floor, a table, two plastic chairs, a cracked mirror on the wall. Everything was covered with a fine, light-brown layer of termite dust.

We were not alone. "Something's eating our soap," Maud said. The bar was grooved by narrow, sharp incisors.

"Mice," I explained. "They love to eat soap."

That was fine. Maud grew up in Indonesia. She doesn't mind mice. Unfortunately, something was eating the mice.

Early one morning, a few days after we arrived, our resident boa, hunting mice on the roof rafters, slipped and landed with a squishy plop on the floor two feet from Maud's head. Maud is terrified of snakes. I've rarely seen her move so fast. The snake, a bit dazed by the fall, lay quietly in a heap, still holding its captured mouse. I picked it up, the dark shiny skin silky smooth, and carried snake plus prey outside.

"There are snakes in our room!" Maud complained to the head warden.

"Yes," he said in an indifferent, "so-what" tone. "They catch mice."

"One snake fell from the roof," Maud said. "It nearly hit me."

Now the warden seemed concerned. "Was the snake hurt?" he asked.

Maud got no sympathy. "In the houses there are only good snakes," the warden said. "They catch mice. You have cats. We have snakes."

"Emanuel tells me you are not afraid of dragons," the chief warden told me.

"Not with Emanuel around," I said.

We had a perfect guide. Emanuel had been a park ranger for fifteen years. The dragons were his life. He admired them, knew their behaviour, loved to talk about them. He was very protective since he knew his salary would cease if his client was eaten.

Like all rangers, Emanuel carried a stout, forked stick to ward off an attacking lizard. He rarely used it. "If you are careful, nothing happens," he kept repeating.

But even with all his care and experience we exposed ourselves frequently to potential attacks. Hidden among brush, the earth-coloured, log-like lizards are extremely difficult to spot. On many occasions I saw the dragon at the last moment, at three feet or less, and stared startled into the black, unblinking eyes of the hidden animal, my adrenalin level soaring.

But nothing happened. In all the weeks, not one of the dragons in ambush attacked us. And dragons in the open, basking in the morning sun, were amazingly tolerant and indifferent to our presence. I knelt a few feet in front of them. They only glanced at me. We touched the rough, granular skin. They did not budge. Not once did they assume the typical threat posture of an angry dragon: standing with lowered head, back arched, eyes glaring, the short, thick, powerful tail turned aside to slash abruptly, like a scythe, at the enemy.

"They can break your leg," said Emanuel.

When one of the great lizards walked directly toward me with a typical bow-legged, swinging motion, its terrifying appearance and my knowledge that these seemingly slow, sluggish lizards can accelerate in an instant to a top speed of 5.6

metres per second (18 feet per second) invariably broke my nerve and I ran.

An angry dragon is impressive. We were walking from one valley to another through dense, scratchy brush, when we heard a violent hissing, like an old-time locomotive letting off steam. It was an unreceptive female dragon being courted by a large male. He approached. She arched her back and hissed. He flickered his tongue over her side and hip. She hissed louder and lashed out with her tail. He tried to mount her, but she turned abruptly, raked him with sharp claws, and he backed off.

If mating is successful, the female lays an average of eighteen large (about the weight of hen's eggs) smooth, leathery-shelled eggs. She digs a burrow to hide her eggs. They hatch after about eight months and the hatchlings head instantly for the nearest tree, for the number one enemy of baby dragons is cannibalistic adult dragons.

The young are beautiful: lithe, long-tailed, with dark, alert, shining eyes. Their snake-smooth skin is flecked in orange, yellow, black and white, a cryptic colour pattern that blends to perfection with the light-dappled foliage and bark of trees. They eat insects, small lizards, geckos, and occasionally leave their arboreal havens to hunt grasshoppers on the ground. There, they are shy and skittish and with good reason. One that I followed was suddenly attacked by two racing six-foot adults. The baby dragon zipped up a tree and I jumped aside.

When they are one or two years old and about 1 metre (3 feet) long, the juveniles leave the trees, eat carrion when they can find it, and hunt mice, rats, and snakes, including the many poisonous snakes that are common on Komodo Island.

The dragons reach sexual maturity when they are about five years old and 2 metres (6 feet) long. They are massive and can no longer climb trees. They hunt primarily large animals.

The adult dragons we watched were active in daytime and slept all night. Komodo is just south of the equator. The sun sets at about 6:30 p.m., and at 7:30 p.m. the dragons fell into a deep sleep. They sleep so soundly, that Auffenberg "obtained tick samples from their skin, attached plastic bands to their toes, moved their feet and nails, took temperatures from their skin surfaces" without wakening the dragons.

They rise before dawn, walk slowly to a favourite basking area, lie spread-eagled and soak up the warming sun. Once warm, they go into hiding near a game trail or amble slowly through the underbrush, then dash ahead to catch a lizard, snake, or rat.

Long sleeps, slow movements, raising and lowering body temperature as required, make it possible for the Komodo dragon to survive on about one-tenth of the energy required by a mammalian predator of comparable size.

A Komodo dragon needs, on average, only a half kilogram (a pound) of meat a day and a meal a month will keep a dragon alive. But, given the opportunity, their meals are enormous. They eat with ravenous rapidity at the rate of 2 kilograms (5 pounds) per minute and can consume 80 per cent of their weight in one meal. They have been described as "super-efficient eating machines."

Deer have a fatal habit of following favourite paths. The dragons lie in ambush near these trails. The typical attack is a lightning lunge, a powerful ripping, cutting bite that often severs the Achilles tendon and instantly cripples the deer.

The dragon does not hold its prey. The deer flees, but loss of blood and severe, rapidly spreading septicemia caused by the dragon's bacteria-swarming saliva, will usually kill it within an hour or two. The great lizard, its long tongue flickering along the scent trail follows the doomed deer. Their sense of smell is phenomenal. "The greatest proven distance from which we have attracted lizards to bait is approximately 11 kilometres [7 miles]," wrote Auffenberg.

The dead deer, consequently, attracts not only the dragon that slew it, but dragons from far and wide and they usually consume a 181-kilogram (400-pound) stag, provided it lies in the shade, in less than four hours. Dragons eat the entire prey: skin, meat, intestines, hoofs, bones, head. Only the sharp deer antlers remain, and the head of an adult water buffalo is too big to swallow.

This rapid and total consumption of prey foiled our efforts to see feeding dragons. Drenched in sweat, Emanuel and I walked for weeks and weeks and never found a kill, only the trampled, bloody areas where prey had recently been eaten and nearby bloated dragons, resting and digesting. Until the day when we found the dead deer at dawn and dragged it into a clearing in the forest.

The first dragon at the deer carcass ripped, sliced, and gulped chunks of meat with rapid efficiency. Dragons don't bother to chew. It was one of the largest dragons in the area, about 2 metres (8 feet) long. A second dragon approached. It was smaller, slimmer, and very cautious. It eased in on the opposite side of the feeding lizard, touched the carcass with its tongue, then bit and cut.

After an hour, four dragons of various sizes were eating the deer. They ignored each other. They neither threatened nor hissed. They sneezed often and loudly, licked their blood-smeared lips, and then ate again with fierce urgency.

Normally they would have quickly devoured the entire deer. But since we had,

with malice aforethought, dragged the dead deer into a large open area, the toiling dragons overheated rapidly in the broiling sun and soon all four had to stop eating. They walked to the nearest shaded area and lay there, mouths wide open, panting.

Flicking its long, forked tongue, a Komodo dragon tests the air for smells that will lead the huge lizard to prey or to carrion.

No sooner had the large dragons left to cool their overheated bodies, than a whole bevy of minor dragons appeared. They obviously had waited nearby for this opportunity and now they came running. This is a disconcerting aspect of dragon watching. They blend so well with their environment that they appear and vanish with startling abruptness.

The smaller animals lacked the strength to sever large pieces. Bracing their sharp-clawed forefeet against the carcass, they ripped off bits of meat. They were distinctly nervous and when one of the large dragons lumbered back to the feast, the smaller animals scattered and vanished.

In a fearsome display of power, the large dragon twisted the hind leg, now nearly stripped of meat, jerked violently backwards a dozen times, tore the entire limb from the body, and swallowed it.

In the afternoon, sated and sizzling, all big dragons rested in the shade and finally a few juveniles came to feed, quick and nervous. They pulled off shreds of meat, tendons and sinews, stripping the bones. Two Brahminy kites sat in a nearby tree but did not dare to come to the carcass because of our presence. Jungle crows, less shy, hopped in to eat the spilled paunch content and coagulated blood, startling the small, nervous lizards with their abrupt movements.

In the bluish haze of evening, the large dragons returned to demolish the remains of the carcass. They wrenched the ribs loose and swallowed them. They broke the spinal column and gulped it down. One took the head and attached neck vertebrae and dragged his trophy into a thicket. There were sharp cracks as the dragon somehow broke the antlers off.

I peered cautiously into the dense, tangled brush and there, pushing himself up, was the dragon, straining with all his power to swallow the entire head of the deer. That was the end of the dragons' feast. Thus had dinosaurs hunted and feasted millions of years ago. Our dragons went to sleep and we walked through the dark forest back to our camp.

Chapter 5

KODLUNARN ISLAND, CANADA
The Arctic Island of Golden Hopes

O N MAY 31, 1578, in the twentieth year of the reign of Queen Elizabeth I and eighty-six years after Columbus discovered America, a fleet of fifteen ships left England bound for a tiny arctic island that the Inuit to this day call Kodlunarn (the white man's island). It was the largest arctic expedition of all time and the lure was gold.

The queen herself and several of her noble courtiers had invested heavily in this venture to the 6-hectare (15-acre) island in the remote Arctic. The Elizabethans called Kodlunarn Island (in today's Frobisher Bay, Baffin Island), the Countess of Warwick Island and on it, they believed, was enough gold, "to satisfy all the gold gluttons in the world."

It was Canada's first mining venture, the first gold rush, the first expedition to what is now the Canadian Arctic. It was also North America's first great mining fraud. The "gold ore" quarried on Kodlunarn Island by Cornish miners with "great

travail" and for the miserly wage of ten shillings per month, was worthless. It was, in fact, amphibolite flecked with mica. It glittered, but it was not gold.

It had all begun, three years before, in 1576, as quite a different quest: England's first attempt to find an arctic Northwest Passage to the immense wealth of China and the Spice Islands of the Pacific. Spain and Portugal had pioneered the southern routes around Africa and South America to the wealth of the East and

now, with overwhelming power and overweening pride, claimed sole rights to the southern passages.

Elizabethan England's mariners and merchant adventurers, busy, bustling, and expanding, wanted a share of the far-eastern wealth. One man who believed that there was a "new and nearer passage to Cataya [China]," was Martin Frobisher, a tough, gruff captain of limited education but great daring. His spelling was atrocious but his seamanship was superb. According to his shipmate and chronicler of all three arctic voyages, George Best, Frobisher told friends that "a voyage [to China] was not only possible by the Northwest, but also...easie to bee performed."

That erroneous belief was based on optimism and ignorance, but Frobisher was certainly the right man to try the near-impossible. Born in 1539 to a family of Yorkshire gentry, he was raised by an uncle, Sir John York, a London merchant-adventurer busy in the Africa trade. Young Frobisher was fifteen when he joined his first trading venture to West Africa. A crew of 140 men left London; only forty returned. Fever and fighting killed the rest.

By age twenty, Frobisher was captain. He switched from trading to raiding and piracy. At twenty-five, he was one of England's most famous pirates; so notorious, Frobisher was near the top of the list made by Philip II, king of Spain, of Englishmen he wanted caught and hanged.

Beyond the risks and profits of piracy, this dour and daring Yorkshireman did have a dream: to find the Northwest Passage and fame because he told George Best, "it was the only thing in the world that was left yet undone."

Others shared his dream and the hope of immense wealth if a northern passage to China was discovered. Foremost among Frobisher's patrons were the London merchant Michael Lok and Ambrose Dudley, the wealthy Earl of Warwick. Together with others, they raised the 875 pounds sterling needed to launch a modest expedition: two small, tubby, high-pooped 20-ton barks, the *Gabriel* and the *Michael*, each with a crew of eighteen men, and an even smaller pinnace with a crew of four. Rations for a year were adequate but modest. They only splurged on booze and beer: three hogshead (about 600 litres [159 gallons]) of aqua vitae and five tuns (or casks) of beer, enough to give each sailor a gallon of beer each day.

The Inuit call it Kodlunarn Island, the "white man's island." On this little arctic island, hundreds of Englishmen mined "gold ore" in 1577 and 1578. Explorer Martin Frobisher even planned to colonize the island.

The small fleet sailed in June of 1576 north and west across the Atlantic Ocean. Near Greenland they were hit by a dreadful storm. The pinnace sank with all hands, the *Michael* turned and fled back to England, but Frobisher in the *Gabriel* persevered and on July 20 they reached a "great gutte...dividing as it were two mayne lands or continents." They thought they had found the passage to China and Frobisher called it Frobishers Streytes, just as the Portuguese explorer Magellan had named the southern route to the Pacific after himself. It was, in fact, a great bay, today's Frobisher Bay of Baffin Island.

To the Elizabethan sailors it was a region of marvels, vast barren lands and snow-streaked hills and in the sea "mountaines of yce" (icebergs). On August 19, they spotted what they at first believed to be a group of porpoises or seals or "strange fishes," but what turned out to be men in skin boats, Inuit who, wrote Best, "be like Tartars, with long black haire, broad faces...and tawnie in colour."

At first, sailors and natives got along fine. They traded: small mirrors, beads, baubles, and bells for fresh meat, fish, and furs. But then, against Frobisher's orders, five sailors went ashore, vanished and were never seen again. In retaliation, and as a curiosity to show to the folks back home, Frobisher, a man of brawn and guile, lured an Inuk close to the ship by holding out a tinkling bell, then "grabbed the man, and plucked him out of the sea by main force, boat and all."

Before sailing back to England, Frobisher picked up a heavy, coal-black stone "in token of Christian possession" of the newly discovered land.

In London he gave the stone to Michael Lok, his main merchant-backer. Lok took it to three government assayers. All three said it was worthless.

At this point, the story gets murky. Not satisfied with three definite noes, Lok took his rock to John Baptista Agnello, an Italian assayer and alchemist and, lo, he found the stone to be rich in gold. How come, asked Lok, that the other assayers did not detect the gold? "*Besogna sapere adulare la natura*" (nature needs a little coaxing), replied Agnello. Modern historians believe he may have adulated nature quite a bit, that, in fact, he "salted" the sample.

News spread fast: gold had been found in the north, in the new land, which Queen Elizabeth named Meta Incognita (the unknown destination). Funds for a new expedition were quickly gathered. Even the queen, notoriously tight with her money, invested one thousand pounds sterling. She promoted Frobisher to high admiral and gave him the 200-ton ship *Ayde*. With two other ships, Frobisher sailed in May 1577, together with 143 men, thirty of them miners.

They reached Frobisher Bay and on July 29 came to anchor, wrote Best, "vnder a smal Ilande whiche now is called by ye name of that right Honorable and vertuous Lady, Anne Countesse of Warwicke." This was tiny Kodlunarn Island, about 6 hectares (15 acres) in size, measuring 1148 by 1312 feet (350 by 400 metres).

It was, they decided, just the island they were seeking because "upon this Ilande was found good store of Ore, which in the washing helde golde plainly to be seene." Gold fever gripped all of them and from Frobisher down all men "both better and worse" dug feverishly.

The Inuk they had kidnapped and taken to England in 1576, had been a great but brief success. He showed off his speed and skill as a kayaking hunter and, while the queen watched, darted royal swans. But he died within weeks, lacking immunity to European illnesses.

Now Frobisher, still hoping to recover his five lost men, kidnapped three more Inuit—a man, a woman, and a child—in an effort to exchange prisoners. Nothing came of it. The natives by now were understandably wary and hostile. One day they ambushed Frobisher and some of his men. They shot an arrow into the admiral's buttocks and, said Best, he fled "rather speedily." The Inuit captives were painted by John White, a young artist member of the expedition, and their portraits are now in the British Museum.

The toiling miners and sailors on Kodlunarn Island amassed in three weeks 200 tons of ore in the holds of their ships. On August 22, wrote Best, "[W]e plucked down our tents, built bonfires upon the top of the highest hills, and marched around the island with the flag flying. We fired a farewell volley of shot in honour...of the Countess of Warwick, for whom the island was named, and so departed." Inuit watched it all from nearby hills. They must have been amazed and puzzled.

In England, everyone was delighted with their success. The queen invited Frobisher to Windsor Castle and thanked him for his great achievement. The usually crusty and truculent sailor knelt meekly and kissed her hand.

The "gold ore" from Kodlunarn Island was taken to Bristol Castle and the Tower of London. Commissioners examined the ore and reported "ye voyage gretly worthy to be advanced again." It was estimated that each ton of ore from Kodlunarn Island contained seven pounds sterling fifteen shillings worth of gold, and sixteen pounds sterling of silver. Transport from Meta Incognita cost eight pounds sterling per ton and refining ten pounds sterling per ton, leaving a

Deep trench dug by Elizabethan miners on Kodlunarn Island, hoping for gold and wealth. The ore contained glittering mica, but it did not contain gold.

profit of more than five pounds sterling per ton of ore shipped from the far north.

The Company of Cathay, now a regular joint stock corporation, with a charter from the Crown, prepared for the next voyage to the island of gold. There was no more talk of exploration or the Northwest Passage. The investors, including again the queen, subscribed nearly seven thousand pounds sterling for the third voyage and Queen Elizabeth presented Frobisher with a gold chain.

In 1578, Frobisher led a fleet of fifteen ships. His orders were to proceed directly to Kodlunarn Island and mine 2,000 tons of ore. He was also to land a prefabricated fort on the island and establish there a settlement where 120 men would spend the winter.

Four hundred men took part in the venture: sailors, soldiers, surgeons, miners from Cornwall, musicians, an assortment of "gentlemen," and one

Spanish spy who had been instructed by his government to make maps and to obtain ore samples.

The fleet stopped briefly at South Greenland. Frobisher went ashore, took possession of Greenland in the name of his queen and named the country New England. Storm and ice destroyed one ship, the 100-ton bark *Dennys*. The crew was saved, but with the ship sank part of the prefabricated fort for the arctic island colonists.

After passing herds of large whales "that were as plentiful as porpoises," the fleet arrived at Kodlunarn Island at the end of July. They set up tents, built a smithy, and constructed a furnace for the "goldfiners" to assay ore.

The small arctic island was now so crowded that Frobisher had to issue some strict sanitary decrees. No one was allowed to wash his hands in the island's spring and "for the better preservation and health of everyone, no person or persons shall do his easement anywhere except under the cliffs, where the sea may wash the same away." First offenders were to be imprisoned in the bilges for fourteen hours. The second time they were fined twelve pence.

Anticipating today's environmental concerns by more than four hundred years, Frobisher ordered that "no person or persons of any nature or condition shall cast out of their ship or ships any ballast or rubbish into the road where these ships are now riding."

Some of the ships had been damaged by ice. Sailors and miners dug a deep trench into the side of Kodlunarn Island as a sort of dry dock where ships could be hauled ashore and repaired. Since part of the fortress building had sunk, Frobisher, probably to the great relief of the 120 colonists, decided to abandon the settlement venture.

Instead, his men built a house of "lyme and stone" and filled it with "many barrels of meale, pease, and griste" in order to "fraight our ships full of Ore whiche we holde of farre greater price." In the house, they also left gifts for the Inuit: bells, mirrors, lead toys, whistles, even loaves of freshly baked bread. With touching optimism, and believing they would return, they started agriculture on this barren, rocky arctic island. They "sowed pease, corne and other graine to proue the fruitfulnesse of the soyle against the next yeare."

As things turned out, there was to be no next year. When the mariners and miners returned with their precious hoard, nearly 2,000 tons of "gold ore," the unpleasant news awaited them that it was worthless.

Frobisher fell from favour until he redeemed himself ten years later as one of the principal captains responsible for the defeat of the Spanish Armada and earned a knighthood. The Company of Cathay went broke and the unfortunate Michael Lok, chief promoter and financial backer of the three expeditions, ended up in debtor's prison where he had plenty of time to ponder "the prouerbe, all that glistereth is not golde."

Much of the "ore", mined on Kodlunarn Island with so much toil, travail, and loss of life, was used, according to a contemporary report, "to repayre the high-wayes."

For 285 years, no one knew the location of Frobisher's Countess of Warwick Island. Then, in 1861, the American explorer Charles Francis Hall abandoned the whaling ship, which had taken him north, to go and live with the Inuit of the Frobisher Bay area. There, he learned that, after nearly three centuries, the Inuit had preserved an amazingly accurate oral tradition about the Frobisher expeditions.

An old woman told him that "a great many years ago white men with great ships came. The first year one ship came, the second year three ships, and many ships the third year." The Inuit recalled many details, such as the disappearance of five of Frobisher's men and the kidnapping of Inuit by the English. When Hall asked where Frobisher had dug for gold, the Inuit unhesitatingly said "on Kodlunarn Island" (white man's island).

On Kodlunarn Island, Hall found two great trenches and the ruins of two houses. The Inuit told him that one of these trenches, sloping down into the sea, was used by the white men to repair their ships.

Hall discovered pieces of metal and glass on the island, various pottery shards, and lots of coal. He collected all the relics he could find and later donated them in equal portions to the Smithsonian Institution, which threw nearly all of it out during a housecleaning frenzy in 1953, and to the Royal Geographical Society in London, which catalogued all items and then mislaid them irretrievably.

Kodlunarn Island was again briefly visited in 1927 by the Rawson-MacMillan Sub-Arctic expedition from Chicago. They found merely a few shards, lots of coal, the trenches, and ruins of two houses.

In the summer of 1965, I went to northern Baffin Island with a small team of scientists and technicians to study narwhal, that strange arctic whale whose male carries in its forehead a single, tapered, torqued ivory tusk that can be up to 3 metres (10 feet) long. For about a thousand years that tusk was sold in Europe, Asia, and the Middle East as the miracle-working "horn of the unicorn," worth ten times its weight in gold.

On his second voyage, in 1577, Martin Frobisher found on a shore near Kodlunarn Island a dead "sea unicorn...having a horn two yards [two metres] long...wreathed and straight like a wax taper." He presented the ivory tusk to his queen, who prized it as a "jewel."

In 1965, I had already written several articles for *The Beaver*, the magazine of the venerable Hudson's Bay Company (incorporated on May 2, 1670, during the reign of King Charles II of England) whose full name was "The Governor and Company of Adventurers of England Trading into Hudson's Bay," younger sister to Michael Lok's ill-fated Company of Cathay.

Informed that I was going to Baffin Island, the company asked me to photograph its stores at Frobisher Bay, then a nascent town on southern Baffin Island at the head of the eponymous Frobisher Bay, with a population of less than a thousand people. Now called Iqaluit, it is the capital of the vast Nunavut Territory and has a population of more than five thousand.

Inuit children, round-faced, dark-haired, and happy, played on the steps of the store. I was sitting quietly and photographing them when someone tapped me on the shoulder.

"Are you Fred Bruemmer?" he asked.

"Yes."

It was Bryan Pearson, long-time northern resident, entrepreneur, impresario of the town's spring festival and, later, mayor of Frobisher Bay: sardonic and opinionated, he was a man who liked to organize.

"You want to go to Kodlunarn Island?" he asked. Bryan the promoter, a sort of latter-day Michael Lok, was thinking about possible future tourism and publicity.

"I'd love to. But I can't. I must be on the plane to northern Baffin Island in ten days," I said regretfully.

"No problem," Bryan assured me. "I'll have you back in eight days. Don't worry. I'll fix everything. We leave tomorrow morning." And so, on short notice, started the third white man's expedition to Kodlunarn Island since Frobisher left it in 1578, his thirteen ships laden with "gold" that later turned to dross.

We were five: Bryan Pearson; Simonee Michael, a young modern Inuk, president of Inook Limited, then Canada's only Inuit company and, shortly after our trip, the first Inuk elected to the territorial legislative assembly; John Rae, then a summer student and assistant manager of Inook Limited, and a future politician of note; Ioola, a traditional Inuit hunter, quiet, kind, and competent; and I, writer and photographer, in my third of thirty years of arctic travel.

Compared to future large, elaborate, and well-funded expeditions to Kodlunarn Island, especially the 1974 "Frobisher IV" expedition of Toronto's Royal Ontario Museum, and the 1981, 1990, 1991, 1992 Smithsonian Institution expeditions, ours was a very modest venture with a total budget of two hundred dollars.

Our major expense was about 900 litres (200 gallons) of gas to run the 15 h.p. outboard motors during the 700-kilometre (435-mile) round trip in two open, 6-metre (20-foot) freight canoes. But gas then cost only forty-four cents a gallon (about eleven cents a litre) even in Frobisher Bay. The two Inuit, well-equipped with guns and ammunition, planned to hunt en route and "live off the land." We three *kabloonait* (white men) preferred to live off supermarkets and came with boxes of cans, 5 kilograms (10 pounds) of potatoes, and half a kilogram (1 pound) of onions.

Frobisher left England on his first voyage in search of the Northwest Passage to China on June 15, 1576. Our two canoes left Frobisher Bay at high tide on June 15, 1965. Our travels in the bay, like Frobisher's 389 years before us, were ruled, to some extent, by the tides which, with 13-metre (44-foot) neap tides, are among the highest in the world.

We travelled into the past. To the northwest of us was the Hall Peninsula, to the southwest was Meta Incognita Peninsula named by Queen Elizabeth I.

The land was vast, mountainous, and bare, majestic in its barren emptiness. The bay was dotted with rugged, ice-rimmed islands. We stopped briefly at one islet. The Inuit gathered eider duck eggs and shot four ducks for supper.

We were near the Arctic Circle and a few days past the summer solstice. Day merged into luminous night. We set up our tents at an old and now-abandoned Inuit camp site. Bleached kayak skeletons lay on the rocks, the lines still elegant, the joints still a marvel of craftsmanship.

Frobisher had seen flotillas of kayaks. The chroniclers of his voyages gave Europe the first descriptions of these superb hunting craft. With a sailor's admiration for the speed and dexterity with which the Inuit paddled their

kayaks, George Best wrote, "[T]hey rowe therein with one ore, more swiftly a great deale, than we in our boates do with twentie." Perhaps the most beautiful hunting boat ever designed by man, kayaks in this region had been made obsolete by motor-driven canoes.

In 1578, more than four hundred Englishmen camped and mined "gold" on this tiny arctic island. In this trench sloping to the sea, Inuit oral tradition says, white men hauled ships ashore to repair them.

The next day we zigzagged through extensive fields of pack ice. Similar ice fields, storm-driven, had damaged many of the ships of Frobisher's fleet. We passed shimmering icebergs, the "mountaines of yce" that had impressed Elizabethan sailors so much.

In the evening, we stopped in a sheltered bay and camped near history: the stone remains of ancient Inuit winter houses and, nearby, remnants of a nineteenth-century American whaling station. Large, verdigrised kettles lay on the rocks, the try-pots in which whale blubber had long ago been rendered into oil, and huge square metal tanks in which the whale oil was stored before being taken home to New England.

Frobisher had seen vast pods of huge bowhead whales. Scottish and

American whalers hunted them to the verge of extinction. We saw many seals and walruses, but in eight days of travel we did not see a single whale.

Late in the evening of the third day, near the southern tip of Hall Peninsula and the entrance to "the great gutte" that Frobisher named Frobisher Streytes, the hoped-for passage to China, we passed Cape Sarah, turned into Countess of Warwick Sound and there, small, flat-topped, inconspicuous, one island among thousands along this coast, was Kodlunarn Island, the Elizabethan island of golden hopes.

We camped on Kodlunarn. Before coming to Baffin Island I had read George Best's detailed account of Frobisher's three voyages and now, in an oddly dream-like way, the island seemed familiar. We camped not far from the east shore on a gravelly plain. Our tents stood undoubtedly on the spot where Frobisher's four hundred men had set up their tents.

Just north of our camp was the "gold mine," a great trench, 27 metres (88 feet) long, 6 metres (20 feet) wide, and 1.5 metres (5 feet) deep. To the east, on a rise above the sea, was Best's Bulwark, once a lookout-fortification to ward off attacking Inuit (they wisely did not come close to Kodlunarn).

Near the island's highest point, 18 metres (61 feet) above sea level, lay piles of stone, the ruins of Frobisher's smithy and the house of "lyme and stone" his men built and filled with barrels of flour and peas, and toys and trinkets for the Inuit.

On the north shore, a steep trench sloped sharply down to the sea. "That's where the white men repaired their ships," said Simonee.

"How do you know?" we asked.

"Our old people say so," said Simonee.

Charles Francis Hall in 1861 had marvelled that "the Esquimaux traditionary history, extending back for centuries, is wonderfully accurate."

Apart from the trenches and house ruins, there was little left from Frobisher's time on this small, desolate, barren, rock island. We found lots of coal (perhaps from Newcastle!), a few small chips of glass and pottery shards, a piece of crumbling brick and, on trench rocks, the striae left by the tools of Cornish miners.

After supper in the tent, talking and drinking mugs of tea, I asked Simonee a question that intrigued me.

"What did your people think of the white men who came in many ships to this island, dug up lots and lots of rock, carried it to their ships and sailed away again?" Simonee smiled. "They could not understand. To them that was the greatest mystery. For our people wood and metal were rare and precious. These white men had lots of wood and metal. All they wanted was rock." He laughed. "They probably thought it was some sort of magic or that the white men were a bit crazy!"

Next day was gloomy. While the others continued to search Kodlunarn for Frobisher relics, Ioola took me across a narrow channel, dropped me off at Tikoon Point, then continued into Lincoln Bay (named in 1861 by Hall) to hunt seals.

Inuit probably lived at Tikoon Point when Frobisher came to Kodlunarn Island. George Best mentions a nearby Inuit encampment. But, fearing the aggressive whites armed with calivers, they had fled inland. Stone tent rings covered the area, and the bleached bones of seals, walruses and caribou, remains of long-ago Inuit feasts.

I climbed a steep valley to the top of Tikoon Point and emerged on a wide plateau with bright yellow arctic poppies and snow beds in the lee of rock ridges. Far below me lay the Countess of Warwick Sound and, dark and bleak beneath a lead grey sky, Kodlunarn, the white man's island.

Where I now stood, Inuit had no doubt stood 387 years ago and had looked down in puzzled amazement. Thirteen ships, their sails furled, lay at anchor near the small island. Teams of men mined "gold ore." Others carried the ore in wicker baskets to shore and loaded the holds of their ships with it.

Masons built a house of "lyme and stone" and "we left a variety of English toys in the house" to allure the natives "for we intended to return." The bakers baked bread. Smiths hammered busily in the smithy. The "goldfiners" tested ore in their furnace on the island.

Captains gathered for council meetings and, wrote Best, "Mr. Selman, the notary, recorded their decisions so that Her Majesty, the Lords of the Council, and the Adventurers might be satisfied." Finally, their "ships loaded with gold ore," the fleet left the Countess of Warwick Island on the last day of August 1578. They never returned.

A rifle shot broke my reverie and brought me back to the present. Ioola, the seal hunter, was coming back to fetch me. It was time to leave this arctic "isle of gold" and return to Frobisher Bay.

Chapter 6

FALKLAND ISLANDS, UNITED KINGDOM
Islands of Sheep, Birds, and War

IN 1492, Columbus discovered the New World.

In 1493, Pope Alexander VI divided the New World between Spain and Portugal.

Divvying up worlds was easy in those days: the pope drew a north-south line from pole to pole across the Atlantic Ocean, 100 leagues [483 kilometres or 300 miles] (changed to 370 leagues [1787 kilometres or 1110 miles] in 1494) west of the Cape Verde Islands. It gave Brazil to Portugal and the rest of the New World to Spain, and that's why Brazilians today speak Portuguese and all other South Americans speak Spanish.

That papal bull gave the yet-to-be-discovered and later British-owned Falkland Islands to Spain, creating conflicting and colliding claims to these "miserable islands," as Charles Darwin called them, situated near the southern tip of South America and home to two thousand people, six hundred thousand sheep, fifty thousand seals, and millions of birds.

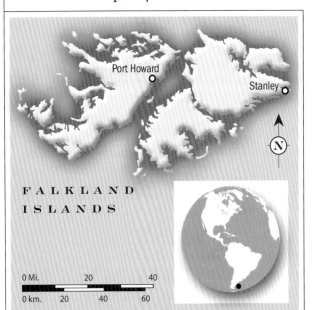

FALKLAND ISLANDS

Port Howard

Stanley

N

0 Mi.   20   40
0 km.   20   40   60

The result was a nasty war in 1982 between Argentina and Great Britain for possession of "that little ice-cold bunch of land," as a puzzled and annoyed President Ronald Reagan called the Falklands.

Britain won, but at a price: nine hundred British and Argentinian soldiers died in the war. Many more were wounded. The war ruined Argentina's already faltering economy and cost Great Britain two billion U.S. dollars, one million dollars for every Falkland

Island man, woman, and child.

British historians say the Falkland Islands were first seen and "discovered" by Captain John Davis in 1592, blithely ignoring the fact that these islands near the Strait of Magellan are already shown on a 1522 Portuguese map.

Davis was one of those far-roving Elizabethan sailors who combined spectacular voyages of exploration with piracy and plunder. Searching for the Northwest Passage in 1586 and 1587, he explored and mapped the coasts of Baffin Bay, Greenland, Arctic Canada and Labrador. Davis Strait between Greenland and Canada is named after him.

Four years later, in 1591, he sailed south. On August 14, heading for the Strait of Magellan, he was caught by a fierce storm and "was driven in among certain islands. We most firmly believe these islands had never before been seen by civilized man.... In position, they lie about fifty leagues eastward of the mainland and are somewhat northerly of the Strait of Magellan." Having marked the islands and their strategic position near the passage to the Pacific on his chart, Davis sailed on. In 1605, in the Strait of Malacca, he was killed by Japanese pirates.

Stanley, the neat, colourful capital of the bleak, wind-swept Falkland Islands. For eleven weeks in 1982, the town and the islands were occupied by Argentine troops.

In 1690, the English captain John Strong landed on the islands and named the channel dividing the two main islands Falkland Sound, after Viscount Falkland, then First Lord of the Admiralty. The name was later given to the entire Connecticut-sized group of about two hundred islands.

The most important phase of the Falkland's convoluted history began in 1759 in then French-owned Canada with a wealthy nobleman, Louis Antoine de Bougainville, who later became an admiral, a senator, the first Frenchman to sail around the world, and the man after whom the beautiful bougainvillaea plant is named. He was aide-de-camp to the Marquis de Montcalm and since, as Montcalm said, "he has more money than he knows what to do with," he used his wealth to bribe Indian tribes near Montreal to stay neutral in the French-English war for Canada.

The French lost, Montcalm was killed, the English got Canada, and a very angry Bougainville returned to France determined to thwart the English elsewhere. To forestall British expansion in the south, he decided to settle the Falkland Islands.

Sinking his entire fortune into the venture, Bougainville sailed in 1763 with two ships from the town of Saint-Malo to the islands he named after the town Îles Malouines, and the Spanish, and now the Argentinians, call the Islas Malvinas.

Heavily laden, the ships carried all that was needed to establish a colony: hundreds of barrels with seeds and plants, cattle, horses, pigs, goats, poultry, and about eighty colonists, including two refugee families from Acadia (Nova Scotia).

They reached the Falklands in February of 1764, built houses of stone and sod and a small fort and called their settlement Fort Louis, after their king, Louis XV of France, and in memory of the great Fort Louisbourg on Canada's Cape Breton Island, built by the French, destroyed by the British.

Unbeknownst to Bougainville and his struggling settlers on the east side of the Falkland Islands, his nemesis, Commodore John Byron (grandfather of the poet Lord Byron), the very man who had supervised the destruction of Louisbourg, founded, one year after Bougainville, in 1765, an English settlement on the west side of the Falkland Islands. He called his settlement Port Egmont and claimed all the islands in the name of his king, George III.

When the Spanish found out that "their" islands had been settled by France and Britain, they were not amused. "We are sole owner of these islands," they said. Under pressure, Bougainville sold his settlement and all rights and claims to Spain for twenty-five thousand pounds sterling in 1767. Then Spanish ships and troops arrived from Buenos Aires and turfed the British out of Port Egmont in 1770. Britain threatened war. Spain backed off. The English settlers returned, ran out of funds in 1774, left again, and the Spaniards reoccupied the islands. By then, Commodore Byron had long gone to become governor of Newfoundland.

Succeeding Spanish rule in 1820, the United Provinces of the Rio de la Plata (later called Argentina), despite being in a nearly constant state of civil war, found time to declare themselves owners of the Islas Malvinas.

Too busy to bother with settlement, Argentina leased the islands to an odd entrepreneur, a Frenchman named Luis Vernet, who had studied business in Philadelphia, had been a long-time merchant in Hamburg, Germany, and now wanted to be ruler of the Falklands. In 1824 he founded a fairly successful colony with German, English, and Spanish settlers and some thirty indentured black labourers. All might have gone well had not Vernet, unwisely, picked a fight with the United States.

Annoyed by the presence of many sealing vessels at "his" islands, Vernet seized three American-owned ships. The corvette USS *Lexington* happened to be in Buenos Aires. Urged on by the local U.S. consul, Captain Silas Duncan took his warship to the Falklands, charged Vernet with piracy, wiped out his settlement, and declared the islands *res nullius* (belonging to no-one).

That really riled Argentina. Its foreign minister, Manuel V. de Maza, charged, with fury and drama, that Señor Duncan had "carried his turpitude and ferocity to the last extremity, destroying with unspeakable ferocity the Islas Malvinas colony."

While the United States and Argentina traded first insults and then broke off diplomatic relations, the Falklands were visited by the youthful Charles Darwin, in 1833, then near the beginning of his five-year study voyage aboard the *Beagle*. Darwin was not impressed. "After the possession of these miserable islands had been contested by France, Spain, and England, they were left uninhabited," he wrote. "The government of Buenos Ayres then sold them to a private individual [Luis Vernet], but likewise used them...for a penal colony."

Darwin went riding with gauchos, hunting wild cattle, descendants of cattle brought to the Falklands by Bougainville. The hunt was exciting, but Darwin disliked the monotonous moorland. "An undulating land with a desolate and wretched aspect, is everywhere covered by a peaty soil and wiry grass," he noted.

Despite such a bleak description of the real estate, Britain was determined to own it. It sent another naval expedition to the Falklands on January 3, 1833 and claimed "the right of sovereignty over these islands."

Settlers from England and Scotland arrived and Pax Britannica settled over the isolated, much-disputed islands. The first colonists lived primarily off the islands' animal wealth. They hunted feral cattle and pigs, killed seals and whales, clubbed two million tubby penguins and rendered their fat into oil.

Until the Panama Canal was opened in 1914, ships bound to and from the west coasts of South and North America used the notoriously stormy Cape Horn route around the tip of South America. Battered ships limped into the harbour of Stanley, the Falkland's only town and now its capital, to be repaired, revictualled, or wrecked.

In the 1850s, several, mostly Britain-based companies bought much of the Falklands' 1.2 million hectares (3 million acres) of outback and divided it into vast sheep ranches with locals as ranch hands. It takes five island acres to feed one sheep and eventually six hundred thousand sheep roamed the islands. Wool became the Falklands' wealth and sole export. Life on the islands drifted gently through the generations, simple, peaceful, British-rural.

After World War II, Great Britain dismantled its empire and sort of lost interest in the remote Falklands. As Britain's love waned, Argentina, which had always and fervently claimed Las Malvinas as part of its *patria*, courted the reluctant islanders.

Argentina had geography on her side. The Falklands are 483 kilometres (300 miles) east of Argentina and 12,874 kilometres (8,000 miles) southwest of Great Britain. Regular and cheap air traffic began to link the long-isolated islands with Argentina. In 1971, Britain and Argentina signed a communications agreement. Islanders went on shopping trips to Argentina. There was talk the islands might be "co-ruled" by the two claimant nations. Argentinians referred to it all as their "charm offensive."

And then, abruptly, in 1982, Argentina decided to skip the wooing and resort to rape. The reason was political. Argentina's brutal military junta led by General Leopoldo Galtieri had already murdered at least ten thousand of its opponents at home in the infamous *Guerra Sucia* (Dirty War). Unemployment soared. The inflation rate rushed past 130 per cent. The economy was near collapse. Then Galtieri had the bright idea to do what dictators do when they're in trouble: be patriotic and start a war.

On April 2, 1982, more than eleven thousand Argentine troops invaded the

Falkland Islands that were defended, but not for long, by eighty-four British soldiers. Argentina was ecstatic. *"Islas Malvinas Recuperadas,"* (The Islas Malvinas Have Been Recovered) headlined the Buenos Aires newspaper *Crónica.* In Stanley, as Argentinian troops marched into town, the local radio station first played "Strangers in the Night" and then Burt Bacharach's rendition of "Close to You."

In Argentina, Galtieri was a national hero. But not for long. He had misjudged two important people: Britain's Prime Minister Margaret Thatcher and President Ronald Reagan. Thatcher, the "Iron Lady," dispatched a task force of nearly a hundred ships and five thousand elite soldiers to the Falklands. Reagan, although baffled why anyone should fight over "that little ice-cold bunch of land," sided with Britain and imposed economic sanctions against Argentina. The war was over in seventy-four days.

British troops took more than ten thousand prisoners and shipped them back to Argentina. Argentina took one prisoner (a pilot) and shipped him back to Britain. General Galtieri was fired and later sentenced to twelve years in prison.

The Falkland Islanders were glad to be rid of the "Argies." The occupation had been grim but not brutal. Three island women died, tragically by misdirected

Penned sheep await shearing. About one hundred island ranching families own a total of more than six hundred thousand sheep. Wool, once the sole wealth of the islands, now takes second place to lucrative fishing industry.

"friendly fire." After driving for two months on the right-hand side of the road, because during the occupation the Falklands belonged to Argentina, the islands' 371 cars and trucks could drive again on the left-hand side.

Many things changed after the war. Britain created a mighty military base manned by more than two thousand soldiers. The Falkland Islands Development Corporation, financed by the British government, bought most of the islands' huge sheep ranches owned by absentee landlords, broke them up, and sold sections to local ranchers.

Prosperity came to the formerly frugal Falklands. Flocks of birders arrived, for the Falkland Islands, said the famous American ornithologist Olin Sewall Pettingill, "are the most exciting place for birdlife in the southern oceans." For the great tourist liners en route to Antarctica a stop at the now-famous Falklands became *de rigueur*.

Britain, suddenly assertive about the rights of its long-neglected colony near the southern end of the earth, declared in 1986 a 277-kilometre (150-nautical-mile) exclusive fishing zone around the islands and gave it muscle with ships of the Falkland Islands Fisheries Protection Service. Fishing ships from European and Asian nations, catching five hundred million U.S. dollars' worth of fish and squid each year in the seas around the Falklands, now had to obtain licenses and pay hefty fees. Within one year, the islands' income rose from eighteen million dollars to more than fifty-four million dollars.

Things are fine now on the Falklands. But one ancient problem remains. Far-away Britain may own the Falkland Islands, but nearby Argentina, inheritor of Spain and the pope's 1493 largesse, keeps insisting that it has sole rights and absolute sovereignty over the Islas Malvinas.

Our cruise ship from Argentina to the Falklands had two captains. The year was 1975 and the Argentinian Department of Tourism had invited me and twenty-four other writers from a dozen nations to share a cruise with four hundred fifty Argentinian tourists to the Islas Malvinas and the Argentinian portion of Antarctica. It was a voyage of pride and prejudice.

In charge of the difficult contingent of foreign writers was a tactful, tango-smooth, dark-haired public relations man named Hernando Schmidt.

"Please," he pleaded, "don't say 'the Falkland Islands'. They are the Islas Malvinas. They are Argentinian islands. They belong to Argentina."

"Since when?" asked a Swedish reporter.

"Since 1493!" Señor Schmidt said proudly.

That caught nearly all of us by surprise. Schmidt patiently told us about the pope who in 1493 had so generously divided the New World between Portugal and Spain and consequently the Islas Malvinas were now a part of Argentina.

"According to that ruling the United States belongs to Spain," an American writer remarked.

"Why does our ship have two captains?" a French journalist wanted to know.

"Because it is a Greek ship, registered in Panama, and under charter to the Argentinian Tourist Department. We have a Greek captain and an Argentinian captain," Señor Schmidt explained.

"How do they speak together?"

"In English," Señor Schmidt said curtly.

Our naval trichotomy soon led to problems.

For the Argentinian tourists the visit to the Falkland Islands was part patriotic pilgrimage, part shopping spree. They came to see "our Malvinas" and planned to buy unlimited cheap liquor, cigarettes, radios or cameras, all duty-free since according to their government, they were in Argentina.

They rushed ashore in Stanley with the eagerness of Boxing Day shoppers and then got a nasty jolt. Although it was a weekday, most shops were closed by patriotic islanders, in a snit because our ship did not fly the British flag.

According to a recently signed British-Argentinian agreement, an Argentinian ship visiting the Falkland Islands did not have to fly the British flag, but was not allowed to fly the Argentinian flag either. Our ship, although under Argentinian charter, was registered in Panama and therefore should have flown the British flag. It didn't and, in a pique, the islanders closed their stores.

Like jilted lovers our tourists returned, filled with that profound sadness and rancour of disappointed shoppers. Our ship gave an angry hoot, raised the bright blue-white-blue flag of Argentina and steamed south toward Antarctica.

Twenty years later, in 1995, I returned to the Falkland Islands. This time I came alone and for three months, to photograph birds and seals. I was working on a book about the seals of the world. Three species live on the Falklands: the elegant southern fur seal; the powerful, shaggy-maned southern sea lion; and the aptly named southern elephant seal, the giant of all seals. Males weigh up to 3,628 kilograms (8,000 pounds).

The Argentinians had come and gone, but they had left a lethal legacy:

120 mine fields planted with death. They buried more than twenty thousand mines. Most were made of plastic that cannot be located with metal detectors. Two British soldiers lost their legs trying to remove mines. To avoid more casualties, they fenced the minefields. Skull-and-crossbones signs warned against trespassing.

Penguins liked that. Since humans were excluded, they thought of a minefield as a nice quiet place to raise children.

A major penguin-upon-high-explosives colony was near Stanley. I walked to it on my second day in town. I liked Stanley: British suburbia transplanted to the subantarctic, neat clap-board houses with brightly painted roofs. Many had large and lovingly tended gardens, growing flowers, potatoes and vegetables, for veggies from Britain came by plane and were expensive. Until the 1982 war, the isolated islanders were nearly entirely self-sufficient. Mutton was, and is, their main food. They call it "the 365," for mutton is eaten every day of the year.

I passed the squat and massive Christ Church Anglican Cathedral, the southernmost cathedral in the world. A giant arch stands in front of it, made of four blue whale jaw bones. The Whalebone Arch was erected in part as a memento of the islands' whaling days, but mainly to commemorate the 1933 centenary of British rule in the Falklands.

More than a million black-browed albatrosses breed on uninhabited Steeple Jason Island. Immensely rich in marine life, the sea around the Falkland Islands provides food for vast bird colonies.

During the 1982 war, the Argentinians occupying Stanley, and expecting a frontal assault, plastered the beach and dunes nearby at Yorke Bay with thousands of plastic mines. Now barbed wire enclosed the mined area and the place is known as Penguin Walk, with worried humans outside and unconcerned penguins inside the fence.

Watching penguin family life upon a deadly minefield was eerily fascinating. They marched up from the sea, stomped blithely across sand and buried mines, greeted neighbours, bowed to acquaintances, talked with mates, and fed teenage chicks, all in an area marked by bright red signs saying DANGER—MINES. The mines, however, were designed to kill or maim humans, including children, not gentoo penguins weighing 5 to 6 kilograms (12 to 13 pounds).

Of the Falklands' two thousand inhabitants, about one thousand five hundred live in Stanley (plus the military guarding "Fortress Falkland") and five hundred live "in camp" (a term derived from the *el campo* of Spanish gauchos) in the 1.2-million-hectare (3-million-acre) outback region. Many of the smaller islands are owned and inhabited by only one sheep-ranching family.

Only a few sheep were kept on Sea Lion Island, the southernmost inhabited island of the archipelago. The income of this island came from tourists, mainly European birders, plus a few from the United States. They stayed at the island's pleasant lodge, and oohed and aahed in ecstasy all over the little island, for it is a birder's paradise with more than forty breeding species. In the evening after supper, they gathered in the comfortable lounge with its glowing peat fire, re-lived the day's thrills, compared notes, and indulged in gentle but exultant one-upmanship.

A bit apart from the happy birders, but not aloof, sat the newly appointed governor of the Falkland Islands, Richard Ralph, with a post-prandial coffee and brandy.

"Where were you before being appointed governor of the Falkland Islands?" I asked.

"I was British ambassador to Latvia, living in Riga, the capital," he said and was about to elucidate, since few people know where Latvia is. I interrupted him.

"I was born in Riga, Latvia," I said. "I'm Baltic German." And then we exchanged the proper platitudes about the smallness of the world.

The governor was on Sea Lion Island as part of a tour of his new domain and to check on the lodge's suitability for a soon-to-arrive royal guest. After laying wreaths at war memorials, meeting a lot of soldiers, and shaking hands with many of her mother's loyal island subjects, Princess Anne, the Princess Royal, her royal duties done, wanted to rest a bit on Sea Lion Island and hobnob for a change with penguins and seals.

The princess, no doubt, would love the penguins. Most people do. She would probably be fascinated but less enchanted by the giant elephant seals, for many were moulting and now looked revolting.

They were once heavily hunted for their blubber and more than a million were killed by "elephanters" and their fat was rendered into oil.

Now protected, the giant seals lay on a beach not far from the lodge on Sea

Lion Island and suffered through their annual moult. They sloughed off the entire epidermal layer, skin and hair, in large mouldy-looking patches. It is an exhausting process, and the elephant seals, lethargic at the best of times, were now nearly comatose. To conserve heat (and energy), they lay together in tight, malodorous groups, and peeled slowly from nose to tail.

This was of interest to several opportunistic birds. The pure white sheath-bill, an odd bird of the Far South, looks like a cross between a gull and a pigeon. It is primarily a scavenger and picked up bits and pieces of skin that peel off the resting giants.

The little brownish tussock birds, native to the Falklands and to Tierra del Fuego, were already more adventurous. They fluttered up to the sleeping behemoths and chipped off bits of flaking skin or pecked dried snot from a seal's nose.

Boldest were the caracaras, the rowdy pirates of the Falklands. They live on these islands and nowhere else in the world and Charles Darwin in 1833 was fascinated by these avian thugs. "They are very mischievous and inquisitive.... They are noisy, uttering several harsh cries, one of which is like that of the English rook; hence the sealers always call them rooks."

The Falklanders call them Johnny Rooks. They are among the rarest birds on earth. Only a few hundred live on the Falkland Islands. They are protected but not loved, for they are a naughty gang of raucous rascals delighting in mischief. They pestered the elephant seals and they plagued me.

Normally noisy, these long-legged, powerful raptors looked sleek, sneaky, lean, and mean as they approached a blissfully sleeping elephant seal. They tip-toed close and tore off pieces of moulting skin. The seal roared "ouch!" then fell asleep again, and the caracaras sidled up for another piece of skin.

They also thought it very funny to fly up from behind, rip the hat off my head and drop it far away. That was annoying, but I was more fortunate than another victim, the Falkland Island naturalist and artist Tony Chater. They pinched his binoculars and "from a few hundred feet, dropped them into the South Atlantic."

The caracaras are hooligans in paradise. I watched them on many of the islands. They were sometimes annoying, often amusing and always amazingly tame. The "extraordinary tameness" of the caracaras and most other Falkland Island birds had already intrigued Darwin in 1833. The birds are still delightfully tame and trusting, placing the Falklands among those rare magic islands of the world, where most animals are not afraid of humans.

Chapter 7

SAN MIGUEL ISLAND, CALIFORNIA, U.S A.
The Island of Elephant Seals

SAN MIGUEL ISLAND off California is to seals what France's Côte d'Azur is to the very rich: a perfect breeding place, sunny, warm, and exclusive. The sand is soft, the beaches wide, and the paparazzi rare. Access to San Miguel Island for photographers and other humans is severely restricted during the seals' breeding season.

Six seal species live upon the beaches of this remote, dun-coloured, 5,665-hectare (14,000-acre) island, more than upon any other island in the world. Two of these seals were once believed extinct: the marvellously elegant, foxy-faced Guadalupe fur seal, and the mighty northern elephant seal, 2-ton animals, the second largest seal on earth, surpassed in weight and size only by its close cousin, the southern elephant seal of the subantarctic regions.

For the European invaders of California, these seals that look like bloated blimps were easy prey. They had little fear of humans, and were slow, lethargic, and easy to kill. A large, blubber-wrapped male yielded about 757 litres (200 gallons) of valuable oil for the lamps of America.

Ruthlessly hunted for more than seventy years, the giant seals were believed extinct by the end of the nineteenth century. In 1884, an American biology book sadly called the northern elephant seal "one of the bygone wonders of the animal world."

Today, about forty thousand elephant seals carpet the breeding beaches of San Miguel. All may be descendants of one single bull, the sole male survivor of the species in the 1880s, the Adam of all northern elephant seals. When Burney J. LeBoeuf of the University of California at Santa Cruz, the foremost expert on elephant seals, took blood samples from many seals, he found them to be as similar as the blood samples of identical twins.

San Miguel is one of eight Channel Islands in the Santa Barbara Channel, only 160 kilometres (one hundred miles) west of Los Angeles. During the last ice age, which reached its peak about eighteen thousand years ago, ice sheets covered about 11.1 million square kilometres (4.3 million square miles) of North America and about 3.1 million square kilometres (1.2 million square miles) of Europe. More than 27.2 million cubic kilometres (17 million cubic miles) of water were locked within this monstrous mass of ice and the level of the world's oceans was about 122 metres (400 feet) lower than it is now.

At that time, the four northern Channel Islands formed one immense superisland. It was a strange place: while elephant seals lolled upon the beaches, elephants grazed upon the nearby plains. These were island elephants, only about 2 metres (6 feet) tall, pygmy cousins to the giant mammoths that lived in southern California at that time.

With the waning ice age, the vast ice caps melted, sea levels rose slowly by 122 metres (400 feet) and the superisland split into four separate islands: Anacapa, Santa Cruz, Santa Rosa and, farthest west, San Miguel. The climate changed. The dwarf mammoth of San Miguel and other islands became extinct and so did the mainland mammoth.

The elephant seals survived. At the beginning of the nineteenth century, the northern elephant seal bred from Cabo San Lázaro, near the southern tip of Baja California, to Point Reyes, just north of San Francisco, a distance of slightly more than 1,600 kilometres (1,000 miles). Scientists estimate that the original population exceeded one hundred thousand animals.

Then came the slaughter, the "elephanting," as it was called. For the Spanish, Russian, and American invaders of California the huge, blubber-wrapped elephant seals were simply oil. Before the use of petroleum lamps became widespread in the 1860s and 1870s, the world burned animal or vegetable oils in its lamps, or used expensive candles. The animal oil came mainly from killed whales. After 1810, some of it came from elephant seals.

With its high-quality oil, the slow-moving elephant seals offered

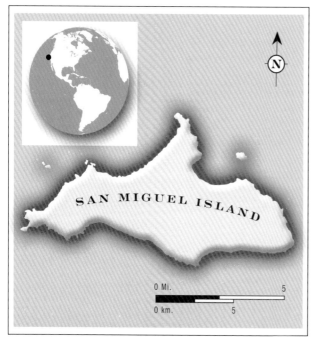

SAN MIGUEL ISLAND

0 Mi.   5

0 km.   5

easy fortunes. Russians and their Aleut slaves began the hunt. Some Spanish and American "elephanters" joined them on California's killing grounds.

The oil rendered from elephant seal blubber lubricated machinery, water-proofed garments, fired streetlights, and thickened paints and soaps.

"A fat [elephant seal] bull," recorded the whaler-scientist Charles M. Scammon in his classic 1874 book *The Marine Mammals of the Northwestern Coast of North America*, "yielded 210 gallons [795 litres] of oil," enough to fuel one lamp for four years.

California's gold rush and population boom kept the demand for seal oil high. In 1840, one San Diego merchant wrote to a prospective client that "if you want some lamp oil, I can supply you with 30 to 40 gallons[113 to 151 litres] of good elephant oil at a dollar per gallon. I think it burns equal to or better than sperm [whale oil]."

Profits could be further enhanced with the sale of an odd side product. The Chinese paid high prices for the elephant seal's long, flexible whiskers (and those of fur seals and sea lions). They were perfect for cleaning opium pipes.

The huge, lethargic seals made an easy quarry. "The

Once believed extinct, northern elephant seals have made a spectacular comeback. They began to resettle San Miguel Island in 1925. Now forty thousand crowd its breeding beaches.

method of capturing them," wrote Scammon, "is thus: The sailors get between the herd and the water; then, raising all possible noise by shouting and at the same time flourishing clubs, guns and lances, the party advances slowly toward the rookery. The onslaught creates such a panic among these peculiar creatures...that they climb, roll and tumble over each other." Many were trampled to death, especially females and pups. The rest were clubbed and lanced until they died.

Methodically, the killers wiped out seal colony after seal colony, including the huge and ancient elephant seal rookery on San Miguel Island. In his book *The War Against the Seals*, American historian Briton Cooper Busch estimates that between 1810 and 1860 about 250,000 northern elephant seals were killed. By 1860, the species was considered "commercially extinct."

In 1880, one more small elephant seal colony was discovered. About four hundred animals survived on a remote, sheltered beach of Baja California near Isla de Cedros. Delighted, seal hunters rushed in and killed them all. With that, the magnificent northern elephant seal seemed truly extinct.

In 1892, rumours reached Charles Haskins Townsend of the Smithsonian Institution that a few elephant seals might live on a remote, uninhabited volcanic island in the Pacific—Mexico-owned Isla de Guadalupe, 240 kilometres (150 miles) west of Baja California.

Townsend organized an expedition to Guadalupe Island and found eight elephant seals on a small, crescent-shaped beach beneath a 914-metre (3,000-foot) cliff. He promptly shot seven of the animals, "the last of an exceedingly rare species," because "few, if any specimen were to be found in the museums of North America."

That was the elephant seal's nadir. Scientists estimate that between twenty and one hundred seals survived the elephanters and the museum hunters. Those that escaped the slaughter were probably at sea or perhaps had sought refuge in Guadalupe's jagged lava caves.

Now that the final refuge of elephant seals had been discovered, they appeared doomed. Another museum expedition was planned to kill the last animals and exhibit the stuffed specimen of "an extinct species." A fertilizer company hoped to make some money by "cleaning up" the few remaining elephant seals.

At the last moment, the California Academy of Sciences intervened. At its urging, President Alvaro Obregon of Mexico gave total protection to the *ele-*

fante marino and, in 1922, declared the Isla de Guadalupe a wildlife reserve. Mexico took a no-nonsense attitude toward conservation: a squad of soldiers was posted on the island with orders "to shoot anyone molesting the animals."

For a few years, that pathetic remnant of a once numerous and widespread species hovered on the brink of extinction. Then, thanks to total protection, first by Mexico and then also by the United States, the giant seals began to make a spectacular comeback.

At first, they clung to the security of Guadalupe Island. But as its beaches became too crowded, they spread and began to recolonize the islands off California and Baja California that they had inhabited before hunters wiped them out. In 1925, a few elephant seals occupied again their ancestral beaches on San Miguel Island. Today the island is home to the largest colony of northern elephant seals in the world.

From about fifty survivors in 1892, the elephant seals increased to 1,500 in 1930; 13,000 in 1957; 48,000 in 1976; 70,000 in 1984; 100,000 in 1988; and to more than 150,000 today. They now probably exceed their pre-hunt population and occupy again their entire former range. To Burney LeBoeuf, who has studied elephant seals for more than thirty-five years, this spectacular recovery "is one of the most remarkable achievements documented for any marine or terrestrial mammal."

All 150,000 of today's elephant seals are probably descended from a single male, the grand sire of the species. Elephant seals are polygamous. When only about fifty were left in 1892, one alpha bull may have controlled all surviving females and fathered all their offspring, bequeathing his progeny a limited genetic base. As a result, LeBoeuf's studies have revealed, today's northern elephant seals are, in many respects, as similar as identical twins.

They may be closely related, but as the elephant seal populations spread, members of far-flung colonies began to form separate, discrete entities whose members developed regional dialects. Just as Bavarians and people from Hamburg are both German but, when they speak their dialects, can barely understand each other, the seals from widely separated colonies have developed local lingoes peculiar to their group; an evolutionary achievement once thought to be confined to humans and a few species of birds.

The rhythmic, resonant, metallic calls of elephant seal males, which can be heard for more than a mile, vary considerably in pulse rate, pitch, intensity, and timbre. The animals of a rookery recognize each other perhaps by sight but definitely by voice. "The pulse rate of males within a population is remarkably constant," writes LeBoeuf, "but average pulse rate varies considerably between populations. Males on Año Nuevo Island, for instance, have a pulse rate half that of males at San Nicolas Island, which is about 531 kilometres (330 miles) to the south." Elephant seals from afar first seem confused by the way the locals talk, then either leave or quickly adopt the regional dialect. Thus, scientists believe, over time separate populations evolve that, in the distant future, may barely be on speaking terms.

No seal species in the world has been so intensively studied as the northern elephant seal, and the more scientists learn about this goliath of all seals, the more amazed they are by its astounding feats.

Not only do new colonies evolve distinct dialects, but

A hungry elephant seal pup calls loudly for its mother. Fed on immensely fat-rich milk, the pup will weigh about 136 kilograms (300 pounds) at the time of weaning.

these seals can also dive deeper than any marine mammal, to depths that ought to crush them. Both males and females make two marathon migrations every year, swimming a total of 19,311 kilometres (12,000 miles) for the females and 20,920 kilometres (13,000 miles) for the males. They stay underwater for up to two hours, a length of time that ought to kill them but evidently doesn't. They surface rapidly from abyssal depths, breathe quickly and dive again—and again and again, and keep this up for days, weeks, even months. These superseals are "breaking every record in the book," said LeBoeuf.

All these amazing revelations about this seal that nearly vanished from our earth and that, most of the time, looks about as exciting as a flat tire, are quite recent. They have been achieved with increasingly efficient, durable, crush-proof, miniaturized and very expensive recording devices affixed to the massive seals with epoxy glue. (It does them no harm. At the next moult, the seals slough off both skin and recorders.)

Scientists had long assumed that elephant seals are deep and long-duration divers. A scientific paper published in 1968 reported that they could dive to a maximum depth of 42 metres (138 feet). The same year the famous French oceanographer Jacques-Yves Cousteau filmed the "rare" elephant seal, that "giant amphibian, an enormous mass of flesh and fat," and reported with *bouche bée* amazement that "they are able to remain underwater for at least fifteen minutes, dive to a depth of a thousand feet, and travel for over a mile beneath the surface."

Recent studies by LeBoeuf and others have shown that elephant seals can do much better than that. They are, in fact, as one scientist recently remarked, "the greatest diving champions on earth." Most of their dives slant down to 518 to 548 metres (1,700 to 1,800 feet), but recently one seal carrying a recorder dived to a record depth of 1,569 metres, or 1.5 kilometres (5,150 feet, or nearly a mile).

At that depth the seals swim in a deadly world of total darkness and the colossal crushing power of about 160 atmospheres. That's more than a ton of pressure per square inch! Long before he reaches that depth, a human diver would die a terrible death: he would be crushed as if in an all-encompassing vise, his body would cave in, the ribs would buckle and break, his eyes would be forced from their sockets.

Elephant seals do this routinely and they can stay underwater for up to two hours. They dive, swim and hunt, yet do not breathe for two hours. That's another record. A highly trained human can dive for a few minutes. A few whale species can remain underwater for nearly an hour. But no mammal can equal the diving time of elephant seals.

And these seals that on land often look like lethargic, skin-encased blobs of blubber, make the greatest migration of all sea mammals. Recent studies carried out by the marine mammal expert Brent S. Stewart of the Hubbs Marine Research Center in San Diego, with whom I spent several seasons on San Miguel Island, show that the elephant seals migrate, mostly underwater, from their breeding and moulting beaches off California to marine areas in the vicinity of Alaska's Aleutian Islands. That's like swimming across the Atlantic Ocean, from New York to London—and back again!

These are astounding physiological feats and one naturally wonders why these record-setting seals swim the deepest, the longest, the farthest. The answers, most scientists assume, are to avoid enemies and access ample food.

Their only natural enemies are killer whales and great white sharks. By diving deep, elephant seals avoid both. And they reach submarine regions containing hundreds of species of squid and fish that are hunted by no other mammal and are not even exploited by humans. It is a rich realm where only elephant seals hunt.

That may account, in part, for the amazing success of these seals that once teetered on the edge of extinction and now cover again in thousands their ancestral breeding beaches on San Miguel Island.

We left Los Angeles with its churning, rushing millions in the morning. One hour later, our small chartered plane banked sharply and landed on a flat, dry lake bed in the centre of San Miguel Island. We unloaded our supplies, the plane roared off, and Brent Stewart and I were alone, the only humans on this 5,665-hectare (14,000 acre) island that belongs to the U.S. Navy. It was marvellously quiet and peaceful.

We lugged our supplies to the modest research building near the west end of the island and then fetched water from the nearest island spring, the same spring where, long ago, island Indians had obtained their water. They were the Chumash Indians who, according to the anthropologist Robert F. Heizer, like other early California Indians, had "solved one of mankind's most vexing problems—how to live in peace and understanding with other nations."

There was a darkish mound not far from the spring, a midden, one of many on San Miguel, an ancient garbage dump of the early islanders. Their seas were rich, the living easy. They fished from 7-metre (25-foot) canoes, made of driftwood planks, sewn with fibre cordage, and caulked with asphalt. They hunted the abundant sea mammals. They collected mussels, oysters, clams, scallops, and, to judge by the blue-black middens, vast amounts of abalones. They hunted elephant seals and, thousands of years ago, may have also hunted the island elephants. The dwarf elephants died out and so, after being "discovered" by Europeans, did the peaceful Chumash Indians.

Sailing north from Mexico in 1542, Juan Rodriguez Cabrillo, a Portuguese navigator in the service of Spain, explored California. He landed on San Miguel, found the natives friendly and helpful and gave their island the ominous name Isla de Posesión (Island of Possession). He sailed further north, past San Francisco Bay, returned to San Miguel, and died there, probably of a gangrene infection. He may be buried on the island, though his grave has never been found.

To the friendly Indians of San Miguel who had lived so long in peace, contact with another world was fatal. Fighting foreigners and alien diseases led to their extinction.

The elephant seals survived, barely, and then made a stunning comeback. I walked up a dune near the island's west end, the soft yellow of the sand garlanded with deep-green mats of the crystalline ice plant. As I reached the crest, I saw before me a spectacle of stunning magnificence: a vast world of seals, acres and acres covered with seals, the greatest northern elephant seal colony in the world.

The huge males with their pendulous, trunk-like noses, to which elephant seals owe their name, had arrived in early December. They were swathed in fat, with a blubber layer up to 15 centimetres (6 inches) thick. These 2- to 3-ton seals galumphed ashore with but two things on their mind: to fight and to fertilize as many females as possible. One scientist has called elephant seal males "sex-obsessed mating machines."

I sat on the soft sand and watched for days the battles of the bulls. "Few animals fight as fiercely and violently as bull elephant seals," wrote Burney LeBoeuf.

A challenger humped ashore, 5 metres (16 feet) of fat and fury, and roared, a strange, pulsing, metallic battle cry. Despite their mass, the blimp-like bulls were amazingly fast and flexible. They reared high, like Brobdingnagian

Bloody battle of the bulls. Immensely powerful, the 2-ton males hack at each other with dagger-sharp canines. To the victor goes a harem of females.

cobras, and hacked and slashed at each other's neck and chest with lightning speed and long yellow canines. Blood streamed from the fighting males. The weaker bull began to yield, backed up, turned abruptly, and fled into the sea.

To the victor of these mighty, primal battles went a section of the beach and all the females on it. Being an alpha bull had its perks, but it was not an easy life. Top bulls fought often, did not eat or drink for up to three months, mated frequently, and rarely slept. They lost about 680 kilograms (1,500 pounds) in a season and, exhausted, toppled from alpha to omega. Only rarely, Brent Stewart told me, does a beach master reign for more than one year. Still, his is a genetically productive reign. Studies have shown that a mere 4 per cent of all males impregnate 85 per cent of the females.

Apart from the vast elephant seal rookeries were the colonies of other pinnipeds: fusiform harbour seals, vigilant and wary; sienna-brown Steller's sea lions, largest of the world's five sea lion species, with massive males that can weigh a ton; elegant Alaska fur seals that established in the late 1960s a now flourishing colony on San Miguel Island; and California sea lions, graceful on land and sublime in the sea, body-surfing in the long Pacific swells.

One day while watching California sea lions, I noticed one animal that looked different and realized with a sudden thrill that I was looking at one of the rarest seals on earth: the Guadalupe fur seal.

Long ago about one hundred thousand of these seals lived on Guadalupe Island and on islands off California. They were wrapped in lustrous, deep-pile fur and that was fatal. Sealers killed them all. In 1890, the Guadalupe fur seal was declared "extinct." It remained "extinct" for nearly sixty years, when a single male was spotted on one of the Channel Islands. Like the elephant seals, a few Guadalupe fur seals had survived the slaughter, perhaps breeding in remote sea caves. Now they number more than four thousand and some have moved to San Miguel.

We lived in this world of seals for many weeks. The island was lovely, the crowded human world on the mainland, just east of us, seemed very far away. On the beaches a new generation of elephant seal pups was being born. Suckling the richest milk known, as thick as cream and containing 55 per cent fat, the pups expanded visibly. They gained about ten pounds every day and soon looked like rotund, flippered blimps.

It had been a close thing. A century ago, only about fifty northern elephant seals survived. Now more than forty thousand lay on the San Miguel beaches, the great sanctuary of the seals.

Chapter 8

SANTORINI ISLAND, GREECE
The Island that May Have Been Fabled Atlantis

FOUR THOUSAND YEARS AGO, on the large Mediterranean island of Crete, there flourished Europe's first great civilization: the fabulous Minoan culture of the Bronze Age. It was master of the sea, the world's first great maritime power.

Homer, the greatest poet of antiquity, wrote in the eighth century BCE in the *Odyssey* about the long-ago glory of Crete and its Minoan culture: "There is an island called Crete, set in the wine-dark sea, lovely and fertile and ocean-rounded. Those who live in this island are many...there are ninety cities there. Among the cities is mighty Knossos; its king was once Minos, who every ninth year took council with Zeus himself."

And suddenly, abruptly, at the zenith of its power and brilliance in about 1645 BCE the Minoan culture collapsed, snuffed out, it is now believed, by a horrendous natural catastrophe: the explosion of the volcanic island of Santorini, some 110 kilometres (68 miles) north of Crete. It was the greatest volcanic explosion in recorded history. Its furor, and the tsunami it unleashed, changed the history and fate of the Middle East. On Crete, it wiped out Europe's first great artistic, commercial, and maritime civilization. It may have led to the destruction of fabled Babylon. It altered the history of Egypt.

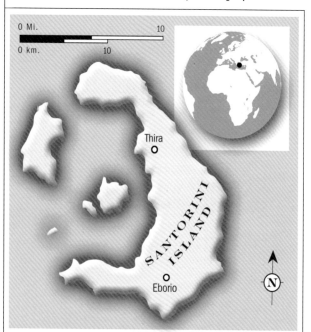

Writing in the fifth century BCE, Herodotus, the famous Greek "Father of History," said that "Crete...in ancient times was occupied entirely by non-Greek people." They may have been Carians from Asia Minor and, starting about 3000 BCE, they became the master mariners of the Mediterranean. Egypt and Mesopotamia, at that time, had flat-bottomed ships suitable only for river navigation. The Minoans of Crete are credited with the invention of the keel that gave their ocean-going ships strength and stability.

They travelled, traded, and became immensely rich. Their houses were ornamented with superb frescoes. Their kings built magnificent palaces with bathrooms that, four thousand years ago, had plumbing and drainage. Being sole masters of the sea, the Minoans feared no invasions. Their palaces were not fortified, their cities not encircled by ramparts and battlements.

Knossos, the main Minoan town, with nearly one hundred thousand inhabitants, was then the largest city in Europe and may have been at that time the largest city in the world. The Minoans founded many colonies, including one on Santorini. It was then a nearly circular island, its volcanic cone rising to a height of more than 800 metres (2624 feet). The Minoans called it Strongyle (Round Island).

This was the golden age and suddenly it ended. "After some fifteen centuries of peaceful rise to civilization and the enjoyment of its fruits," wrote Professor Peter Warren, an authority on Aegean history, "Minoan Crete suffered an enormous disaster around the mid-fiftheenth century BCE, after which the island never again rose to its former splendor."

Minoan Crete with its glorious culture faded into fable until, early in the twentieth century, it was unearthed and named by the British archaeologist Sir Arthur Evans. He excavated the 1,500-room palace of Knossos and found evidence of a long-vanished culture that had been amazingly rich and sophisticated. He named it the Minoan culture after King Minos, the legendary founder of Knossos. And he was deeply puzzled why this culture, at the very peak of its power, had ended with shocking abruptness.

In 1939, the Greek archaeologist Spyridon Marinatos proposed a solution to this riddle that is now widely accepted: the end of Minoan culture on Crete and on Santorini came with the explosion of Santorini's great volcano in 1645 BCE, followed by immense earthquakes, devastating tsunamis, and a deathly pall, as ash, spewed kilometres-high into the stratosphere, blocked out the sun and smothered fields and harvests from Crete to Asia Minor. Santorini itself was covered by a 61-metre- (200-feet-) thick layer of ash, pumice, and magma.

The Minoan inhabitants of Santorini, then called Strongyle, probably had ample warning of the impending disaster. Earthquakes shook the island and demolished houses. The people fled by ship, probably to Crete only 110 kilometres (68 miles) away. They took all their valuables and their domestic animals, for archaeological digs on Santorini have yielded lots of pottery but, unlike the similarly buried Roman city of Pompeii, no ornaments or human or animal remains.

The island shook. Immense amounts of plutonic gases lay compressed beneath its cone. They exploded with cataclysmic force, throwing up 10 cubic kilometres (6.25 cubic

Fira, the island capital, and a tourist boat glow in the early night. Centre of a great culture four thousand years ago, Santorini may have been Plato's marvellous kingdom of Atlantis.

miles) of ash, magma and pumice, hurtling magma pieces 35 kilometres (22 miles) high into the air. Stupendous plumes of ash and pumice rose into the stratosphere. It was the most powerful volcanic explosion in the past ten thousand years.

Half the round island flew into the air. The vast outpouring of magma created an immense void, the sea poured in and formed an 82-square-kilometre (31-square-mile) caldera, the second largest on earth, flanked by a crescent of remaining land: today's Santorini, 72 square kilometres (27 square miles); its sister island Thirasia, 10 square kilometres (4 square miles); and tiny Aspronisi Island.

To better envision the far-reaching devastation caused by a volcanic explosion of such magnitude, Professor Marinatos compared it to the more recent explosion of the island of Krakatoa. In August 1883, this 13-square-kilometre (5-square-mile) volcanic island that rose 813 metres (2,667 feet) high out of the Sunda Strait between the great islands of Java and Sumatra in the Netherlands East Indies (now Indonesia), exploded with a bang that could be heard 4,827 kilometres (3,000 miles) away.

It created a tidal wave, or tsunami, more than 30 metres (100 feet) high, travelling at a speed of more than 80 kilometres (50 miles) per hour. It swept away villages and coastal towns and killed more than thirty-six thousand people. (On Dec. 26, 2004, a submarine earthquake off Sumatra created a tsunami that killed more than two hundred thousand people in southeast Asia.)

Santorini's explosion, Professor Marinatos estimated, was at least four times more powerful than the explosion of Krakatoa.

The resultant tsunami destroyed the coastal settlements of Crete.

Harbours were flooded, the great fleets of Minoan ships were crushed. It was the death blow to a great and ancient culture, an early empire that had ruled the sea.

Recent studies indicate that the explosion of the Santorini volcano and the immense plumes of ash that darkened the sky, brought on a far-ranging domino-effect of disasters. Global cooling caused by the volcanic pall resulted in crop failures, not only on Crete, but in far-away Asia Minor (now Turkey). The world was dark. Ash smothered the fields. Livestock died. The people starved.

The famished and warlike Hittites of Anatolia (Turkey), led by their king, Mursilis, rushed south into Syria and Mesopotamia to obtain food. They looted stored grain and cereals and sacked cities, including Babylon, and another ancient civilization vanished. There was crop failure and famine even in Egypt, far south of Santorini, and the ruling dynasty crumbled.

The explosion of Santorini 3,500 years ago, brought an ever-widening circle of woe and war to the ancient world and, wrote Professor Marinatos, "altered the course of Western civilization."

The explosion and collapse of much of Santorini also spawned one of the world's most durable legends: the island of Atlantis, a once-perfect world, that sinned and was punished by the gods. It was destroyed by a terrible explosion and sank into the sea. C.W. Ceram in his famous book *Gods, Graves and Scholars,* states that "approximately twenty thousand volumes have been written on the Atlantis theme." That's a lot of books about a place that may have never existed.

All these books are based upon the same vague evidence. In the fifth century BCE, the great Greek philosopher Plato described Atlantis in two of his famous dialogues, *Timaeus* and *Critias.*

The existence of Atlantis, said Plato, was revealed to Solon, the wise Athenian statesman and lawgiver, when he visited Egypt. There, priests in the venerable city of Saïs, consulting ancient hieroglyphic records, told him the story of Atlantis, the perfect city, on the perfect island, in a perfect world.

The island was rich and fruitful. Vineyards covered the slopes. The fields yielded ample harvests. "The entire area was densely crowded with habitations" and the harbour was "full of vessels and merchants coming from all parts."

The rulers of Atlantis "had such an amount of wealth as was never before possessed by kings and potentates." Poseidon, god of the sea, was patron of Atlantis and the walls of his immense temple "they covered with silver, and the pinnacles with gold."

The rulers and the ruled of Atlantis created the utopian society: a wealthy society, a peaceful society, a just society. As it reached its pinnacle of perfection, however, the people of Atlantis, being human, became arrogant and aggressive, cruel and corrupt, venal and depraved. They no longer worshipped the gods, and in anger the gods destroyed them.

"There occurred violent earthquakes and floods and in a single day and night of rain all your warlike men in a body sunk into the earth, and the island of Atlantis in like manner disappeared, and was sunk beneath the sea."

Plato's story of Atlantis bred over the centuries a plethora of wacky theories and quite a few way-out but bestselling books.

The simple truth, claimed Professor Marinatos, and many scientists agree with him, is that Atlantis, the story of a great civilization wiped out in a burst of brimstone and fire, is based on ancient Egyptian accounts, long lost, that told of the eruption of Santorini and its collapse into the sea, of the "Great Flood" that followed, the terrible tsunami that destroyed the wealthy, artistic Bronze Age Minoan culture of Crete, Europe's first great civilization.

The plane from Athens banked and beneath us lay Santorini: the great, deep-blue caldera and, rising from it, the sheer, russet-red crater cliffs of the island, with the whitewashed houses of the two main towns, Fira and Oia, clinging to the crater's edge like cubistic swallows' nests.

It was late October; the summer waves of tourists had ebbed home. We rented a nice, small apartment inland, far from the costly caldera view. The owner had a cousin who would be glad to rent us a car. Santorini's population, we found, consists largely of cousins who will be glad to rent or sell you something. Tourism and the distinctive and delicious island wines are today the basis of Santorini's prosperity.

The car-rental cousin had worked for years in Chicago. "I've got a bargain for you," he said and produced a cheap but badly dented car.

I was back in minutes. "The clutch slips," I complained.

The cousin spread his hands with that wonderfully expressive sweep used by the Greeks. "So! What do you expect from a bargain?" he exclaimed.

I got used to the slipping clutch.

In the evening, photographers visiting Santorini cluster at the west end of Oia, near the remnants of an old Venetian fortress, to take pictures of the sunset. It is a postcard-pretty view, and variants of it are on dozens of postcards:

White houses and blue-domed orthodox churches of the village of Oia cling to the crater rim. In 1645 BCE, half of Santorini vanished in a volcanic explosion and was replaced by the sea-filled caldera at right.

the vast caldera a Homeric wine-dark, the steep crater cliffs umber and sombre-red in the rays of the setting sun. Oia, white and weird, the loveliest town of Santorini, appears glued to the rim of the crater, a long-stretched agglutination of white houses and blue-domed churches.

We ate on the terrace of one of the many tavernas overlooking the caldera. The water of the crater sea, deep red in the sun's afterglow, was broken by the dark outlines of two late-born islands in the caldera's centre.

After the furious outburst of 1645 BCE, Santorini lay quiescent for more than a thousand years. In 197 BCE and again in 46 CE, the island shook, the caldera, like some witch's kettle, hissed and boiled and bubbled, and a new volcanic island arose, called Palaia Kameni (Old Burnt), for its ochre and sienna-streaked rocks were born in fire and fury.

Another thousand years passed. Earthquakes shook Santorini again in the fifteenth century. The island heaved and shuddered and in the caldera another fiery island was born: Nea Kameni (New Burnt). Wisps of smoke still seep out of its fissures and tourists bathe near it for the water is warm and smells of sulphur. "It is good for you!" guides assure the visitors.

More centuries passed and Santorini was quiet and peaceful. Until 5:30 a.m. on July 9, 1956. At that moment, without warning, an earthquake struck, 7.8 on the Richter scale. In forty-five seconds, two thousand island homes, more than two thirds of all Santorini houses, were reduced to rubble and fifty people were dead. The taverna where we ate, the towns of Oia and Fira, all had been rebuilt since 1956.

We dined in the company of five cats. Santorini, like much of Greece, is cat country. Nearly every restaurant has its gang of beggar cats. Ours were experts. They sat quietly relaxed but attentive during soup. When the main course arrived, finger-long fried *marides*, delicious whitebait from the surrounding sea, the cats began to beg, faintly at first, then with growing insistence, a chorus of piteous meowing: "Please! Please! Please!" They got the heads, tails and bones, scrunched them quickly but daintily and then lost interest. Tourists, they knew, do not share dessert.

Dessert was very sweet and of Turkish descent, a souvenir of the time when Santorini was part of the Ottoman Empire and under Turkish rule from 1537 to 1830. The Turks have long gone but have not been entirely forgotten. The scarecrows on the island fields, I noticed with amusement, are dressed as Turks.

In its long history, Santorini has had many masters and many names. To its Minoan inhabitants it was Strongyle (the Round Island). After the great explosion of 1645 BCE, the island was no longer round. Only a jagged crescent

The famous fresco of the Fisherman and His Mackerel Catch *was painted nearly four thousand years ago and preserved by a thick layer of volcanic ash. The beautiful naked boy may have been bringing offerings to a temple.*

remained, capped with up to 60 metres (200 feet) of tephra, compacted volcanic ash.

Weathered ash is fertile. Santorini must have recovered quickly, for twenty years after the catastrophe, when Phoenician sailors settled it briefly, it was called Kalliste (Most Fair). They were followed by Doric people who came island-conquering from the Greek mainland and named the island Thera after one of their mythological kings. Today, that remains the island's official name, but islanders and visitors generally prefer to call it Santorini.

The Dorians ruled for a thousand years, their capital, also called Thera, perched on a high plateau above the city. It was a wealthy city with an open-air theatre that seated 1,500. A neatly chiselled phallus on a stone still points in the direction of the city's long-ago "House of Pleasure."

Three empires rose and fell and left their vestiges on Santorini: the flamboyant but short-lived realm of Alexander the Great; the rigorous, road-building empire of the Romans; and the Byzantine Empire, which bestowed on the island its Orthodox faith and its numerous, beautiful, usually blue-domed churches.

Byzantium crumbled, Venice took over the island group known as the Cyclades in 1207 CE and divided the spoils among its nobles. The new lord landed first on the small island of Thirasia on the northwest side of the caldera, near the church of Aghia Irini (Saint Irene), an early Christian martyr. To the Venetians, she was Santa Irene, the patron saint of the island, and after her the island was called Santorini.

Then came Turkish rule from 1537 to 1830: corrupt, extortionate, but oddly tolerant. As long as the islanders paid lots of taxes, their Osmanli rulers left them alone.

In 1830, Santorini became part of independent Greece, a remote island of poor fishermen and vintners. The island's main export, a gift from the 1645 BCE explosion, was pozzolana, also called Santorini Earth, volcanic ash and tuff mixed with slaked lime that produced a mortar so iron-hard and water-resistant, Ferdinand Marie de Lesseps used it in the nineteenth century to build the Suez Canal.

Santorini, poor and peaceful, awoke from its slumbers when the tourists came: a trickle in the 1960s, a steady stream in the 1970s and 1980s, and now a massive flood, attracted by Santorini's fascinating history, its stunning colours, and by Akrotiri, its buried Minoan city, the "Pompeii of the Aegean."

On the south coast of Santorini where, on a clear fall day, one can see Crete looming on the distant horizon, there once stood a Minoan city. It was, like Knossos on Crete, a wealthy Bronze Age trading city. Warned by the earthquakes that preceded the 1645 BCE eruptions, the citizens fled by ship, taking along their livestock and their most valuable possessions.

The volcano exploded, the remaining portion of Santorini was covered by a thick blanket of ash and pumice and its city lay buried, sealed, and forgotten for 3,500 years.

In 1967, the veteran Greek archaeologist Spyridon Marinatos, at that time Greece's inspector general of antiquities, guided by the "instincts archaeologists develop in the field," began an excavation near the present-day village of Akrotiri.

Slowly the remains of the ancient Minoan city emerged. A wealthy city, its streets flanked by two- and even three-storey houses. We visited it often, fascinating excursions into the distant past that often was not that different from the present. "The finds show that the street-level rooms were often used as stores," our guide explained. "The upper floors were probably inhabited by the owners." It was a way of living and doing business in the same building that was once common in Europe and is still common in many Middle Eastern cities.

The discovery of a perfectly preserved Bronze Age city, wrote Professor Marinatos, "offered fascinating glimpses into the life as well as the death of the Minoan Age." Tragically, it brought its discoverer both worldwide fame and death. On October 1, 1974, Professor Marinatos was killed by the crumbling wall of a building. His grave, always graced with flowers, is near the ancient city he found.

The houses of the wealthy in the ash-sealed city were often decorated with superb frescoes, masterpieces of art, the colours marvellously fresh and vivid after 3,500 years. In one house, perhaps once owned by a successful captain, the three walls of the main room were ornamented by a 6-metre (20-foot) long panorama painting of a fleet returning in triumph, probably from Africa. Lions chase gazelles. Dolphins arch high out of the sea. A long procession of large, canopied ships, packed with oarsmen, passes two cities. The inhabitants crowd the shores in joyous welcome.

The original frescoes, shattered by earthquakes, have been restored and are now at the National Archaeological Museum in Athens. But perfect copies are on Santorini and they are a delight. The ancient pictures are full of grace and vitality. Two young boys are boxing; it is the first known depiction of gloves. A young fisherman carries a rich catch of mackerel. He is naked, as was then customary when approaching an altar. So the fish may be his gift to the gods.

I loved the animals. A bird darts through the air above a spring scene of lilies, its rust-red throat and deep-forked tail the perfect image of *Hirundo rustica*, the common swallow that builds its mud-cup nests in the barns and byres all over Europe.

Some paintings were equally beautiful but puzzling. I recognized the animals in a large fresco immediately: Beisa oryx, a large antelope with very long, slightly curved horns. I have photographed it often in Kenya. Another fresco shows a troop of cheeky blue monkeys raiding a garden.

These pictures are so vivid and alive, and so accurate, the artist must have seen the animals. But where? Did he see and sketch them during a Minoan trading trip to Africa? Or did these animals, now restricted to Africa, range into Europe in those days? Lions, after all, were then common in southeastern Europe, and the Middle East. They were the bane of herders (King David, the Bible tells us, slew a lion when he was a shepherd youth) and a favourite trophy of hunting kings. Monkeys then roamed Europe. (A remnant population of European macaques still lives on the Rock of Gibraltar.)

So perhaps these "African" animals, so vivid and elegant in the frescoes, lived in Europe at the time. Created with marvellous verve by unknown artists, the Akrotiri frescoes are among the most beautiful paintings ever made, pictures from a long-ago world on the island that may have been Plato's Atlantis.

Chapter 9

SABLE ISLAND, CANADA
Island of Dead Ships and Wild Horses

OR FOUR-AND-A-HALF centuries, Sable Island, 160 kilometres (99 miles) east of Nova Scotia, was the island most feared in all the Atlantic Ocean. Alexander Graham Bell who visited Sable Island in 1898 to search for the bodies of friends lost in the sinking of the liner *La Bourgogne* called it, "One of the world's most terrible traps for sailors."

More than four hundred ships perished on Sable Island and on the shoals and bars that surround it. The wrecks and the bodies of thousands of drowned sailors were slowly buried by the island's shifting sands. As the death toll mounted, Sable Island became widely known as the "Graveyard of the Atlantic."

Sable Island is a narrow, treeless crescent of sand, 37 kilometres (23 miles) long, barely a mile wide, its highest dunes rising to about 24 metres (80 feet). It is the remnant, scientists believe, of a once-vast land that may have extended from the Grand Banks to the United States. Certain insect species are found on Sable Island and at Cape Cod in Massachusetts, and nowhere else in the world.

A rising sea after the last ice age slowly drowned this land. Sable Island, a sinister scimitar of sand, is the summit and remnant of this once-vast and now-vanished land. Submerged sand bars extend into the sea from either end of the low, often fog-shrouded island. The whole, surrounded by shifting shoals and shallows, forms an 85-kilometre- (53-mile-) long lethal trap for ships. "The deadliest piece of real estate in the country," the Canadian writer and historian Pierre Berton called it.

Sable Island was so deadly because it lies at the vortex of powerful ocean currents. Swirling gyres and eddies sucked ships, groping blindly through the fog, toward the fatal shores. Storms were frequent and vicious. The average wind speed on Sable is 33 kilometres (21 miles) per hour. The winter gales that shriek and rage across the flat island have reached 209 kilometres (130 miles) per hour.

And Sable, fog-hidden and storm-haunted, lay in the path of two major shipping lanes: the Great Circle Route from New England to Europe, and the route from the Gulf of St. Lawrence and the Maritimes to Europe. From its discovery by Europeans in 1500, Sable was destined to be the isle of death.

The Portuguese, master mariners of the age, discovered the low sand island in 1500. Pedro Reinel, a pilot "of much fame," showed it on his 1505 map of the just-discovered New World. He called it Santa Cruz. It, and tiny Funk Island off Newfoundland, which Reinel called Y dos Aves (Island of Birds), were among the very first parts of Canada to receive European names.

The Portuguese named it. They also realized that the long but fog-hidden island (then perhaps twice as long as it is now) was a terrible danger to ships. As was their custom, they released cattle and pigs on the island as food for shipwrecked mariners.

Sir Humphrey Gilbert heard of this when he claimed Newfoundland for his queen, Elizabeth I of England. Red-haired and hot-tempered, Gilbert, half-brother of Sir Walter Raleigh, was a flamboyant Elizabethan man: soldier, sailor, explorer, adventurer, courtier, schemer, dreamer, and charmer. He had lost fortunes on alchemical get-rich-schemes, trying to turn iron into copper and lead into quicksilver.

Hoping to recoup his losses, Gilbert planned to seize and settle large portions of the New World. He led a fleet of five ships to Newfoundland and sailed into St. John's harbour, already a centre of Europe's fishing fleets. On August 15, 1583, in the presence of thirty-six ships "of all nations," twenty Spanish and Portuguese and sixteen French and English, he took formal possession of Newfoundland for England.

While in St. John's, a Portuguese captain told Sir Humphrey that "some thirty years past they [the Portuguese] did put into the Island [Sable] both neat and swine which were multiplied

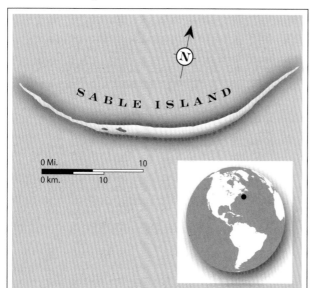

SABLE ISLAND

0 Mi.   10
0 km.   10

exceedingly." ("Neat" is an old English word for cattle.)

Being short of food, Gilbert sailed for Sable to stock his ship with beef and pork. A storm "blew vehemently," thick fog shrouded the sea, and through the pall they heard "strange voyces," possibly the loud and large walrus herds then living on Sable. The warning came too late. The largest ship, the 120-ton *Delight*, struck a shoal. Huge waves pounded and smashed the ship and nearly a hundred sailors drowned. They were the first recorded victims of Sable Island.

Gilbert's was not a successful venture, but it annoyed and alarmed England's rival, France. To forestall any further English expansion, King Henri IV of France, with that gracious largesse of kings giving away what does not belong to them, gave title to "Canada and adjacent territories" to a Breton nobleman, Troïlus de Mesgouez, marquis de la Roche.

Before colonizing Canada, the marquis decided to settle Sable Island (called Isle de Sable, the island of sand by the French). Since volunteers for the venture were scarce, the marquis recruited his fifty-odd settlers from the prisons of France. He put them ashore on Sable in 1598 together with some provisions. Then a violent storm blew his ship all the way back to France. There his creditors had him thrown in jail.

The abandoned colonists built crude cabins with timbers from wrecked ships or, as a contemporary historian reported, lived "like foxes in sand pits." They hunted seals, walruses, and the Portuguese cattle. And they quarrelled. As Marc Lescarbot, the lawyer-historian at Port Royal remarked with icy logic in 1606, they fought *"et coupe la gorge l'un à l'autre, tant que le nombre se racourcit de jour en jour"* (they cut each other's throat so that their number diminished daily).

When, after five years, it occurred to King Henri to find out what had happened to the colonists, the rescue ship from France found only eleven survivors. Dressed in sealskins, with shoulder-length hair and long beards, the men were presented at court. They looked, said one amazed courtier, like ancient river gods. The king gave each man a pouch with fifty *écus* (gold coin). He also granted all of them a full pardon.

As shipwrecks on Sable became more frequent, they also became a potential source of profit. Boston merchants in the seventeenth century regularly sent expeditions to Sable Island to loot wrecks, save survivors, and slaughter the wild cattle, descendants of the cattle the Portuguese had left on Sable more than a century before. At times, the island herds were large. In 1633, John Rose, a shipwrecked sailor out of Boston lived several months on Sable and estimated that about eight hundred head of cattle roamed the island.

The men from Boston also hunted seals and the walruses who had on Sable Island, at the latitude of Milan, Italy, their southernmost colonies. John Winthrop, first governor of the Massachusetts Bay colony, wrote in his *History of New England* that, in 1642, "the merchants of Boston sent out a vessel again to the isle of Sable, with 12 men, to stay there a year. They brought home 400 pairs of sea horse [walrus] teeth which were esteemed worth 300 Pounds Sterling...also 12 tons of oil and many skins."

In 1738, Andrew LeMercier, Huguenot pastor of Boston had the idea of establishing on Sable, far from sin and city, a colony of French Protestants. He petitioned Nova Scotia's governor in council to rent him land for this pious project. Settling the island, he pointed out, would be a "Great Advantage...to His Majesty's Unfortunate Subjects...so unlucky as to Suffer Shipwreck near to Or upon the Island of Sable."

Harsh climate and marginal food have produced a distinct island breed of horses, small, stocky, with thick fur and long manes and tails. After storms, they stand in the surf and eat the washed-out, nutrient-rich rhizomes of marram grass.

As an earnest of his good intentions, LeMercier wrote, he had already sent to Sable in 1737, "Horn Cattle, Swine, Sheep and so forth...in order to Succour, Help and Relieve such as may be shipwrecked there." (By about 1700 the efficient Boston hunters had killed all the Portuguese cattle.

They had also wiped out the once-great walrus colonies on Sable Island.)

LeMercier's colony on the foggy, storm-lashed island was to consist of one hundred Huguenot families. That plan failed, probably to the profound relief of his parishioners. But the pastor did send a few workmen and their families to the island. They lived there for fifteen years. LeMercier, who himself wisely avoided living on Sable, spoke of his men's existence with the pushy charm of a promoter. In summer, they had large gardens "and looked after the cattle." In winter, "they go and kill Seils [seals] and boil their Fat into Oyl, as well as that of Whales which now and then are cast away dead upon the Beach." The people lived well, he claimed, made some profit and, he added piously, had "the pleasure of saving often Men's Lives."

Finally the pastor would not, or could not, pay the penny-an-acre quit-rent. In 1753, he abandoned his settlement plans, leaving on the island: "90 Sheep, between 20 and 30 Horses, including Colts, Stallions and Breeding Mares, about 30 or 40 Cows, and 40 Hogs." The horses he left are the ancestors of the "wild horses" that now roam Sable Island.

Toward the end of the eighteenth century, the feared island was claiming an average of ten ships each year. Its reputation, always bad, became increasingly sinister. Wreckers established themselves on the island. They lit false beacons to lure additional ships to their doom and, rumour had it, murdered survivors systematically to obtain their valuables and, incidentally, eliminate witnesses. "Every year adds to the calamities occasioned by this dreadful Island," wrote the Nova Scotia journalist John Howe. It was high time, he urged, to create on Sable Island "some establishment under the sanction of government."

The final straw was the loss on December 22, 1799 of the 280-ton snow *Frances* carrying the personal furniture and goods of Prince Edward, Duke of Kent, commander-in-chief of His Majesty's forces in North America (and future father of Queen Victoria). Nineteen sailors died in the wreck, as well as the ship's surgeon, Dr. Copeland, his wife and children, twelve of the duke's magnificent horses, their coachman, and four young stable boys.

This tragedy, one of so many on Sable Island, was exacerbated by lurid tales. Sealers who had lived on the island left hurriedly, their schooner reportedly laden with royal luggage. The men had also, it was alleged, robbed the bloated corpses on the beach and hacked a finger off Mrs. Copeland's hand to get her rings. She henceforth haunted the island, and the lady with the bloodied hand became the most famous ghost of Sable Island.

That did it. Wreckers and sealers were expelled from Sable Island. In 1801, the Nova Scotia House of Assembly voted six hundred pounds sterling to establish a lifesaving station on Sable and settle three families there.

The lifesavers patrolled the island, saved sailors, tried their hand at some ecologically disastrous farming, and introduced all sorts of animals that did the island no good. About 1804, they released pigs. They fattened nicely and the families looked forward to wonderful feasts. But when they discovered the main reason why the roaming pigs were so fat, it cut their appetite. The pigs had turned ghouls, digging up and eating the corpses of drowned sailors. The pigs were shot. The drifting sand covered them.

Rats abandoned sinking ships and scurried ashore. The settlers released rabbits. Rats and rabbits multiplied prodigiously until their number reached plague proportions. To control both, cats were imported. They ate rats and rabbits, but also the island birds. Foxes were imported. They ate cats, rats, rabbits, and the settlers' chickens. Finally, a gang of tough terriers was imported. They decimated rats, rabbits, cats, foxes, and were then returned to the mainland.

In the nineteen-century ship traffic between North America and Europe increased and so did the number of ships trapped and killed by Sable Island, an average of fifteen wrecks every year. The importance of the lifesaving station was so well-recognized that during the 1812 war between Great Britain and the United States, President James Madison ordered that "the public and private armed vessels of the United States are not to interrupt any British unarmed vessel bound to Sable Island and laden with supplies for the humane establishment there."

Near Sable three powerful ocean currents meet: the Labrador Current and the Belle Isle Current bring masses of cold water from north and east. The Gulf Stream contributes warm water from the south. Where their waters meet and mix, they produce fog, shrouding Sable Island for weeks at a time—nine weeks one recent summer. Within that fog lies the low island, deadly and invisible.

Joshua Slocum, the first person to sail around the world single-handedly, passed Sable in 1895 and wrote, "I was in a world of fog, shut off from the universe." He swerved wide "to be clear of land and shoals...[of this] Island of Tragedies."

Tales of tragedies and heroism, death and despair crowd the diaries kept by successive superintendents of the Sable Island lifesaving station. In 1854, the 715-ton barque *Arcadia*, carrying a large cargo of glass, iron and silk, and 147 German passengers from Antwerp to New York, struck Sable Island.

The rescuers made six trips with their surfboat through the crashing waves and saved more than eighty people. Then they had to stop and superintendent Matthew McKenna wrote, "When night came on and we had to haul up our boat, the cries of those left on the wreck were truly heart rending. In the hurry of work families had been separated and when those on shore heard the cries of those on the wreck at seeing the boat hauled, a scene was witnessed that may be better imagined but cannot be described."

During the night, the storm abated. Next morning, the remaining passengers and crew were saved. A few days later, another storm struck and the *Arcadia* "was broken in a thousand pieces."

Some diary entries border on the fabulous. In 1846, the superintendent Joseph Darby recorded a marvellous tale of oil on troubled water. The schooner *Arno* "was running down right before this tremendous gale...[and it seemed] incredible that any vessel could live to come so great a distance through such mountains of broken water."

As the ship came close, Darby saw that, miraculously, the sea before the ship turned "smooth as glass." The *Arno* had barrels of oil on board. The crew spread it over the tumultuous waters and it made "the surface smooth before her and left a shining path behind." Thus the *Arno* sailed safely through the raging sea to shore and all her crew was saved. As the Italians say so nicely, "*Si non é vero, é ben trovato!*" (It may not be true, but it's beautifully said.)

Decades passed. Hundreds of ships, deflected by currents and blinded by fog, crashed into the deadly sand island. Ernest Baker, a Nova Scotia fisherman, visited Sable in the early twentieth century and found its beaches covered with the cargo of destroyed ships. "And the wrecks! You couldn't hardly walk for the wrecks, especially on the northeast end."

Forty years later, thanks to sonar and radar, ships could "see" and skirt the fog-hidden island. In 1947, a radio beacon was installed on Sable Island. That same year the Panamanian freighter *Manhasset* struck the south shore and pounding waves destroyed the ship. After 450 years of disasters and death, it was Sable Island's last victim. Twelve years later, the Sable Island Humane Establishment was closed. Only a weather station remained on the island.

A violent era ended. Sable became a sanctuary, home to thousands of seals, herds of wild horses, and a multitude of birds, among them the rare, sand-yellowish Ipswich sparrow, which nests on Sable Island and nowhere else in the world.

Only three wrecks, all off-shore, were visible when I first visited Sable Island in January 1967. The mast of the *Manhasset*, the last ship to die near Sable, rose like a symbolic cross above the waves. A few years later, wreck and mast had vanished. Nothing on Sable, I quickly learned, is permanent, except the wind and the waves and the fog.

The dunes move. The very island moves. Waves and wind gnaw away at the island's west end, and wind and waves build up the island's east end. In five centuries, Sable Island has shifted about 16 kilometres (10 miles) from west to east.

Dr. Arthur Mansfield of the Fisheries Research Board of Canada and I had come to Sable Island to study grey seals, then, with a total population of less than five thousand the rarest seals in Canada. All along the Atlantic coast these seals were avidly killed by fishermen and bounty hunters. Only on remote Sable Island were the seals safe.

They lay on the sand in "family" groups, dark, 317-to-362-kilogram (700-to-800-pound) males possessively guarding tan-coloured, dark-dotted females and their large-eyed pups, wrapped in silky-soft lanugo, the white natal fur. About three hundred grey seal pups were born on Sable Island that winter. We tagged most of them to learn about their later life, their wanderings, and their fate.

Survivors returned to the safety of Sable Island. The colony grew. Now more than fifty thousand grey seal pups are born each winter on Sable Island. It is the largest grey seal colony in the world.

The lighthouses near the east and west ends of the island had been automated. We lived in the long-abandoned lighthouse keeper's home near the island's east end, a sturdy house, its shingled walls the silvery grey of aged, sand-polished wood.

It stormed. We sat in the warm kitchen of the old house and listened to the dull, rhythmic roar of the surf. Outside, the air was brown with flying sand. A herd of horses, a stallion, four mares, and their foals, huddled in the lee of our house, heads low, their rumps turned into the raging wind. Nestled cozily into the deep-pile fur of one of the horses sat three starlings, keeping their feet warm.

These were the descendants of the strong Acadian work horses the Huguenot pastor LeMercier released on Sable Island more than 250 years ago, plus some horses brought in the nineteenth century from the mainland "to improve the island breed."

After World War II, some Ottawa bureaucrats decided to remove the "useless" island horses and turn them into something useful, like dog food and glue. That news, not surprisingly, produced shrieks of outrage from environmentalists

and horse lovers, and the bureaucrats hurriedly backed off. In 1961, the Canadian government passed a law that "No person shall molest, interfere with, feed or otherwise have anything to do with the ponies on the island."

Clay pipes, hand-forged nails, and shards of ancient vessels lie on the sand of Sable Island, relics from the more than four hundred ships wrecked on the island's low, often fog-shrouded coast.

The population fluctuates. In 1967, there were 181 horses on the island. Some years later, they had increased to 340. Then came a cruel winter, cold and stormy, and more than two hundred horses died. Only the toughest, the fittest survived.

Such ruthless selection has produced a distinctive Sable Island type: small, stocky and short-eared, with heavy dark-brown fur and long, black forelock, mane and tail. Most horses have the dark dorsal stripe that, eons ago, was the distinctive marking of the wild horses of Eurasia.

We passed several herds each day. Some horses were tame and curious. They walked up to us to say "Hello!" Others were very shy. When we came within 91 metres (100 yards), the lead stallion whinnied a warning and the herd galloped away, their hoofs thudding on Sable's sand, long manes flowing in the wind.

On this island of sand, the wind covers, the wind uncovers. After a storm, I noticed bone sticking out of the sand. I dug the sand away and a great walrus skull emerged, brittle and mineral-stained, the long ivory tusks amber-brown, a memento of the time, before their extermination, when large walrus herds lolled on the beaches of Sable Island.

A dune moved, and parts of an ancient house emerged. Hand-forged, rust-eaten nails lay on the sand, pottery shards, broken dishes that came from England, clay pipes, and chips of amethyst-coloured glass, knives with bone handles, and a lead musket ball. An exquisite little ship's lantern emerged from the sand, its glass sandblasted and matte, its metal frame so eaten by the corrosive salt air, it crumbled at my touch.

There could be treasures on Sable Island. I never found anything more precious than clay pipes, but Christel Bell who, with her husband Norman, lived for many years on Sable, had found, after storms, a few Spanish gold coins on the beach.

"An American came with a metal detector," Norman Bell, who ran the island's power station, told me. "He didn't find any treasure. But he sure found a lot of old nails."

Treasure of a different sort has been found near Sable Island: vast amounts of natural gas. The search for off-shore oil and gas near Sable began in the early 1960s. Success came in August of 1971, when Mobil Oil Canada, drilling on the extreme west spit of Sable Island, brought in a gusher, the first producing off-shore well on the Atlantic seaboard north of the Gulf of Mexico.

Now giant rigs rise from the shallow sea near Sable, the region that once was so deadly to ships, and natural gas deposits that may amount to trillions of cubic feet flow to the furnaces and factories of energy-hungry North America.

I returned to Sable Island for many years: in winter, the breeding season of grey seals; in spring for the breeding harbour seals that also have large colonies on this sanctuary island. I lived in the old, wind-scoured house near the island's east end. It stood in the way of a wandering dune. Slowly sand surrounded the house, engulfed it, crushed it. The last time I visited Sable, "my" house had vanished. But nearby, in a wind-scooped gully, the remains of an ancient ship were beginning to emerge from the sand.

JUAN FERNANDEZ ISLANDS, CHILE
The Island Where Robinson Crusoe Lived

THE REMOTE JUAN FERNANDEZ Islands in the Pacific Ocean were once home to the man who was Robinson Crusoe, and to a multitude of seals. Crusoe, the world's most famous castaway, was in reality Alexander Selkirk, a fiery-tempered Scot from Largo in County Fife who spent more than four years alone on this island. His adventures inspired Daniel Defoe, "the father of modern journalism," to write the classic *The Life and Strange Surprizing Adventures of Robinson Crusoe.*

Selkirk survived and was eventually rescued. The seals with whom he shared the island, the elegant, endemic Juan Fernandez fur seals, fared worse. Sealers came, mostly from New England, and killed and killed and killed. In less than a century they massacred more than four million seals and when they were finished the once-crowded lava beaches were empty. By 1860, the Juan Fernandez fur seal was considered "extinct." A century later, a few survivors were rediscovered.

The volcanic Juan Fernandez Islands, two main islands and a spattering of islets, soar in steep-cliffed grandeur from the sea near the western edge of the Humboldt Current, which sweeps cold, food-rich water north along the west coast of South America. The uninhabited islands were discovered in 1563 by the Spanish navigator Juan Fernandez. He stopped briefly and put goats ashore as future provender for

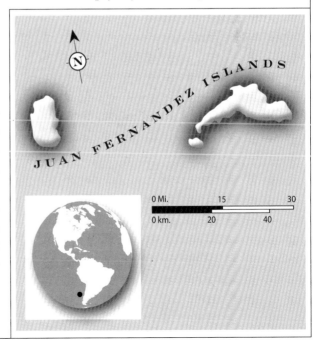

Robinson Crusoe's cave. The real-life Crusoe, the seaman Alexander Selkirk, lived alone on this remote island from 1704 to 1709. He survived by hunting feral goats.

ship-wrecked sailors. It was a common practice of the time. Later, the descendants of those goats provided the marooned Selkirk with food and clothing.

With little imagination the main islands were initially called Màs a Tierra ("close to land," referring to South America 643 kilometres [400 miles] away), and Màs a Fuera ("farther out," 160 kilometres [100 miles] farther west). In 1966, the Chilean government renamed the islands after their most famous resident. Màs a Tierra is now Isla Robinson Crusoe; Màs a Fuera is Isla Alejandro Selkirk.

Selkirk was born in 1676, the seventh son of John Selcraig (as the name was then spelled), Largo's cobbler and tanner. Records agree that young Alexander was the village's vile-tempered tough. After one nasty fight, he evaded justice by going to sea.

He returned two years later, a good sailor but still quick to anger and flare. His brother laughed when, by mistake, Alexander drank some salt water and gagged. He thrashed the brother, and then his father and sister-in-law when they tried to stop him. That earned him a public and humiliating rebuke in the kirk next Sunday. Disgruntled, he went to sea again.

In 1703, Selkirk joined a two-ship privateering venture commanded by one of the era's strangest men: William Dampier, full-time pirate, part-time explorer, naturalist, anthropologist, author of a brilliant treatise on hydrography, bestselling writer, and the only man of his time to have sailed three times around the world.

They sailed in September 1703. Dampier commanded the 320-ton *St. George*. Selkirk was sailing master (first mate) aboard the 120-ton *Cinque Ports* with a crew of sixty-three and a young, tyrannical captain, the twenty-one-year-old Thomas Stradling, "a man," wrote a contemporary, "of ferocious and quarrelsome temper." It was not a happy voyage.

They zigzagged down the east coast of South America, plundering Spanish ships, looting coastal towns. They survived the gales off Cape Horn and sailed storm-battered and bickering into tranquil Cumberland Bay of Màs a Tierra, to take on water and wood, repair the ships and harvest the turnips that Dampier had planted on a previous voyage in 1683 and which had "now overspread some acres of ground."

The captains quarrelled and Dampier sailed off in a huff. Aboard the *Cinque Ports,* rebellion brewed. Stradling wanted to sail on, rob, pillage, collect booty. Selkirk claimed the ship, riddled by wood-boring teredo worms, was not seaworthy. They argued. When the captain, pulling rank, insisted on leaving, Selkirk in a fit of fury, and believing many of the crew would follow him, demanded to be set ashore. Stradling, glad to be rid of his mutinous mate, agreed immediately.

It was October 1705. Alexander Selkirk was twenty-eight years old. A boat took him ashore together with his clothes and bedding, a firelock gun, some powder, bullets, tobacco, a hatchet, a knife, a kettle, a Bible, a flask of rum, and "his Mathematical Instruments and Books."

The boat pulled away. Selkirk stood alone on shore. None of the crew had joined him. Suddenly the true horror of the situation struck him. In desperation he waded out into the surf and shrieked and pleaded. Stradling was pleased. He jeered. The crew laughed. The ship sailed away. (Much later, Selkirk learned that his warning had been accurate. Shortly after abandoning him, the leaky *Cinque Ports* sank off Peru. Most men drowned. Captain Stradling and a few survivors ended up in Spanish prisons.)

The first eight months, Selkirk later told his rescuer, Captain Woodes Rogers, were terrible. He was consumed, he told Rogers, by "Melancholy, and the Terror of being left alone in such a desolate place." He lingered near shore, hoping, praying the ship would return. It didn't. He ate only enough to keep alive. At times, in despair, he came close to committing suicide.

Gradually he rallied. He explored the rugged, heavily forested, steep-sided 93-square-kilometre (36-square-mile) island. He built two huts with "Piemento Trees, cover'd them with long Grass, and lin'd them with the Skins of Goats," which he killed with his gun as long as the powder lasted.

Food was not a problem. Massive sea turtles crawled up the beach. They were easy to kill, delicious to eat. On the ebb, tidal pools were acrawl with "craw-fish," the large "Juan Fernandez lobsters," really a clawless crayfish (and today the islands' number one export). Fish were plentiful but, wrote Rogers, "he could not eat 'em for want of Salt, because they occasion'd a Looseness."

At first he made fire with steel, flint, and tinder. Later he learned how to produce fire by friction with a simple but efficient fire drill. In one hut he cooked, worked, and slept. In the other he sang psalms, played, and read the Bible "so that he said he was a better Christian while in the Solitude than ever he was before."

His main food was goat. During his four years on the island, he killed more than five hundred. At first he shot them. Then, a strong, vigorous, agile man, he raced "with a wonderful Swiftness thro the Woods and up the Rocks and Hills," outran the goats and killed them with his knife. Cooked with the abundant turnips Dampier had planted in 1683, seasoned with the fruits of the pimento tree, which were as good as the "best Jamaica pepper," he made a sort of spicy goat goulash. It was his favourite meal. Wandering through the dense forest of his island, he also discovered a sort of medicinal black pepper "which was very good to expel the wind, and against Griping of the Guts."

Years passed. His shoes wore out. His feet became calloused and hard as leather. His clothes fell apart in the warm, moist climate. He made a coat and cap of goat skins, stitched together with goat-skin thong, using a nail as an awl.

At first, cats and rats from ships, ran wild upon the island and were a pest. The rats "gnaw'd at his Feet and Clothes while asleep." He tamed the abundant cats "so that they would lie about him in hundreds." With a bit of coaxing, his cat friends "soon delivered him from the rats."

The lonely man also tamed some young goats "and to divert himself would now and then sing and dance with them and his Cats."

Now resigned, physically and mentally amazingly fit, Selkirk was never sick, but had one terrible accident. He raced after a goat, caught it at the very edge of a precipice and both goat and man tumbled over. He fell on top of the goat. That saved his life but "stunn'd and bruised...he lay there 24 hours" and then slowly, painfully dragged himself back to his hut, which was a mile distant. It took him more than a week to recover.

He became reconciled to his island existence and its solitude. But the intense hope of rescue never left him. Every day he climbed a 548-metre (1,800-foot) cliff (now called Mirador de Selkirk [Selkirk's Lookout]) and scanned the sea, hoping to spot a saving sail.

A few ships passed in the distance. Two ships landed. Both were Spanish and, more than exile and loneliness, Selkirk dreaded the Spanish "for he apprehended they would murder him, or make a Slave of him in the Mines."

Four years and four months passed. And then, on February 2, 1709, while Selkirk stood high on his lookout, two British ships, the *Duke* and *Duchess* in need of fresh water, sailed into Cumberland Bay. They were commanded by a famous and rather classy pirate, Woodes Rogers. He was now on a privateering spree around the world, sponsored by Bristol merchants, and made such a pile of money, he subsequently leased the Bahamas. Later, as first royal governor of the Bahamas, the ex-pirate gone legit, became the dreaded scourge of Caribbean pirates.

Now, Rogers dryly reported, "our Pinnace returned from shore, and brought abundance of Craw-fish, with a Man cloth'd in Goat-Skins, who look'd wilder than their first Owners." Very much the wild man from the woods, Selkirk "had so much forgot his Language for want of Use, that we could scarce understand him."

One man knew him. The ever-sailing William Dampier was navigator of the expedition. Selkirk, he assured Rogers, "was the best Man" on the *Cinque Ports*. Rogers, impressed, immediately agreed "with him to be Mate on board our ship."

Saved, shaved, newly clad in clothes, and now mate aboard the *Duke*, it took Selkirk a while to adjust. He had trouble with shoes and "his Feet swell'd when he came first to wear 'em again." After four years of fresh goat stew and lobster, he found the ship's salt pork diet revolting. But the two-year pirating voyage was so successful that when Selkirk returned to Britain in 1711, his share of the booty came to eight hundred pounds sterling.

He was now wealthy and he soon became famous. His story was widely published in magazines, broadsheets, and pamphlets. The prolific author Daniel Defoe heard the tale and enhanced Selkirk's life into the Robinson Crusoe adventure. To provide native colour, Defoe changed the locale to the Caribbean, kept the goats but added cannibals, and provided Crusoe with his famous Man Friday, the native servant whom he acquired on a Friday.

Selkirk, the real-life Crusoe, had trouble with civilization. He returned to Largo, his native village, a grouchy recluse. He moped and pined for a paradise lost. "Oh my beloved island!" he once exclaimed. "I wish I had never left thee!"

A misfit on land, Selkirk returned to sea. He died on December 13, 1721 off the coast of Africa, probably of typhus. He was forty-five years old.

Years after Selkirk left, death came to his "beloved island." Sealers arrived to butcher the fur seals that covered the dark lava beaches like a living carpet. One of the few men to describe the immense colonies before the sealing started was Selkirk's one-time commander, William Dampier. He visited Màs a Tierra in 1683. There, he wrote, "seals swarm as thick about this Island, as if they had no other place in the World to live in; for there is not a Bay nor Rock that one can get ashore on, but is full of them...Here are always thousands, I might say possibly millions of them."

Dampier may have been right. In a recent review, based on seventeenth- and eighteenth-century kill and sales figures, the Chilean scientist Daniel Torres of the Instituto Antartico Chileno concluded that "the total population toward the end of the seventeenth century exceeded four million animals."

For New England sealers, this was a call of fortune. They sailed to the Juan Fernandez Islands in winter, the seals' breeding season, when the great beaches were covered with males, females, and pups. The men moved in among the densely packed animals, smashed skulls with five-foot hickory clubs, and flayed the twitching corpses. Amasa Delano, one of the sealing captains, reported that "some men could skin 60 seals an hour."

The men marched on, killing, skinning, salting the precious pelts, and hauling them to their ships. The beaches, before so full of life, were now covered with bloody corpses and with hungry, screaming pups next to their skinned mothers. They cried for days and then they died of starvation.

During peak years in the early eighteenth century, men from up to fourteen ships killed seals season after season. They were devastatingly efficient. Some pelts were shipped to Europe, but the bulk went to Canton, China, where the dense lustrous fur was highly prized. Captain Delano "made an estimate of more than 3,000,000 that has been carried to Canton from thence [the Juan Fernandez Islands] in the space of seven years. I have carried more than 100,000 myself."

In Canton, the fur seal pelts were often exchanged for bales of silk and chests of tea. Owners, masters, and agents profited greatly. Each sealer, for his dangerous and brutally hard work, received one skin in a hundred, or between one hundred twenty and two hundred dollars after a successful voyage that might last nearly a year.

After more than a century of slaughter, the Juan Fernandez fur seal was on the edge of extinction. When Captain Benjamin Morrell of the American Merchant Service visited the islands in 1834, they were "nearly without seals." In the years that followed, the odd sealer still passed to kill the few remaining animals. By 1850, the great breeding beaches were empty. The Juan Fernandez fur seal was listed as "extinct."

A hundred years later, rumours reached Chile that seals had been sighted near the Juan Fernandez Islands. In

Elegant Juan Fernandez fur seal. Millions were killed by sealers. By the 1850s this fur seal was listed as "extinct." A remnant population was discovered in 1965. It may have survived in sea caves. Now about ten thousand of these beautiful fur seals breed again on the Juan Fernandez Islands.

1965, the Chilean scientist N. Bahamonde visited the islands and discovered two hundred seals. In 1968, an American expedition, led by marine biologist Kenneth Norris confirmed that there were seals near the islands and these were indeed the "extinct" Juan Fernandez fur seals.

We had crayfish for supper, the famous Juan Fernandez lobster, fresh from the sea, the meat a delicate pink, firm and delicious, with Chilean white wine, and fresh salad from the garden. The hi-fi filled the dining room with the glorious music of Mozart. It was our first evening on Isla Robinson Crusoe, the island Selkirk had known as Màs a Tierra.

We had left Santiago, Chile, population six million, at ten in the morning and were now in San Juan Bautista (St. John the Baptist), population six hundred, the only settlement on the Juan Fernandez Islands. The flight had been easy. Two-and-a-half hours in a twin engine Piper Cub, Maud, my wife, a young German tourist, I, and, taking up most of the space, the crated motor for a fishing boat. We had a brief glimpse of a tortured volcanic land, jagged and torn, soaring up into the clouds and then we landed with a roar and stopped abruptly because the runway is short and ends in a several hundred foot drop into the sea.

A launch brought us in ninety minutes from the airport to the settlement, past sheer volcanic cliffs alternating with deep-green valleys. Señora Green from the Hosteria Villa Green picked us up at the pier with a wheelbarrow for our luggage. The town had only fourteen cars, plus three more at the airport.

We sat in the garden, filled with flowers and flowering bushes, and talked with our host, Señor Reynold M. Green Rojas, a gentle man in his eighties, who loved classical music, very erect, with an exquisite, old-fashioned Spanish politeness.

"Before the airport was built," he said, "we were very isolated. Only six or seven ships came each year to collect lobsters. Forty, fifty years ago we caught a lot of lobsters, eighty thousand and more each year. And they were big. Some were nearly a metre long and weighed 4 to 5 kilograms (10 to 12 pounds). Now they are smaller and the fishermen do not catch many. Six or seven a day is considered a good catch."

A jewel flickered through the air and I realized with a thrill that I was seeing one of the rarest birds on earth, the tiny, endemic Juan Fernandez hummingbird (*Sephanoides fernandensis*). The male, garnet-red, whirred from flower for flower. Soon after we saw his moss-green mate.

"Scientists say only 250 of those birds exist," said Señor Green, then added with quiet pride, "One pair is always in our garden because we have so many flowers."

We walked up to the Mirador de Selkirk, 1,800 feet up—and up and up! Three kilometres. Selkirk, the man who outran goats for supper, "raced up the mountain," wrote Woodes Rogers. We did it slowly. The landscape looked oddly ancient, with thickets of deep green firs and gnarled, twisted trees festooned with mosses. The island is a World Biosphere Reserve. It is a botanist's paradise. Of 140 native island plant species, 101 grow nowhere else on earth.

We reached the lookout, a saddle between soaring mountains, covered with rain forest, half-hidden by shifting, drifting greyish clouds. Here Selkirk had stood, day after day, year after year, staring into the distance, hoping, praying for deliverance, alone upon this wind-swept col. It was this lonely vigil that inspired the British poet William Cowper to begin his poem about Selkirk's solitude with the famous line, "I am monarch of all I survey."

A lobster fisherman gave me a lift to Puerto Inglés. As we crossed Cumberland Bay, he pointed down. "That's where the *Dresden* sits," he said. In World War I, the German *Panzerkreuzer* (cruiser) *Dresden* was cornered by three British battleships in Cumberland Bay. Rather than surrender, the captain, Carl Gustav von Lüdecke, sank the ship, after first evacuating the crew. "She's upright on the bottom," said my fisherman. "And still in pretty good shape. Full of moray eels."

One young officer aboard the *Dresden* was *Oberleutnant zur See* (Naval Lieutenant) Wilhelm Canaris. Later Admiral Canaris and head of the German Abwehr (military intelligence), he aided anti-Nazi resistance. He was hanged by the Gestapo on Hitler's orders in April 1945, a few days before the end of World War II.

There is a shallow grotto at Puerto Inglés where Selkirk reputedly lived. Further inland, another Selkirk "home" was discovered in January 2005. In the earth floor the explorer Daisuke Takahashi found the tip from bronze navigational dividers, one of the "Mathematical Instruments" Selkirk took ashore on that fateful day in October 1705 when he left his ship.

Robinson Crusoe Island is split by a central mountain chain into dramatically disparate halves: the north shore gets a lot of rain and is covered with dense rain forest; the south coast is storm-lashed and desert-dry. That's where the fur seals live.

It is a spectacular setting: an immense amphitheatre of black lava beach beneath steep cliffs, the rocks smoothly polished by the fur seal legions of ages past. Now the immense breeding beaches, once covered by millions of seals, were nearly empty. A few clusters of fur seals lay here and there, like the last thousand survivors of the human race in the vastness of a one-hundred-thousand-seat stadium.

Sweat-soaked and scared, carrying a heavy packsack with food, water, and camera gear, I climbed every day down the steep cliffs at Bahia Tierras Blancas, the chalky rock weathered and friable. One problem with being past seventy is that one definitely does not enjoy climbing down crumbly cliffs!

However, the seals on the beach beneath were worth the effort. An extensive arc of lava rocks and reefs protects this beach from the great Pacific waves that shatter against them in explosions of spray and spume. In 1817, a sealer in a shallop was thrown against these rocks, and, according to a witness, "one thigh bone and one arm were the only parts of the body that could be found." Yet fur seals glide in with ease.

San Juan Bautista, the only settlement on Isla Robinson Crusoe in the Pacific, 600 kilometres (372 miles) due west of Santiago, Chile. Alexander Selkirk was marooned on this uninhabited island.

Their breeding season is in October. Now it was December and the harem clusters had long dispersed. Pups slept or played. Females were at sea feeding and returned

at one-week intervals to nurse their pups. Young males were play-fighting.

The great males in their prime were impressive, nearly 3 metres (9 feet) long and weighing about 158 kilograms (350 pounds). They have pointy snouts, bulbous noses, and grizzled manes. The rest of the fur is deep brown-black when dry, or glossy black when they emerge from the sea. At first, the males snarled and threatened me. Gradually they got used to my presence and stared at me with supercilious hauteur.

The females were much smaller: only 1 metre (5 feet long) and weighing 45 to 50 kilograms (100 to 110 pounds). They were all elegance, svelte, lithe, and graceful.

The pups were adorable, with huge shining eyes and outsized flippers. Their short curly hair is jet black above. Tummy and muzzle are cinnamon brown. Most of the time they slept. Some played with each other. A few of the older ones ventured into rock pools for cautious swimming lessons.

When a mother returned from the sea, she called loudly. That call, meaning mom and milk, instantly roused her pup from the soundest sleep. It answered eagerly. The mother came, sniffed the little one to make quite sure that this was really her pup, then stretched out in lovely, languorous repose. The pup, its eyes half-closed in bliss, suckled her cream-thick, fat-rich milk.

Slowly, I merged into the life of this little colony of beautiful animals that had miraculously, probably in remote, inaccessible sea caves, escaped the eternal death of extinction.

Chapter 11

LITTLE DIOMEDE ISLAND, ALASKA, U.S.A.
Island between Two Worlds

SET IN THE CHILL and lead-grey Bering Strait midway between Alaska and Siberia, usually wrapped in dismal fog and haunted by northerly storms, Little Diomede Island seems singularly unattractive. Yet Ignaluk, the island's only village, tacked against a steep mountain slope, with a population that during the past four centuries has rarely exceeded 150 inhabitants, is older than New York, London, Paris, or Berlin.

The village sits atop a giant, frozen midden, the debris of millennia of people who lived on this lonely rock and set forth in their skin boats, as they still do, to intercept the vast throngs of marine mammals migrating through Bering Strait each spring and fall. It was, and still is, one of the richest ocean regions on earth. The Russian naval officer and explorer Otto von Kotzebue sailed past Little Diomede on August 18, 1817 and "immense numbers of whales and morse [walrus] played about us."

To store surplus meat from successful hunts of large marine mammals, mainly walruses, the people of Little Diomede used, and many still use, some of the oldest freezers in the world: meat holes, spacious, stone-lined, ice-cold caverns cut deep into the permafrost mountain side. (Clarence Birdseye, the American inventor and founder of the frozen-food industry, acquired the idea in 1912 watching Labrador Inuit preserve food in similar meat holes.)

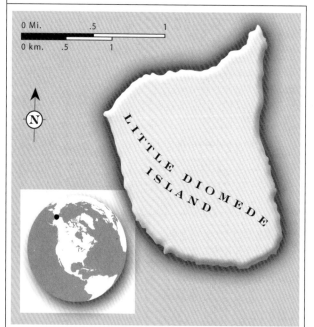

Little Diomede is about 4 kilometres (2.5 miles) long, 2 kilometres (1.5 miles) wide and rises steeply on all sides to its 398-metre (1,309-foot) summit. It is an ancient crag of granite mixed with masses of limestone that, weathered and worn, has shattered into boulders and rocks, covering many slopes—the breeding places of hundreds of thousands of seabirds.

Sheer cliffs rim much of the island. Only at its northwest corner is the slope gentler, grading down to a narrow strip of boulder beach. That is where the village houses cling, tier upon tier, to the mountain side, facing the sister island, Big Diomede (or Ostrov Ratmanova, its Russian name), 5 kilometres (3 miles) west and about three times bigger.

Two or three times a week, while I lived in Ignaluk in the 1970s, a Soviet helicopter would rise from Big Diomede and fly east. After exactly 2 kilometres (1.5 miles) it stopped abruptly, as if it had hit a glass wall, then flew south or north along this line and returned to base.

That borderline, precisely in the middle between the islands, divides two worlds: Asia and America, the United States and Russia and, in the 1960s, communism and capitalism, Russia's far east and America's far west. It even separates today and tomorrow, for here the border coincides with the international date line. When we travelled west across this line on our hunting trips, we moved from today into tomorrow. When we came back, we returned on the previous day.

Little and Big Diomede islands are the remnants of a vanished land: Beringia, the 1,609-kilometre (1,000-mile) wide "land bridge" that connected Asia and America during the ice ages of the Pleistocene. Across that bridge, early humans came from Asia to America, the ancestors of Indians and Inuit, walking perhaps past the craggy mountains whose tops today stick out of the sea as the Diomede Islands.

At the end of the last ice age, vast ice sheets and glaciers melted, releasing their store of water and, like an Arctic Atlantis, Beringia disappeared beneath the rising sea.

Then it became Bering Strait with the two Diomede islands in the middle as handy stepping stones from Asia to America. Living on their rugged rock island between two worlds, the Diomeders were ideally placed to be middlemen in the once flourishing and very ancient trade between Siberia and Alaska.

I saw fragments of this trade and of prehistoric hunts emerge when I lived on Little Diomede. In early summer, village children grubbed with hope, enthusiasm, and old spoons in the midden mud carried down toward the beach by the spring melt. From time to time a happy yell announced a find. It was washed in the nearby sea and avidly examined.

Usually it was just a bit of bone or ivory, a broken harpoon, an ancient lance. Metal pieces were usually rusted beyond recognition. One little girl found a small brass bell, made centuries ago in Europe, still in good condition and now valuable. Chunks of fossil ivory were handed to fathers who carved them into lovely amber-coloured bracelets and pendants.

The kids, happy, muddy, and eagle-eyed found an amazing number of tiny beads. Most were bright blue, some of glass, some of stone, perhaps lapis lazuli. A few were Peking beads from China, others were Venetian beads and some were lovely glass spheres made long ago in Bohemia. All were trade beads of centuries past. Once baubles for natives, the natives were now selling them back for very high prices. The children gathered them carefully. They would be traded for lots of dollars to collectors in the United States and Europe.

Long before Columbus discovered America, Asian and American natives were travelling and trading across Bering Strait. Since remotest times, the Chinese have loved and coveted ivory and jade. Both came from the north: walrus ivory from Bering Strait hunters, jade from Alaska, both traded for Chinese metal goods. As the men in the middle, the Diomeders may have controlled this trade. For a people having the superbly seaworthy, large skin boats known as umiaks (a 12-metre [40-foot] umiak can carry more than forty people or 5 tons of cargo) the one day sail across the 91-kilometre (57-mile) wide Bering Strait was easy.

After achieving the first traverse of the Northeast Passage, the Swedish explorer Nils Adolf Baron Nordenskjöld passed, in 1879, "Diomede Island, the market-place famed among Polar Tribes...and probably before the time of Columbus a station of traffic between the Old and the New World."

But this was also a region of war, and trade was often interrupted. Of all Inuit, noted the Russian scientist Peter Simon Pallas in 1780, the Diomeders were the most "warlike."

From time to time the Ignaluk children unearthed relics of their ancestors' warlike ways: rectangular ivory plates, once part of the warring Diomeders' imbricated body armour. This armour, its ivory plates held together

Tacked to the west-side of steep Little Diomede Island, the village of Ignaluk in America faces Bering Strait and Asia.

by thong or sinew thread, looked remarkably similar to the imbricated metal armour worn in ancient times by Chinese and Japanese warriors.

The Diomeders needed armour. Accounts of fights raging back and forth across Bering Strait sound at times like an arctic version of the medieval French-English cross-Channel wars. Edward W. Nelson of the Smithsonian Institution, travelling in this region between 1877 and 1881, wrote that "in ancient times the people of Bering Strait were constantly at war with one another, the people of the Diomede Islands being leaguered with the Eskimos of the Siberian shore against the combined forces" of Inuit along the American side of Bering Strait. Occasionally, alliances changed and Little Diomeders fought on the American side, against their erstwhile allies on Big Diomede and Siberia.

Early in the eighteenth century the Diomeders were "discovered" and from then on they had new worries and new wars. Shortly before his death in 1725, Czar Peter the Great of Russia looked at his immense but as yet only slightly known eastern realm and wondered what lay beyond Siberia. To find out, he dispatched his veteran Danish-born naval officer Vitus Bering to Siberia.

Bering sailed north from Kamchatka. On August 16, 1728, the name day of Saint Diomede, Bering passed "a high mountain on the right [Siberia's East Cape or Mys Dezhneva]...and on the left and seaward they saw an island which in honor of the day they called Diomede." But the famous sea passage dividing two continents (that Captain James Cook would later name Bering Strait in his predecessor's honour) was, as so often, shrouded in fog and Bering did not see the not-so-distant continent of America.

Occupation followed exploration. During the eighteenth century, Russia gradually seized Alaska. Little Diomede became a Russian-owned island and Cossack tax collectors arrived to explore, make head counts, and levy and collect *yassak* (tribute). (They are remembered. To this day, Diomeders call a disliked white a *gussuk*, a corruption of "Cossack.")

Getting tribute, in the form of ivory and furs, from the recalcitrant and warlike Diomeders turned out to be difficult. In 1732, four years after Bering, the Cossacks Mikhail Gvozdev and Ivan Fedorov crossed Bering Strait from Siberia to the Diomede Islands. They met, says a contemporary account, "with an unfriendly reception." The islanders "refused to pay tribute" and when the Cossacks attempted to land and collect *yassak* by force, they were greeted "by a shower of arrows."

That cooled even Cossack greed. Besides, without the help of the natives it was nearly impossible to land a wooden boat on Little Diomede's surf-lashed boulder beach. Henceforth, they squeezed *yassak* out of meeker natives and left the tough and daring Diomeders alone. (In 1926, the famous American anthropologist Ales Hrdlicka visited Little Diomede. "The natives," he noted succinctly, "look sturdy. No other could survive here.")

When the czarist government in 1779 sent the *sotnik* (Cossack officer) Ivan Kobelev to visit the truculent Diomeders, he was under orders to be friendly and bear gifts (perhaps he came with beads). The population, he reported, numbered 168 men, women, and children. Their food consisted "of whales, seals and walruses" and he found the people "daring and cheerful."

Eighty-eight years later Russia sold Little Diomede, and the rest of Alaska, to the United States for 7.2 million dollars. At slightly less than two cents an acre, it was really quite a bargain, but at first Americans did not see it that way. "Walrussia," was a common name for their new territory. For Little Diomede, which has always been a walrus and ivory island, the term was apt. Americans found the Little Diomeders as intractable as the Russians once did. "The island is terribly isolated," a 1917 government report complained, "and the people are hard to handle."

The 1867 treaty between the United States and Russia stipulates that the border between them shall pass "midway between the island Krusenstern, or Ignalook (Little Diomede), and the island Ratmanoff, or Noonarbook (Big Diomede), and proceed due north, without limitation, into the...Frozen Ocean."

That famous treaty signed in Washington didn't impress the Diomeders. They hunted walruses wherever the hunting was good and simply ignored the new border. Trade between Alaska and Siberia became extensive in the nineteenth and early twentieth centuries and even the rise of the Red Star over Siberia did not change this.

Although Americans were banned from the Siberian coast, the Little Diomeders maintained their Russian connection. Nearly all had relatives and friends on both sides of Bering Strait and the Little Diomeders sailed blithely to Siberia whenever they felt like it.

The Siberians then were short of trade goods but had an abundance of furs and ivory. Little Diomeders took over the needed items and returned with lots of ivory and valuable furs. In 1927, white fox pelts were worth forty-two dollars in Alaska and blue fox furs about one hundred fifty dollars. It was a pleasant, prosperous time.

This happy if somewhat anachronistic state of affairs came to an abrupt end in 1948 when the Cold War reached the Diomedes. The Iron Curtain clanked down and two boats from Little Diomede were caught on the wrong side of it.

That summer eighteen Little Diomeders in a happy holiday spirit sailed to visit their neighbours on Big Diomede Island, only to be arrested by Soviet border guards on arrival. They were confined for fifty-two days, interrogated at length, and fed black bread and watery cabbage soup, a drastic change from their usually copious fat-meat diet. They were released only after repeated protests from Washington and returned home famished and furious. Several men joined the National Guard, prompted more by pique than by patriotism.

For nearly a quarter century the separation was total. To avoid any possibility for clandestine meetings, Soviet authorities resettled the Big Diomede Inuit on the Siberian mainland coast in 1954. American authorities, too, wanted to resettle the people from Little Diomede, hard to service and so alarmingly close to the Soviet Union, near the town of Nome on mainland Alaska.

This was the late 1950s, at the height of the Cold War, and American authorities were still worried and upset about the case of the vanishing man. He came to Little Diomede in the early summer of 1959. A white man, quiet, pleasant. "To study birds," he said. He had a tent along, watched the abundant birds, bothered no-one and kept to himself.

One day, when most of the Little Diomede men were away in their skin boats, hunting walruses, the stranger walked down to the beach with a large sack. From it he pulled a rubber boat, inflated it and paddled across to the Soviet Union. He rounded the southern tip of Big Diomede and was never seen again. No one ever found out who he was and why he had crossed from West to East.

That annoyed the American authorities and they exerted considerable pressure to remove the people from this outpost at the very edge of America. But the people of Little Diomede (population: ninety-one in 1959), stubborn and proud, defied authority and refused to budge from their bleak rock.

And then, in 1975, while I lived in Ignaluk, a little détente came to Little Diomede. One spring day we were startled to see two dark dots, barely visible through the greyish veil of wind-driven snow, coming toward us across the ice from the west, out of the forbidden East.

Half the village piled pell-mell onto snowmobiles and raced out to meet the visitors. They were Victor and Volodia, two blithe spirits in voluminous parkas and beautifully made sealskin pants, sent from a Siberian *sovkhoz* (state farm) to trap arctic foxes and hunt fresh meat, on a contract basis, for the Soviet border guards stationed on Big Diomede.

The visitors spoke Yuit, the dialect of nearly all of Siberia's roughly 1,500 Inuit, which is so different from the Inupiaq dialect spoken on Little Diomede that they could barely communicate with each other. They resolved the problem by speaking Russian and English, using me as interpreter.

What, I wondered, did the border guards have to say about their excursion to meet the Diomeders?

"Oh, they," Victor brushed them off with a wave of his hand, "they don't like it. But what can they do? We are hunters. We travel far. How can they keep track of us? So they said: 'OK, go and meet the people over there. Just be careful. No trouble!' What trouble do they expect? These are our people. They are Eskimo, just like us."

That was the dominant theme of this and frequent subsequent meetings. Alien politics and white men's borders divided them. But they were all Inuit, united by kinship, culture, and tradition.

Children on Little Diomede try to catch gulls. They are on westernmost Alaska and North America. Beyond them is easternmost Siberia and Asia, separated by the Bering Strait and the international date line. On the Siberian side it is already tomorrow.

In the late 1980s, the world changed abruptly. It was the era of perestroika (restructure), and glasnost (openness). The Iron Curtain began to crack and the Diomeders on their remote rock were caught up in the change.

In 1988, Gennadi Gerasimov, a frequent spokesman for Soviet president Mikhail Gorbachev, flew to Little Diomede, the place, he said, "where the West ends." Staring across the ice-bound strait toward the nearby U.S.S.R., he quipped, "This is an ice curtain!" then added, "It really is an experience to see how close we are geographically and still worlds apart in other ways. Let's melt the ice curtain!"

It melted quickly. A year later, in September 1989, U.S. secretary of state James Baker and Soviet foreign minister Eduard Shevardnadze met in Jackson Hole, Wyoming, and signed an agreement that would again permit visa-free travel for Inuit from both sides of the Bering Strait "to see each other as often as they want...and reestablish their family customs and ethnic ties."

Soon after the treaty was signed, Diomeders in their umiaks visited Siberia: to exchange gifts; to have parties; to renew long-broken friendships; to search for relatives; to make new friends. After a politically enforced hiatus of more than forty years, the Diomeders were again, as in times past, commuting freely between two worlds.

When I came to Nome, Alaska, in 1975, for my first many-months stay on Little Diomede, I found that the isolated islanders had an ambiguous fame. All agreed that they were the most successful and most daring walrus hunters in the foggy, stormy sea between Alaska and Siberia. They were, people said, self-reliant and aloof, tough guys, "the Vikings of the Arctic Sea."

"They're special," a social worker in Nome told me. "They're hard, aggressive, independent, proud, hostile toward outsiders, and deeply attached to their island."

The plane from Nome with provisions, mail, and me landed on the winter sea ice near the village. Mail and provisions were welcome. I was not.

"What do you want here?" Tom Menadelook, the village mayor asked. He was gruff and curt. I told him I hoped to photograph the life of his village, that I had already spent ten years living with Canadian Inuit.

"I've got a shack you can rent," Tom said. "There's a stove inside. You can buy heating oil at the store." After that he ignored me and so did most of the villagers.

It was April. Late winter. The men hunted seals at the floe edge, the limit of landfast ice, many miles away. Women and children went "crabbing." With a simple and ingenious device, used since prehistoric times, they caught large crabs through holes in the ice. They jigged for fish, mostly small, bony sculpin, that were made into fish soup. Soviet helicopters patrolled the border, 2 kilometres (1.5 miles) away. The sun set over Siberia. Children played hockey on the sea ice below the village.

Slowly the village accepted me. Robert Soolook, a hunter in his early fifties, dropped in for tea and talk. "Can you eat Eskimo food?"(Alaskans don't use the term Inuit.) Assured that I could, he said, "Come for supper."

It was a typical Diomede meal, mostly traditional, varied and healthy: walrus meat from last year, preserved in a permafrost meat hole in the mountain side, with seal oil; greens preserved in seal oil; boiled bearded-seal intestine with seal oil and onions; yellowish blubber marinated in seal oil; followed by tea, canned apricots, and homemade bread.

After supper, the talk turned to shamanism. The shamans of Little Diomede had been famous, and the last of the great *angakut* of Diomede, Assikassak, who died in the early 1940s, was perhaps the most famous of all.

"My dad was a real good Catholic," Soolook said, "and he didn't like the shaman. One day the shaman came to our house to borrow something and he and my dad got into an argument. My dad said, 'Oh sure, you can do your fancy tricks in the dark *kasge* [the community hall] but I bet you can't do them here.'

"The shaman just sort of looked at him, took off his parka, took my dad's great skinning knife, the one we use to butcher walruses with, held the handle in both hands and pushed that long knife into his stomach. He turned it in his stomach, some blood flowed and we all stood around and were very quiet. He pulled out the knife, the wound closed and the blood stopped flowing. He put the knife on the table, put on his parka and left. I remember we all stood there, saying nothing. And then my dad picked up the knife and there was blood on it."

Tom Menadelook was *umialik* (captain) of one of Little Diomede's four large umiaks, superbly seaworthy boats of ancient design, covered with split walrus hide. I asked him whether I could join his eleven-men crew as a non-hunting member. He knew I would ask and was brief and decisive: "Yes. You pay for gas and oil like all of us." He gave me one of his rare smiles. "And you get no ivory."

"Ivory," said the islanders, "is our gold." Walrus meat and fat were important, the main food of the Diomeders. Walrus skins were needed to cover the umiaks. But ivory was the Diomeders' wealth, the basis of their cherished independence. Most men and many women were excellent carvers. Ivory and ivory carvings were, to some extent, the island currency: people paid for groceries and heating oil with ivory carvings, used them to settle telephone bills, and bought cards with them on bingo nights. Centuries ago they sold ivory, via intermediaries, to China. Now their ivory carvings were sold for tourist dollars in Nome and Anchorage.

In mid-May the annual walrus migration begins. The two hundred thousand walruses that winter in the vastness of the Bering Sea funnel through the 91-kilometre- (57-mile-) wide Bering Strait to their far-north summer feeding grounds. For the Diomeders the spring walrus hunt was now, as it had always been, the most dangerous, the most vital hunt of the year.

In the umiak, we reverted to an earlier life and the men, who in Ignaluk usually spoke English, now spoke Inupiaq in the boat. We lived with the currents, the wind and the ice. We travelled far in search of walrus.

Little Diomede islanders hunt walruses, their main food, in the dangerous, ice-chocked Bering Strait. They use umiaks, strong, flexible boats of ancient design, covered with walrus leather.

A storm hit us among the ice and we were caught in a maelstrom of turning, churning floes. The men leapt in

and out of the boat, and poled and hauled the umiak through cracks between the crashing, grinding pans. Broken floes rasped against the walrus-skin cover, the flexible frame buckled but did not break. They hauled the boat onto a large floe and we drifted northward toward the Chukchi Sea.

It was a wild night. The storm screamed across the pack. The ice floes heaved and groaned and turned and creaked. Black clouds scudded low across the sky. The men made a windbreak out of tarps, boiled a big pot of *kauk*, year-old walrus skin, fatty, crunchy, and energy-rich. They drank lots of tea, smoked, joked and teased me, curled up on the umiak thwarts and went to sleep. The storm raged on. They did not seem to care or worry. This was their world. This was their life.

We drifted north all night and all next day. When the storm eased, they launched the umiak. The groans and bellows of walruses drifted to us through the fog. Suddenly we saw them. Masses of madder-brown walruses lay sleeping on a floe. In tense silence, the men paddled close, then shot.

Some walruses lay dead on the floe. Others in fear and fury poured off the ice and attacked. One great bull dived, shot up beneath the boat, slashed it with his tusks and water rushed in through the gash. The hunters stuffed a large piece of blubber into the hole to staunch the leak.

We loaded the umiak to the gunwales with meat, fat and ivory, then searched for Little Diomede, our home, somewhere to the south. We reached Diomede in the morning after sixty hours at sea. Men, women, and children unloaded the boat.

I walked slowly up to my shack, made tea, drank it very hot, and fell exhausted on my cot, reeking of blood and blubber. Two hours later Tom banged on my shack. I put on my sea-soaked parka and we were off again, out into the ice and the fog. Little Diomede receded, home of these hunters who lived in two worlds: in today's America and in the ancient hunting culture of their ancestors who had clung to this gaunt rock island for more than two thousand years.

Chapter 12

FUNK ISLAND, CANADA
Island of the Great Auk

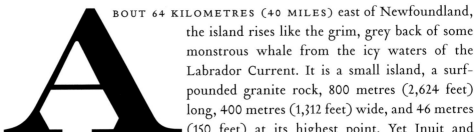

ABOUT 64 KILOMETRES (40 MILES) east of Newfoundland, the island rises like the grim, grey back of some monstrous whale from the icy waters of the Labrador Current. It is a small island, a surf-pounded granite rock, 800 metres (2,624 feet) long, 400 metres (1,312 feet) wide, and 46 metres (150 feet) at its highest point. Yet Inuit and Vikings visited it, and Newfoundland's now-vanished Beothuk Indians risked their lives in frail bark canoes to reach this remote island.

Basque whalers and Breton fishermen probably knew the island long before Columbus discovered America. Polar bears swam far across the sea to clamber up its difficult shore.

It attracted explorers like a magnet. Jacques Cartier stopped twice at the island. Sir Humphrey Gilbert landed on it. North America's first tourist ships sidled up to the island in 1536. And for four centuries hundreds upon hundreds of ships from Portugal and Spain, Britain and France sought out this barren rock in a frigid, fog-shrouded sea. For this is Funk Island, prominently marked on one of the first maps of the New World, the 1505 Pedro Reinel map, as Y dos Aves (Island of Birds), home of the great auk, the now extinct flightless penguin of the North.

"This island is so exceedingly full

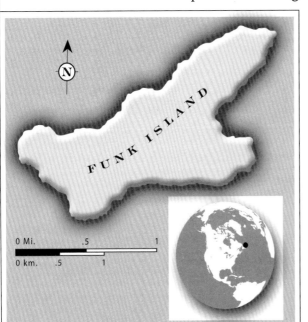

FUNK ISLAND

N

0 Mi. .5 1
0 km. .5 1

of birds that all the ships of France might load a cargo of them without one perceiving that any had been removed," wrote Jacques Cartier in 1535.

The great auk was the original penguin. When I went for the first time to Funk Island more than forty years ago, a folk memory of the great, flightless bird lingered in some of the Newfoundland outports and on Fogo Island. Old people recalled that their ancestors used to go to "the Funks," as they call Funk Island and its surrounding shoals, to hunt "pemwins."

The name "penguin" was later given to the equally stately, flightless birds of the far South. The word, some believe, is derived from the Welsh "*pen*" (head) and "*gwyn*" (white), for the great auk bore two large white marks upon its dark head.

Sir Richard Peckham in his account of Sir Humphrey Gilbert's voyage to Newfoundland in 1583, claimed Funk Island had been discovered by the semi-legendary Maddock ap Owen Gwyneth "from the blood-royall borne in Wales" who is supposed to have visited Newfoundland in 1170 and named many places, including "the island of Penguin [Funk Island] which yet to this day beareth that name." According to a less romantic etymology, the word "penguin" is derived via Spanish or Portuguese from the Latin "*pinguis*" (fat).

The great auk was fat, a stately, portly, upright bird, about 70 centimetres (27 inches) tall, the size of a small goose. It weighed about 4 kilograms (10 pounds). In appearance, it was similar to the penguins who inherited its name: head, back and wings were a deep, glossy black; chest and belly, the purest white. On each side of the head, between eye and bill, the great auk bore a large, distinctive white oval spot (hence the Welsh name "white head").

The wings were short but powerful, good for swimming, too short for flight. The bill was large and strong and both upper and lower mandibles were finely ridged. To that powerful bill the great auk owed its Viking name "*geirfugl*" (spear-bird). In Britain, it was called "garefowl."

The great auk once bred in a vast arc spanning the North Atlantic on about ten small, remote islands, from Britain's St. Kilda Island, to islands off Iceland and south Greenland, to Funk Island off Newfoundland and the Bird Rocks (Rochers aux Oiseaux) in the Gulf of St. Lawrence. Of all the great auk colonies, the one on Funk Island, with probably more than two hundred thousand birds, was by far the largest.

Inuit and Indians hunted great auks since remotest times. Necklaces made of great auk beaks have been found in five-thousand-year-old Indian graves. Newfoundland's Beothuk Indians in their uniquely shaped, keeled and high-prowed birchbark canoes paddled to Funk Island to collect the fat auks and their eggs.

The Labrador trader, trapper, and diarist Captain John Cartwright wrote in 1770, "It is a singular and almost incredible fact that these people [the Beothuk] should visit Funk Island, which lies forty miles [63 kilometres] from Cape Freels and sixty [96 kilometres] from the Island of Fogo." Although the low island is far too far out at sea to be seen from the mainland, "the Indians repair thither once or twice every year and return with their canoes laden with birds and eggs; for the number of sea-fowl which resort to this island to breed, is far beyond credibility."

To both the great auk and the Beothuk Indians death came with discovery. European seamen, explorers, fishermen, and settlers killed the great auk for food and feathers and the Indians for fun or profit.

The first European sailors to visit Funk Island were probably the Basques. That is a reasonable assumption. The Basques, famed in medieval times as whalers and fishermen, were a secretive people: they kept few records and they spoke a language no one else understood. Long before Columbus, they vanished each spring toward the northwest and returned in early winter, their ships laden with whale oil and cod. They had discovered the super-rich codfish banks off Newfoundland and they had no intention to share this secret. They kept very quiet about these voyages and their visits to Funk Island to stock their ships with fresh meat.

The French explorer Jacques Cartier was therefore a bit miffed when, as he "discovered" Canada, he found Basque ships already fishing in the Gulf of St. Lawrence. On May 21, 1534, he stopped at "the isle of Birds [Funk Island]...whose numbers are so great as to be incredible, unless one has seen them...And these birds are so fat it is marvelous...and our two long-boats are laden with them as with stones, in less than half an hour. Of these each of our ships salted four or five casks, not counting those we were able to eat fresh." He went ashore again on July 7, 1535 "and took away two boat-loads [of auks] to add to our stores."

Cartier was not the only one killing great auks on Funk Island. Polar bears, who ranged then much farther south than they do now but were subsequently exterminated in Newfoundland and Labrador, swam to Funk Island. Cartier saw one of them in 1534 and wrote, "Not withstanding that the island lies fourteen leagues [77 kilometres] from shore, bears swim out to it from the mainland in order to feed on these birds; and our men found one as big as a cow and as white as a swan ['*grant comme vne vache, aussi blanc comme vne signe*'] that sprang into the sea in front of them."

In 1501, the Portuguese navigator Gaspar Corte Real "discovered" Newfoundland and called it Terra Verde (the Green Land). He captured fifty-seven Beothuk Indians and brought them to his king at Lisbon. "Their manners and gestures are most gentle," reported a courtier. "The women have small breasts and most beautiful bodies." All were sold into slavery. "The best slaves that have been discovered up to this time," noted Pietro Pasqualigo, the Venetian ambassador to Portugal.

André Thevet, the far-roaming French monk and good friend of Jacques Cartier, his "*grand et singulier ami*," probably heard from Cartier about the marvels of Funk Island and visited it in 1555. "There is so great an abundance of them [great auks] that three large vessels going to Canada loaded each their boats. They drave them into the boats like sheep to the shambles," Thevet wrote in his *Cosmographie Universelle.*

The island of auks was so famous that the first tourist cruise to the Americas headed straight for Funk Island. It was organized in 1536 by Richard Hore, a wealthy London leather merchant. He chartered two ships and talked "six score persons, whereof thirty were gentlemen" into visiting, for a fee, Funk Island and Newfoundland.

Funk Island was a success. They found it "full of great foules...as big as geese" and filled their ships with them.

For more than two centuries, the great auks were herded into these stone pounds and then slaughtered. They supplied the fishing fleets of Europe with food.

They also saw polar bears on Funk Island, "killed some, and took them for no bad food." After the feasts at Funk, the rest of the voyage was dismal. They got lost, starved and a few tourists were eaten by their fellow tourists. That, remarked the famous historian Samuel Eliot Morison, "put an end to the [New World] tourist business...for at least two centuries."

The tourists were incidental. The real allure of Newfoundland was fish. In the seas near it, cod was king. Cod were large then. Most adult cod were a metre (3 feet) long and weighed 13 kilograms (30 pounds), and cod 1.5 metres (5 feet) long and weighing 27 kilograms (60 pounds) were not uncommon. Cod were prolific. At spawning time each adult female laid about ten million eggs. Cod meat was white, delicious, and very rich in protein. The supply was abundant and appeared inexhaustible. When John Cabot "discovered" Newfoundland in 1497, his crew scooped codfish from the sea in weighted baskets.

Salt cod was a staple of European, and later also Caribbean, diet, prized by the wealthy for its whiteness and flavour, praised by the poor because it was cheap. Every spring the fishing fleets of Europe sailed to the seas off Newfoundland. Bird-covered Funk Island was their fresh-meat larder. In 1578, a typical year, 350 Spanish and French, and fifty English vessels caught cod near Funk Island and these fishermen, a contemporary account noted, "doe bring small store of flesh with them but victuall themselves always with these birds."

It was so easy. Superb swimmers, the great auk easily outpaced a boat rowed by six men. On land, the large, flightless birds were slow and very reluctant to leave their precious eggs or chicks. The fishermen clubbed them to death. Or, to save carrying, herded the birds toward shore, bludgeoned them and filled their boats with the carcasses.

The great auks of Funk Island were driven for centuries to boats and slaughtered by European fishermen. In addition, Newfoundland settlers travelled to Funk Island "to load their boats with birds and eggs," Captain Cartwright noted in his diary. "They salt and eat them in lieu of salted pork."

The Beothuk Indians who had made the daring voyage to Funk Island in their bark canoes for hundreds, perhaps thousands of years, no longer dared to visit the island. The last recorded trip was in 1772. Two canoes with Indians approached Funk Island. Fishermen were on the island. "When they [the Indians] came within Musket Shot M'Donald fired his Piece loaded with Mould Shot at one of the canoes," recorded a local historian. "He believes that he wounded some of them."

By the end of the eighteenth century, great auks and Beothuk Indians, both ruthlessly hunted, declined rapidly. The most successful Beothuk-hunter, the trapper Noel Boss, killed ninety-nine men, women, and children. Children were rarely spared. After shooting a group of adults, the fishermen usually rounded up the children and cut their throats.

The last Beothuk, a captive girl called Shanawdihit, died in 1829.

At Funk Island, wrote Captain Cartwright in 1785, "It has been customary of late years for several crews of men to live all summer on that island, for the sole purpose of killing birds for the sake of their feathers; the destruction which they make is incredible."

The great auks were herded into stone pounds, killed, and thrown into large cauldrons of boiling water to loosen the downy feathers and make plucking easier. Some of the plucked bodies were salted. Some were cut up as fish bait. And, since there was no wood on Funk Island, the fat bodies of auks were used to stoke the fires beneath the kettles.

In 1785, Cartwright warned that "if a stop is not put to that practice the whole breed will be diminished to almost nothing."

About 1800, the killing did end. The stately great auk, the penguin of the North that once covered the island "in infinite numbers," had been wiped out on Funk Island.

The great auk survived on a couple of small islands off Iceland. In 1830, Geirfuglasker (Garefowl Skerry), the less-accessible and, for the last auks, safer of these islands, sank beneath the sea in a series of violent volcanic eruptions. Now they bred only on one island, Eldey, the "Fire Island." Fishermen pursued them relentlessly. They killed fifteen in 1830; twenty-four in 1831; thirteen in 1833; nine in 1834; and three in 1840.

On June 4, 1844 a boat with fourteen men set out from Iceland for Eldey Island. Three men jumped ashore and spotted two great auks. The birds ran to the shore. But before they could reach the saving sea, the men cornered the auks, strangled them, and threw the bodies into the boat.

One man, Ketil Ketilsson, returned to the black lava shelf where the auks had first been seen and there lay the pear-shaped, fist-sized egg of a great auk. He smashed it, the last egg of the last of the great auks. The men sold the auks for nine U.S. dollars. Their viscera remain in a museum in Copenhagen, Denmark.

Now all that remains of the great auk is seventy-eight skins in the museums of the world. One skin was recently bought by Iceland's Natural History

Museum for a world-record nine thousand pounds sterling at Sotheby's in London.

The great auk is gone forever. But today Funk Island is again one of the richest, most fascinating, and now-protected bird islands in the world.

After its last auks had been killed, Funk Island was nearly without life. When Dr. Frederick A. Lucas of the U.S. National Museum visited Funk Island in 1887, he found a colony of terns, and other birds only in "insignificant numbers." Since then, slowly at first, and with spectacular speed recently, birds have reoccupied Funk Island. Kittiwakes and puffins are common. Razorbill auks, small cousins of the great auk that are able to fly, nest in rock niches.

Gannets came to the island in the 1930s. Seven pairs nested on Funk Island in 1936. Now their colony numbers thousands of pairs.

Icebergs drift past Funk Island. Once home of the now-extinct great auk, much of the island is now covered with more than a million murres and gannets.

Most dramatic has been the increase of common murres. The first pairs probably came to Funk Island late in the nineteenth century, about a hundred years after the last great auks had been butchered and plucked. By 1936, 10,000 pairs bred on Funk Island; 15,000 pairs in 1945; 150,000 pairs in 1956; and 400,000 pairs in 1958. Now, more than a million murres crowd together in dense colonies—100 to 140 birds per square yard—covering acres on the smooth, rounded rock of the island.

We reached Funk Island in the grey light of dawn after a seven-hour voyage by long-liner from the fishing village of Badgers' Quay on the east coast of Newfoundland. It was a rare calm day. Long, lazy swells rolled against the cliffs and shattered in fans of greenish spray.

A dory brought us to shore and, as

the boat rose on the crest of a swell, we jumped for "The Bench," a narrow ledge on the vertical cliff. Our hands clawed into holds in the rock, the same ledge, the same hand-holds used by Beothuk Indians and Basques, by Spaniards and Portuguese, by Jacques Cartier and Sir Humphrey Gilbert, for here is the best and usually the only place to land.

As we clambered to the top of the island the pungent smell of nitrates and phosphates hit us. It has been estimated that the birds dump daily 100 tons of excrement onto Funk Island. Rains wash most of the guano into the ocean and for miles around the sea is a murky grey. The world "funk" comes from Old English meaning "evil odor or vapor."

The air was filled with murres, legions flying to the sea or returning from it, bullet-shaped black and white bodies hurtling along with the harsh whir of narrow wings, tens of thousands, rushing and racing past with the sound of a mighty storm.

Among the densely massed murres on Funk Island, each bird returning from the sea unerringly finds its mate or chick. The great auks that once covered the island had been exterminated by about 1800.

I walked slowly to the top of the gently sloping island, the granite rock smoothed and polished by rain and wind and the marching, palmate feet of millions of great auks. To my left was a cove and a shallow ravine called Indian Gulch. Paddles, arrowheads and spear points made by Beothuk Indians had been found in this place. Long ago the now-vanished people may have camped there.

I stood on the rounded granite hill. Beneath me, the breeding murres massed. They stood shoulder to shoulder in groups that covered acres, a restless, phantasmagoric mass of black and white, a moving, flickering sea of birds, an op-art picture come to life.

One murre is a very loud and disputatious bird. Now the sound of a million murres engulfed me like a mighty, pulsing, strangely hypnotic force. The harsh, raucous *"arrg-arrg-arrg"* of the adults blended with the shrill, insistent, ceaseless cheeping of the chicks into one overwhelming, all-pervading sea of sound.

Millionfold life was everywhere, and thousandfold death. Pools of stagnant water filled depressions, some a miasmic green, others a strange magenta red. Nearly a third of all eggs were buried in thick, greyish slime or glued to rocks. Muck-smeared murres dragged pathetically in the ooze. Crippled birds hid in rock clefts. Chicks struggled feebly in rock fissures half-filled with the partially decayed corpses of other chicks.

Masses of piled stones marked the ancient pounds into which the doomed auks were driven. Nearby stood the great cauldrons that once were heated with the burning bodies of the fat birds. Some accounts say the fishermen threw the auks alive into the boiling water. Earth layers nearby are still black; they consist of charred, incinerated great auk remains.

Life and death, past and present are concentrated on this small island. About a fifth of Funk Island is now covered by less than a metre (1-to-3-foot) layer of soil, thickly overgrown by hummocky grass. Puffins tunnel their nest burrows into this earth.

It is not earth. I knelt near the puffin burrows. The soil thrown up by the digging birds was full of small, brownish, crumbly bones: the bones of great auks. The cradle of the puffins consisted of the decomposed bodies of millions of great auks. This was the cemetery of the now-extinct penguin of the North.

"It is no exaggeration to say," wrote Dr. Lucas after visiting Funk Island in 1887, "that millions [of great auks] gave up their lives on these few acres of barren rock."

Chapter 13

GALAPAGOS ISLANDS, ECUADOR
Islands of Charles Darwin's Epiphany

OD CREATED THE EARTH in the year 4004 BCE, proclaimed the Irish archbishop James Ussher in 1564. How did he arrive at that precise date? Simple! In a famous four-year chronological study he calculated all the generations since Adam knew Eve, added the time since the birth of Christ and arrived at exactly 4004 BCE. That year, he said, our earth was born and all that is living upon it. Creation was instantaneous and all life-forms on earth were final in form and immutable.

That tenet of faith, held to be true by most people in the Western world, began to crumble in 1835 when a young English naturalist, Charles Darwin, observed on the remote and little-known Galapagos Islands "a most singular group of finches." They are now usually called Darwin's finches. These drab little birds were "the finches that shook the world," wrote the famous ornithologist and bird-guide author Roger Tory Peterson.

No place he visited during his five-year voyage around the world aboard the British survey vessel HMS *Beagle* fascinated Darwin as much as the Galapagos Islands. "The natural history of these islands is eminently curious," he noted. "The archipelago is a little world within itself."

The volcanic islands, Darwin realized, were new. After their fiery birth,

the islands cooled and became crucibles of creation. Here, Darwin felt, "both in space and time, we seem to be brought somewhat near to that great fact—that mystery of mysteries—the first appearance of new beings on this earth."

Darwin, the ever-curious naturalist, was fascinated by the islands' thirteen species of finches. All were small, dusky, and inconspicuous. They were similar in size, but each species had a differently shaped beak. That puzzled Darwin and then, suddenly, came his epiphany, the concept of evolution that was to change our vision of the world.

"Seeing this gradation and diversity of structure [of the beaks]," he wrote in his book *The Voyage of the Beagle*, "in one small, intimately related group of birds, one might really fancy that from an original paucity of birds in this archipelago, one species had been taken and modified for different ends."

In a marvellous flash of intuition, Darwin realized "that no living thing was created ready-made" and, he later wrote to a friend, it was at that moment upon the Galapagos Islands that he decided "to study the origin of species."

Darwin, a cautious, conscientious, and extraordinary diligent scientist, spent the next twenty-four years painstakingly amassing facts and observations that supported his theory of evolution. Finally, at the insistent urging of friends, he published in 1859 the book that altered our perception of the world: *On the Origin of Species by Means of Natural Selection*.

It seems appropriate that this revolutionary revelation should have come to Darwin on the Galapagos Islands, "the greatest natural laboratory in the world," according to Canadian diplomat S.C.H. Nutting, "Las Islas Encantadas," (the Enchanted Isles) according to their Spanish discoverers.

In 1535, two years after the conquest of Peru by Francisco Pizarro and the murder of Atahualpa, last ruler of the Inca empire, the Dominican monk Fray Tomás de Berlanga, bishop of the just-founded city of Panama, travelled by ship from there to Peru. His caravel, becalmed, was caught in the South Equatorial Current and swept some 804 kilometres (500 miles) to the west.

"On the tenth of March [1535] we sighted an island," Fray Tomás wrote to "His Sacred Imperial Catholic Majesty," Charles V of Spain. Going ashore for urgently needed water, the sailors "found nothing but seals, and turtles, and such big tortoises, that each could carry a man on top of itself, and many iguanas that are like serpents."

Like others after him, the bishop was amazed by the tameness of all animals. There were on these islands, he wrote to his emperor, "many birds like those in Spain, but so silly they do not know how to flee, and many were caught in the hand."

On the whole, Fray Tomás did not think highly of the just-discovered islands, "because...[they are] full of very great stones, so much so, that it seems as though some time God has showered stones; and the earth that there is, is like dross, worthless."

Straddling the equator, the Galapagos Islands in the Pacific Ocean, 965 kilometres (600 miles) west of South America, consist of fifteen large islands and more than fifty islets and rocks, with a total area of 7,770 square kilometres (3,000 square miles). The islands are the summits of huge volcanoes risen in cataclysmic, magma-spewing explosions from the bottom of the sea.

Geologically speaking, the islands are new. The oldest rose about two million years ago from the sea. The newest were born in fire and steam less than a million years ago. The islands are cusped with craters; Darwin counted "at least two thousand" of them. Molten magma coursed down the slopes and cooled into weirdly torqued and twisted coils of lava so jagged they can shred a pair of tennis shoes in a day.

To Herman Melville, the author of *Moby Dick*, who visited the Galapagos as a young man on a whaling ship, the islands looked infernally Dantesque "much as the world at large might, after penal conflagration.... In no

Volcanic Galapagos Islands rise from the Pacific Ocean 1,000 kilometres west of South America. On these remote islands, a few immigrant animals evolved into a variety of species.

world but a fallen one could such lands exist."

For millennia after their fiery birth, the islands lay dark and dead and desolate in the deep-blue sea. Then plants and their seeds arrived, bird-borne, seaborne, or airborne. Sea birds came and established rookeries. Through tens of thousands of years, a few land creatures arrived. Small birds were blown to the islands by storms. Reptiles and rats somehow survived the 965-kilometre (600-mile) trip from the mainland on rafts of matted vegetation.

But no large, predatory animals ever arrived. The islands' only mammals are unobtrusive insect-eating bats and mild-mannered vegetarian rice rats. There was no fear, because there was no one to fear. Here was a Garden of Eden, an Age of Innocence where animals did not fear humans.

Ambrose Cowley, British navigator and buccaneer, visited the islands in 1684 and was enchanted: "Turtledoves are so tame they would often alight upon our hats and arms."

Unfortunately, humans are notoriously callous and voracious in paradise. Cowley, after describing so touchingly how tame and trusting the doves were, goes on to tell how he and his shipmates killed them in droves.

That pattern persisted. One hundred and thirty-one years after Cowley, Captain David Porter, USN commander of the frigate *Essex*, wrote in 1815 that the doves "of a small size, and very beautiful plumage...afforded great amusement to the crew in killing them with sticks and stones, which was in no way difficult as they were very tame."

For three centuries after their discovery, the islands were the hideout, haven and larder for pirates, whalers, sailors, and sealers. The pirates, mostly British, plundered Spanish ships. The whalers, mostly American, scoured the oceans in search of their prey, then came to the islands for food, water, and fuel. The sealers hunted the lovely Galapagos fur seals to the very brink of extinction. All filled their ships with *galapagós*, as the Spanish called the giant tortoises after which the islands were named.

The giant tortoises were numerous then. They weigh up to 272 kilograms (600 pounds) and are placid, ponderous, and peaceful. They sleep an average of sixteen hours each day and, given the chance, may live for 150, perhaps even two hundred years. Mighty and antediluvian, they stomp like animated boulders along ancient, tortoise-trampled island paths.

To seamen, the tortoises were easy, delicious, long-lasting, fresh meat, and they provisioned their ships with the unfortunate animals. Wrote Captain

Porter in 1815, "Vessels on whaling voyages among these islands generally take on board from two to three hundred of these animals and stow them in the hold, where, strange as it may appear, they have been known to live for a year, without food or water."

"The buccaneers, whalers, merchantmen and fur sealers probably destroyed at least two to three hundred thousands giant tortoises in just two centuries," wrote the American scientist Craig MacFarland. When he began his study of the giant tortoises in 1971, only about ten thousand survived on all the islands.

Charles Darwin spent five fateful weeks on the Galapagos. Out of his studies of the islands' animals grew his grand theory of evolution by natural selection. Yet Darwin nearly missed seeing the islands because someone important did not like his nose. Years later he wrote, "The voyage of the *Beagle* has been by far the most important event in my life...yet it depended...on such a trifle as the shape of my nose."

Charles Darwin, born into a family of top achievers, at first seemed fated to be a failure or, at best, a modest country parson. Both grandfathers were famous and wealthy: Erasmus Darwin was a celebrated physician, poet, and scientist; Josiah Wedgwood founded the great Wedgwood pottery works. His father, an eminent doctor, thought little of his son who flunked medicine and half-heartedly studied divinity for three years. "You will be a disgrace to yourself and all your family," he predicted.

Only natural history interested young Darwin and at the age of twenty-three, he was offered the unpaid position of naturalist aboard the *Beagle* for its five-year voyage around the world. Then came the last-minute hitch. The *Beagle*'s autocratic, twenty-seven-year-old captain, Robert Fitzroy, a dabbler in phrenology, rejected Darwin because the shape of his nose suggested a lack of "energy and determination." Only the intercession of influential friends secured Darwin the job.

The *Beagle*, a three-masted bark not much bigger than a modern harbour tug, was crammed with provisions and *matériel* for the five-year voyage, plus a crew of seventy-four men. Darwin was given a tiny space in the charthouse. He was extremely prone to seasickness and suffered agonies during the years at sea.

Despite the hardships, Darwin loved the voyage. His curiosity was endless. He filled field book after field book with meticulous notes on the natural history of all the lands and islands he visited.

In 1835, they reached the Galapagos. Darwin was enthralled. "It was most striking to be surrounded by new birds, new reptiles, new shells, new insects, new plants," he wrote. Most animal and plant species were endemic to the islands yet had evolved from mainland ancestors that had arrived on the Galapagos eons ago. Adaptation to island opportunities and demands had changed them over time.

An iguana from the Americas had, on the Galapagos Islands, evolved into a highly specialized and unique marine iguana that feeds on seaweed under water, then basks in groups on the dark lava rocks to warm up its cooled body. "It is a hideous-looking creature, of a dirty black colour, stupid, and sluggish in its movements," Darwin noted. "It is the only existing lizard which lives on marine vegetable production."

Looking like miniature dragons, the crested, sharp-clawed marine iguanas feed on the sea bottom, but seek safety on land. Darwin repeatedly threw one iguana far out onto the water. Each time, it instantly and quickly swam back to him and crawled up "the rugged and fissured masses of lava, which everywhere form the coast." This "apparent stupidity," Darwin astutely observed, "may be accounted for by the circumstance that this reptile has no enemies whatever on shore, whereas at sea it must often fall prey to the numerous sharks."

Sharks, distance and strong ocean currents, discouraged inter-island swimming. As a result, responding to isolation and specific island pressures, different races of the same species evolved on separate islands. The marine iguanas are a dark charcoal grey on most islands. The race living on small, arid Española Island is smaller than marine iguanas elsewhere and magnificently streaked and flecked in deep red and malachite green. Recent studies reveal that these marine iguanas possess another adaptive trait for survival on their hard-scrabble island: when times are tough, their skeleton shrinks and regrows when conditions improve.

Darwin both studied the giant tortoises and ate them. He camped on James Island (San Salvador) with a party of Spaniards who were drying fish and salting tortoise meat. While staying with them "we lived entirely upon tortoise meat...the young tortoises make excellent soup." Near their camp, a reminder of the islands' often violent history, the crew "of a sealing vessel murdered their captain...we saw his skull lying among the bushes."

The tortoises, Darwin noted, are "very fond of water, drinking large quantities." They store the liquid in their large bladders and draw upon it sparingly. That was why tortoises could survive without drinking for a year or more in the holds of ships. Darwin, ever curious, tasted the bladder content of a killed tortoise. "The fluid was quite limpid," he reported, "and had only a very slightly bitter taste."

From the moment he stepped ashore on the Galapagos, Darwin was struck by the fact that it is "the order of reptiles, which gives the most striking character to the zoology of these islands." In a world without mammals, reptiles took their place. "There is no other quarter in the world," said Darwin, "where this Order [of reptiles] replaces the herbivorous mammals in so extraordinary a manner."

Then Darwin realized something even more astounding. It became a vital element in his understanding of evolution by natural selection. He noticed "the most remarkable feature in the natural history of this archipelago; it is, that the different islands to a considerable extent are inhabited by a different set of beings." The giant tortoises, living on separate islands had evolved into separate races. Fourteen distinct island races existed, of which eleven still survive, each adapted to the special demands of its island home.

Giant tortoise of the Galapagos. From a single mainland ancestor, fourteen distinct subspecies evolved. Here, Charles Darwin surmised "the first appearance of new beings on this earth."

The five-year voyage continued. Darwin left the Galapagos reluctantly. "It is the fate of most voyagers, no sooner to discover what is most interesting in any locality, then they are hurried from it," he noted sadly. Still, Darwin had discovered much and he left "astonished at the amount of creative force...displayed on these small, barren, and rocky islands."

Darwin never travelled again. Independently wealthy, he settled at Down House in lovely rural Kent, a quiet, gentle recluse, slowly collating and elucidating the "grand scheme...on which organized beings have been created." His grand design, *The Origin of Species,* was based, in part, on the facts he had gathered on the Galapagos Islands. He died, famous, revered and sometimes reviled, in 1882, and was buried in Westminster Abbey.

In 1959, the government of Ecuador declared the archipelago a national park: the Galapagos National Park. Six years later the Charles Darwin Research Station was opened on Santa Cruz Island, home to scientists from many lands who study the natural wonders of the Galapagos Islands.

Chance moulds our lives. Darwin nearly missed the *Beagle* voyage and the Galapagos Islands because Captain Fitzroy didn't like the shape of his nose. I visited the Galapagos Islands because a scientist friend came down with the flu. "I'm supposed to accompany a tourist group to the Galapagos next week as naturalist leader," he moaned over the telephone. "I can't! I feel awful. Can you take over for me? You can take Maud along."

And so began the first of many trips to the islands Darwin made famous. Like other visitors before us, from Fray Tomás in 1535 to Darwin in 1835, we were amazed and charmed by the wonderful tameness of nearly all island animals. If there ever was a Garden of Eden, it must have been somewhat like this. I poured myself a cup of water on desert-like Española Island and thirsty mockingbirds whirred out of a bush and landed on my hand. They took a sip, looked at me with dark, shining eyes, dipped down, and took another sip.

Blue-footed boobies were courting. Their name comes from the Spanish *bobo*, meaning dunce, and they have bright blue feet of which they are inordinately proud. A he-booby wishing to impress his chosen she-booby did a marvellous little dance routine, while we watched, amused and entranced, from just a few feet away. He lifted alternately and solemnly his large, webbed blue feet in a sort of slow-motion booby cancan, neck and head stretched toward heaven in mounting ecstasy. The female was impressed. When, after the dance and repeated bowing, he presented her with a twig, symbol of a future nest, love, chicks, and domesticity, she accepted it, which in the booby world is as good as a "yes" in church.

Parched Española is also home to the most desert-adapted type of the eleven surviving tortoise races. While its cousins in the lusher highlands of other islands tend to be high-domed and massive, the Española race is light, lean, long-legged, and, for a tortoise, amazingly fast. Its flaring, Spanish-saddle-shaped carapace allows this long-necked race to reach high for sprouting leaves and the succulent beavertail pads of opuntia cacti.

For a while, the strangely-shaped Española tortoise race teetered on the brink of extinction. Thirty years ago only fourteen of them were left: two males and twelve females. Not only had humans killed tortoises, they had also introduced to the islands animals that, as Darwin had predicted, caused "havoc" among trusting animals not "adapted to the stranger's craft or power." Goats, pigs, donkeys, dogs, cats, rats, and cattle went wild, competed with the slow tortoises for food, dug up and ate the tortoise eggs or killed the baby tortoises.

The goats were pushy and prolific. In 1959, one he-goat and two she-goats were released on small Pinta Island. In 1971, their descendants numbered thirty thousand. The Española tortoises were fast. But the goats were faster, smarter. They stripped the meagre vegetation and the tortoises starved.

Now park wardens have killed all goats on Española. The few remaining island tortoises were bred at the Charles Darwin Research Station. More than a thousand young tortoises have been released on their ancestral island. The strangely-shaped Española tortoise race has been saved.

It is a Galapagos paradox that its wild animals are tame and the formerly tame animals are wild and elusive. In all the years we visited the islands, I have only seen three or four goats, and two cats that stared at me for an instant, then vanished like tawny, lethal ghosts. The island birds whose tame nature we so enjoyed, are easy prey for feral cats.

Slowly, beginning with the smaller islands, park wardens are eliminating the destructive alien animals that either eat or out-compete the slower, gentler island residents and threaten their survival.

We saw the success on the little Plaza Islands, which have been returned to their pristine state before humans and their rapacious animal servants came to these isolated islands. Sea lions dozed on our landing pier. They glanced up as we passed, stretched, yawned, and went back to sleep.

I sat down in the shade of a tree-tall opuntia cactus to change film and two of the island's large golden-hued land iguanas marched toward me with interest and ponderous assurance. What do they want? I wondered. It was my yellow film boxes that attracted them. They were the colour of their favourite food, the bright-yellow cactus blossoms.

The opuntia cacti on the Galapagos are a perfect example of Darwin's theory of evolution by natural selection. On islands uninhabited by browsing tortoises or iguanas, the cacti grow in low, ground-hugging clusters. On islands with tortoises or iguanas, opuntia cacti have evolved into 9-metre- (30-foot-) tall cactus trees, their moisture-filled pads high above the munching reptiles.

Darwin's famous finches were everywhere. One, with a powerful, triangular grosbeak bill was busy cracking tough-shelled seeds. A smaller finch with a chickadee-sharp bill probed crevices for insects and their eggs. Another, with a specialized, sharp-edged bill cut pulpy pieces out of an opuntia calyx.

The animals ignored us. A mockingbird sat on my hat. I was, I realized, merely a convenient perch. The two iguanas, golden dragons with crested napes, lay near my feet for a while, then walked away. We humans were incidental, mildly interesting to the animals, inoffensive strangers in this paradise the first explorers called Las Islas Encantadas (the Enchanted Isles).

The dance of the blue boobies. Flashing his bright blue palmate feet, a male blue booby tries to impress a female. Long isolated, the island birds have little fear of humans.

Chapter 14

PRIBILOF ISLANDS, ALASKA, U.S.A.
Islands of Fogs and Fur Seals

THE KILLING FIELDS are no longer used on the Pribilof Islands. The grass on the killing fields is still distinctive. The sward is thick, lush and a deep, rich green. Every summer for two hundred years these fields were fertilized with the blood of fur seals—millions upon millions of fur seals.

The killing began in 1786. It ended in 1984. Between seven million and eight million fur seals were clubbed to death and skinned. America earned more than two hundred million dollars from that slaughter, about twenty-eight times what it had paid for all Alaska in 1867.

Fur seal exploitation led to major quarrels between the United States and Great Britain (representing Canada) and to minor skirmishes between the U.S., Japan, and imperial Russia. The "Seal Wars," as some flamboyant press reports called the fights over fur seals, ended in a 1911 four-nation treaty that controlled and limited the killing of fur seals. It was the first international agreement to protect wildlife.

The Pribilof Islands, hub of the fur seal feuds, and the surrounding Bering Sea are home to some of the largest wildlife concentrations on earth. The region also has some of the world's worst weather.

Near these remote volcanic islands, 1,303 kilometres (810 miles) from the Alaskan mainland, two mighty ocean currents meet and mingle. Here, the warm waters of the Kuroshio (or Japan Current) collide with the icy waters of the Oyashio Current rushing out of the Arctic Ocean through Bering Strait into the Bering Sea.

The violent, churning currents, the sinking and rising layers of warm and cold water, carry a superabundance of nutrients to the sea's surface. Planktonic plants and animals flourish in stupendous numbers, food for higher animals such as fishes and crustaceans, and these in turn feed the vast herds of sea mammals and millions of sea birds that live on the Pribilof Islands.

The titanic clash of ocean currents, one warm, one cold, of the Siberian high with the Aleutian low, produces horrid weather. A University of Alaska study says the Pribilofs have each year forty-two days of heavy fog; eighteen days of snow and sleet; and two hundred days of rain. "Good weather is rare and of short duration," the study notes "and violent gales come from almost any direction."

This is the setting of the fur seal saga, which is a strange and often tragic one. It began in 1741, when Vitus Bering, the Danish-born explorer extraordinaire for Russia's czars, discovered the Alaskan mainland and the Aleutian Islands and claimed it all for Russia.

On the return journey to Kamchatka, Bering's ship broke up on the bleak Commander Islands off Siberia. Bering died and was buried on the island that now bears his name. The survivors spent a gruesome, scurvy-racked winter.

Only one man was happy: the brilliant, young German-born biologist Georg Wilhelm Steller. On this island, he could study animals no European had seen before: a 3-ton sea cow that munched seaweed in the shallows, its skin like the bark of ancient oaks (Steller's sea cow, giant northern cousin of the southern manatees of Florida fame; discovered in 1741, exterminated by 1768!); and a giant flightless cormorant which quickly shared the sea cow's fate.

Thousands of sea otters, which had never seen humans, lolled among the kelp beds near shore, tame and trusting. And in spring the fur seals came in tens of thousands to their island rookeries to breed. Steller built a small hut near a rookery, observed the animals and wrote the first detailed account of fur seal life. The male, he noted, "often has eight, fifteen, or even fifty wives. He guards them with anxious jealousy."

The survivors of the expedition returned to Siberia in a boat made from the remnants of their ships, with a cargo of sea otter pelts. On the fur-hungry Chinese luxury market, each one of these pelts was worth more than a hundred dollars, then the equivalent of a Russian worker's annual salary.

St. Paul Island

PRIBILOF ISLANDS

St. George Island

N

0 Mi.   5   10
0 km.   7.5   15

Siberia's *promyshelniki* (fur hunters), responded instantly to this call of wealth. They were a breed of northern conquistador, grasping, greedy, reckless, and ruthless.

Using any conveyance that could reasonably be expected to float, including *shitiks*, boats made of green lumber, the planks sewn together with thong or osier withes, they rushed to the new land. They robbed and enslaved the Aleuts and sent cargo after cargo of sea otter pelts back to Siberia and on to the markets of opulent China. Imperial ukases from St. Petersburg thundered against "such barbarities, plunder and the ravaging of women." They were ignored. The common saying was, "Russia is great. And the czar is far!" In a few decades, the once-proud Aleuts had been reduced from an estimated sixteen thousand to twenty thousand to a broken, subservient remnant of barely two thousand.

The sea otters declined nearly as swiftly. But around 1750, the Chinese invented a method to remove the fur seal's stiff guard hairs, leaving only the silky, down-soft, deep-pile underwool, so dense (with three hundred thousand hairs to the square inch) that the icy waters of the northern seas never touch a fur seal's skin. Suddenly, fur seal pelts, too, meant fortunes.

The Russians were already exploiting the fur seal rookeries on the Commander Islands, on the Kuril Islands, and on Robben Island off Sakhalin. But the greatest prize as yet eluded them. Each spring about two to three million fur seals could be seen to swim through the straits separating the Aleutian Islands, only to vanish into the fog-shrouded vastness of the Bering Sea.

After a search that lasted three years, Captain Gerassim Pribilof (or Pribylov) found it. On June 25, 1786, the dull roar of a great fur seal rookery guided him through the fog to a small (85-square-kilometre [33-square-mile]) island, which he named St. George after his ship. The following year, on the feast day of St. Peter and St. Paul, he discovered the larger (113-square-kilometre [44-square-mile]) St. Paul Island where, as Rudyard Kipling said in his poem about the fur seals, "they came and went in legions that darkened all the shore."

Pribilof's first cargo of fur seal and sea otter pelts and walrus ivory from the island group later named after him, was valued at 258,018 rubles, well in excess of a million dollars today.

It was a subarctic El Dorado and here the gold was furs. The *promyshelniki* responded instantly and with brutal rapacity. They slaughtered the fur seal legions. They glutted the Chinese market. The waste was catastrophic. Wrote the Russian missionary to the Aleuts, Ivan Veniaminov, later metropolitan of

Moscow: "In 1803, 800,000 seal skins had accumulated...and so many were spoiled that it became necessary to throw into the sea 700,000 pelts."

After this initial free-for-all, the fur seals on the Pribilof Islands became the exclusive property of the Russian-American Company. To kill and skin the seals and cure the pelts, the company imported 137 Aleuts to the uninhabited Pribilof Islands, forebears of the people who live there today.

The Russians also brought Aleuts to the Commander Islands where they mixed with other groups from Russia's far-flung empire brought to these lonely islands to work: Inuit, Kyrgyz, Kurilians, Tlingit Indians, Syrians and Gypsies, plus overseers of Russian, American, Lettish, and Polish origin.

The Aleuts on the Pribilofs, essentially company serfs,

Fur seal bulls guard territories occupied by harems of females. Heavily exploited for two hundred years, the Pribilof Islands fur seal colonies are now protected.

killed about four million fur seals between 1789 and 1867, and cured the pelts
for their Russian masters. At first the killing was indiscriminate and the fur seal
herds declined. Then the Russians realized that by taking only the surplus
males of this polygamous seal society, the herds would not be affected. From
about 1832, they protected female seals and slowly the herds increased again.
Each year sixty thousand to one hundred thousand young male fur seals died
on the Pribilof Islands' killing fields.

It was immensely profitable and the Russian company guarded its seals
with jealous vigilance. Interlopers could be shot, as Rudyard Kipling noted in
"The Rhyme of the Three Sealers":

> Now this is the law of the Muscovite,
> That he proves with shot and steel.
> When ye come by his isles in the Smoky Sea
> Ye must not take the seal.

Muscovite rule over the Pribilofs came to an abrupt end in 1867 when
Russia sold Alaska to the United States for 7.2 million dollars, or less than two
cents an acre. In twenty years, net revenues to the U.S. treasury from fur seal
pelts alone, paid for this vast land, eleven times the size of England.

For the first forty years, the U.S. roughly followed Russian precedent. It leased
the Pribilof Islands, lock, stock, seals, and Aleuts to companies, set a quota of
one hundred thousand seals per year (for the first twenty years; later this was
reduced), and contented itself with collecting a fairly hefty tax revenue.

The companies exploited the seals and their far-away shareholders prospered.
The Aleuts were paid a pittance, which they could only spend at the island
company store and were ruled with mildly despotic paternalism. Visits by outsiders were discouraged. Waldemar Jochelson, leader of the 1909–1910
Kamchatka-Aleutian expedition was given a permit to visit the Pribilofs. Such
permission, he later wrote, was rarely granted because, "The administration of
the islands looks unfavorably on publicity. And indeed, the slaughter of the fur
seals...presents a most painful spectacle."

The seals died. The Aleuts worked. The shareholders profited. The U.S.
treasury collected millions in tax revenues. This cozy setup (except for seals and
Aleuts) might have gone on forever, had not something quite unforeseen happened. Canadians and, later, the Japanese began pelagic sealing on a large scale.

In 1879, sixteen ships, mostly Canadian, killed fur seals at sea. Ten years later, 115 ships were criss-crossing the seals' migration routes along the coasts of Asia and North America, or were lying in wait just off the Pribilof Islands.

In less than thirty years, these pelagic sealers took more than a million fur seals and killed but lost perhaps an equal number. Worst of all, an estimated 80 per cent of all the fur seals destroyed at sea were pregnant females.

The United States retaliated by confiscating some of the Canadian sealing ships. Gatling guns, early machine guns that could fire about six hundred shots a minute, were set up on the Pribilof Islands near the rookeries to shoot Canadian and Japanese rivals.

The Canadian minister of marine and fisheries, Charles A. Tupper, was outraged. This, he declared, was a blatant American attempt "to drive our flag off the ocean in the Northern Pacific." It was time to show some "British pluck and daring."

Britain defended the cause of her Canadian subjects with vigour. President Grover Cleveland had authorized the seizure of Canadian sealing vessels. The British prime minister, Lord Salisbury, protested and ordered four warships to stand ready for action, two in Yokohama and two at the British Columbia naval base of Esquimalt.

For a while Britain and the U.S. glared and dared each other. The press loved it. The remote Pribilofs and the threatening "Seal War" was big news. Finally, in 1893, the whole issue was brought to international arbitration in Paris. Enough reports were written to fill a dozen fat volumes.

While the delegates dined and dawdled in Paris, the killing of seals, on land and at sea, continued at the same frenetic pace, until it finally dawned on all concerned that, if they didn't settle their quarrel, there would be nothing left to quarrel about. On the Pribilofs, where there once had been three million fur seals, only about two hundred thousand were left.

That realization brought about an amazingly quick accord: the First North Pacific Fur Seal Convention signed in 1911 by Japan, the United States, Russia, and Britain (for Canada). Under the terms of the convention all nations promised to abstain from pelagic sealing. In return, Canada and Japan each received 15 per cent of all fur seal pelts taken on land by Russia and the United States. That convention, renewed in 1957 and modified only in detail, remained in force until all commercial sealing ceased on the Pribilofs in 1984.

World War II was good for fur seals and bad for the Aleuts. Fearing an invasion by the Japanese (who did invade the Aleutian islands of Attu and Kiska) the Pribilof Aleuts were abruptly evacuated. They were interned in dilapidated cannery buildings on Admiralty Island off southeast Alaska. It was a miserable time for them.

Until then, they had lived in near-total isolation on their cool, treeless, wind-swept islands. In camp, cramped and hot, many became ill and nearly a fourth of them died. In the 1950s, after repatriation to their home islands, the survivors successfully sued the United States government for having treated them so badly.

With Japanese and Americans killing each other, neither had time to kill fur seals. The beaches of the Pribilofs, their dark lava boulders smoothed and polished by endless flippered generations, were once again covered with fur seals.

The respite was short. After the war, the seal "harvest" was resumed and with an ominous twist. For the first time since 1832, female seals were killed on land. The Aleuts protested vehemently. To them, the killing of females was evil and unwise. Time proved them right, but the advice of government biologists prevailed. Between 1956 and 1968, in addition to the yearly quota of young males, more than three hundred thousand female fur seals were clubbed to death. From that carnage, the seals never recovered.

The herds declined. In 1973, commercial sealing ended on St. George Island. But it was still carried on during the summer I lived on St. Paul Island.

Near the breeding rookeries, but at a respectful distance from the belligerent territorial bulls, the fur seal bachelors hauled out in chummy groups, from a few hundred to well over a thousand. They all were destined to die. Their lovely pelts would become elegant fur coats.

Every morning (except Sunday) in the chill hours before dawn, from June 26 until the end of July, Aleut sealers drove in trucks to one of the rookeries. Fast and noiselessly, they ran between seals and beach and drove a bachelor herd slowly inland, pausing periodically so that the thick-furred seals would not overheat. On level grassy ground beyond each rookery was the killing field. "*Ungisxalgaq*," the Aleuts called it, "the place without hope."

The killing began. In the soft grey light of morning it looked like a superbly orchestrated dance of death. "Stunners," "stickers," "rippers," "pullers" moved in time-tested rhythm and with assembly-line efficiency.

The stunners smashed the seals' heads with 1.5-metre- (5-foot-) long hardwood clubs.

The stickers cut their throats and stabbed their hearts.

The rippers cut the skin around the flippers and along the belly.

The pullers peeled the skins off the carcasses and placed them, steaming warm, on the cool grass.

A skilled crew killed and skinned a seal in about one minute.

Boys ran from carcass to carcass and removed the genitals. Dried, these "seal sticks" were shipped to China where they were greatly in demand. The Chinese believe that powders prepared from them restore or enhance virility.

The killing, veterinary reports agreed, was carried out "with a high level of efficiency" and "in a reasonably humane fashion." But, environmentalists asked, was it ethical to kill thirty thousand or more wild animals just to make five thousand very elegant and very expensive fur coats.

The herds decreased. Public pressure to stop the killing increased. In 1984, 198 years after it began, commercial sealing ended on the Pribilof Islands.

Fur seals die on St. Paul Island "killing fields." Once up to one hundred thousand seals a year were killed for their valuable fur. The islands were exploited first by Russians and later by Americans.

It rained in spring when I arrived on St. Paul Island. It rained nearly all summer. And it rained in fall when I left. Not heavy rain, as a rule. Just a steady light drizzle. The light was soft, diffuse and grey. It was a land without shadows.

I found the island's people strangely tri-cultural: the core was Aleut, wrapped in a many-faceted layer of Russian custom and belief, the whole covered by an American patina. I lived in the village of St. Paul (population then, 470; 525 in 2005) with a charming elderly Aleut couple, Sergie and Nadesda Shaishnikoff (nearly all Aleuts have Russian names).

Sergie and Nadesda, and most older people, spoke Aleut together (containing so many words adopted from Russian that I could follow the gist of a simple conversation). All the young people knew Aleut, but most preferred to speak English.

We ate store-bought American food, but also local specialties: basted roast of seal, marinated murre and kittiwake stew. I felt a bit guilty about the stew made with birds that are a birder's dream: red-legged kittiwakes. They are common on the Pribilof and Commander islands, but exist nowhere else in the world.

On Sundays we went to mass in the Russian Orthodox church of St. Peter and St. Paul, held by the Aleut *batjuska* (from the Russian "little father") Reverend Michael Lestenkof. The service was in Church Slavonic, the ancient liturgical language of Slavic Orthodox churches, which nearly all adult Aleuts could speak. Choir, priest, and congregation sang the mass's magnificent antiphonal chants.

After the service, when it did not rain too hard, St. Paul's young people played baseball or raced their shiny Japanese motorcycles along the 96 kilometres (60 miles) of brick-red scoria roads that snake and twist across the lush green, rolling island, past Polovina (half-way) Hill and Bogoslov (word of God) Hill.

From the main road, others branch off toward the coast, to the island's seventeen fur seal rookeries, to Gorbatch (the hump), to Zoltoi (the golden), to Spilki (the points), or to Morjovi (of the walrus) where walruses once hauled out before all Pribilof Island walruses were killed for their ivory.

The roads to the rookeries were barred. No one was allowed to disturb the breeding seals. For the same reason dogs were, and still are, forbidden on the Pribilof Islands.

I hid in a cleft overlooking the Lukanin rookery, named after a long-ago Russian sealer, the beach Kipling called "Lukannon" in his famous poem about the fur seals' fate:

> The Beaches of Lukannon—the home where we were born!
> The Beaches of Lukannon—two million voices strong,
> The Beaches of Lukannon—before the sealers came!"

The great fur seal bulls, deep brown with grizzled manes, arrived in May. They were magnificent, fat and powerful, about 2 metres (6 feet) long and weighing up to 363 kilograms (800 pounds). Each one of these beachmasters, males in their prime, occupied a large section of breeding beach and fought furiously for its possession with encroaching rival bulls.

Large males faced each other, snarled and roared, and struck cobra-quick at neck and flippers of the enemy. They overheated and stopped, panting puffs of musky vapour. Territories shrank as new bulls muscled in. Territorial borders, invisible to me but very real to the males, were established.

The small, sleek females, weighing only 40 to 54 kilograms (90 to 120 pounds), arrived in late June and early July. Certain territories attracted them. The massive owners seemed to exert little allure. But once females were upon a beachmaster's property, he guarded them with huffy jealousy. Most pups were born within twenty-four hours after their mothers came ashore.

At first, the beach beneath my hiding place appeared to me as utter chaos. It was densely packed with a dark mass of moving, arguing, roaring adult seals and glossy-black, big-flippered bleating pups.

In reality, the beach consisted of distinct territories, each ruled by a beachmaster, surrounded by a harem of from one or two to more than eighty females. There was a vast and ancient synchrony but very little harmony.

The females were gregarious but often ill-tempered and snarly. Devotedly maternal to her own pup, a female thought nothing of picking up a hungry stray pup and throwing it, squalling, yards away. The females were forever moving, sneaking off and their territorial male was non-stop busy, huffing, growling and shaking his head, his normally drooping Genghis Khan whiskers abristle, rounding up wandering wives and arguing with neighbouring males. In their violent, jealousy-prodded rushes across their territory, mighty 363-kilogram (800-pound) seal bulls galumphed blithely over any 10-pound pup in their path.

The pups were pliable and agile and they usually survived. One of the first lessons they learned was to scramble frantically out of the way when Big Daddy came barging along.

The females mated within a few days of giving birth and soon after swam far out to sea, to feed and replenish their milk reserves. Some were away for fourteen days.

For two months the beachmasters reigned. They did not eat, they did not drink, they fought a lot, they mated often, and they rarely slept. When they left, some had lost more than 90 kilograms (200 pounds). It's tough to be an alpha male. Most males plummet from alpha to omega in just two seasons.

As the first fierce winds of fall screamed over the island, the females, their duty done, began to leave. Weeks later, hesitantly at first, the pups left their natal beaches for the food and the dangers of the sea, because there, as Kipling said in his "seal song," "The White Seal": "And summer gales and killer whales / Are bad for baby seals."

The once-vast seal herds of the Pribilofs keep decreasing. Some blame humans and overfishing, others blame killer whales. The islands' fur seal population was 2.1 million in 1951. It had decreased to 871,000 by 1986. It declined to 628,000 in 2005. Alaska sea otters have declined by 75 per cent since the 1980s, the great Steller sea lions by more than 80 per cent.

It's all the fault of the killer whales, some claim. They once killed the abundant whales. Now that whales have become rare, the argument goes, they kill sea otters and the pinnipeds, including fur seals and sea lions.

Others blame overfishing by the fleets of many nations. Since the 1960s they have removed 150 billion pounds of fish from Alaskan waters.

Commercial sealing ended more than twenty years ago. But the seals keep declining on the Pribilofs. Some of the ancient seal rookeries where fur seals once "came and went in legions that darkened all the shore" are now empty.

BELCHER ISLANDS, HUDSON BAY, CANADA

Arctic Islands Ruled Briefly by Religious Hysteria and Murder

ON MARCH 13, 1941, the Hudson's Bay Company head office in Winnipeg received an urgent wireless message from Ernest Riddell, one of its Arctic post managers: "THREE MURDERS HAVE BEEN COMMITTED ON BELCHER ISLANDS. ADVISE IMMEDIATE POLICE INVESTIGATION." The message was at once relayed to the RCMP in Ottawa.

It was wartime. The islands were far away and barely known. Planes were scarce. Before the police could act, a second, even more urgent message arrived: "THERE HAVE BEEN MORE MURDERS. COME IMMEDIATELY."

That winter a messianic cult had been born on the remote Belcher Islands. A portion of the islands' small Inuit population was in a state of advanced hysteria and religious frenzy. The mixture was deadly.

These islands in Hudson Bay, about 160 kilometres (100 miles) off its east coast, had been named after Captain James Belcher who was employed by the Hudson's Bay Company in the early 1700s. The 1910 admiralty chart showed them as a spattering of islets.

That year, Robert Flaherty, explorer and, later, cinematographer who gained world fame with his film *Nanook of the North*, met on Charlton Island in James Bay an Inuk, George Wetaltuk, who had been born on the Belcher Islands. Wetaltuk spoke of "big islands" to the north and drew a map of them which guided the Flaherty expeditions.

Lacking caribou, Belcher Island Inuit made their parkas of eider duck skins. About twenty-five duck skins were needed to make one parka. It was very warm but lasted only one year.

When Flaherty finally reached the Belcher Islands with his schooner *Laddie* in 1914, he was amazed "how remarkably accurate the map is!" that Wetaltuk had made for him. The weirdly contorted islands, gaunt rock ribs rising from the dark sea like some harrowing geological fever graph, covered 12,950 square kilometres (5,000 square miles), five times the size of the Grand Duchy of Luxembourg. Yet until Flaherty visited and mapped them, they were practically unknown.

According to Belcher Island Inuit lore, their ancestors came from the Ungava Bay region about two hundred to three hundred years ago, "at a time when there were already white traders in Hudson Bay." They crossed the peninsula, hunting caribou, and arrived in spring in the vicinity of Great Whale River (Kuujjuarapik) on the east coast of Hudson Bay. Indians attacked them. The survivors fled to sea, and reached, eventually, the Belcher Islands.

There were probably Thule-culture Inuit living on the islands then (the Belchers are rich in Thule-culture camp sites) and it seems likely the newcomers intermixed with them. The island dialect they speak differs considerably from that of eastern Hudson Bay and Hudson Strait. "They speak like children," say the mainland Inuit with just a touch of condescension.

As a home, the bleak, barren, wind-swept islands appear uninviting. Flaherty's report reads like a weatherman's nightmare: "From October till early December winds...of up to 50 miles an hour [80 kilometres an hour] were almost constant." The average January temperature was −26°C (−16°F), with winds of up to 112 kilometres (70 miles) an hour; "calm days were unknown." February was as bad, and summer doesn't sound cheerful either: "From mid–June to late fall exceedingly heavy gales...occurred in every week." Plus rain. Plus fog. "Days of sunshine were rare."

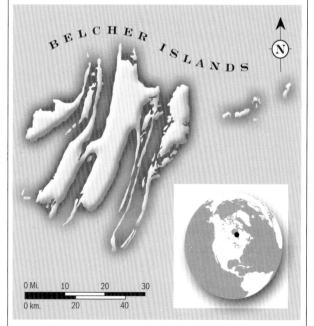

But the islands were (and are) rich in game. White whales cavorted among the islands in large pods. To the north, walrus were common. Ringed seal and bearded seal were immensely numerous and in the great, 69-kilometre-(43-mile–)long Kasegalik Lake (seal lake) lived freshwater harbour seals. Eider ducks by tens of thousands nested on islets and skerries, and near the islands' myriad lakes Canada geese brooded their eggs. In addition, the lakes were rich with char and, in fall, the sloughs and vales were carpeted with cloudberries and crowberries.

One essential ingredient to the Inuit's ability to survive arctic winters was missing: there were no caribou on the Belcher Islands. According to the islanders, caribou had once been common. Then, probably in the 1880s, came a winter of heavy snows. In March, it turned mild and rains poured down, turning the snow into waterlogged mush. Suddenly the wind veered to the north, the temperature dropped abruptly, the wet snow froze and the islands were enveloped for weeks in a glittering, hard carapace of ice. The caribou scraped and scratched in vain. They could not reach the lichen below the ice mantle and all perished.

Thus, the Belcher Island Inuit lacked one item considered essential for survival in the Arctic: caribou pelts for winter clothes and sleeping robes. But the ingenious Inuit solved the problem. They made their winter clothes of eider duck skins.

It took twenty to twenty-five bird skins to make a *mitvin* (eider duck parka), derived from *miterq* (eider duck). Hood and cuffs were trimmed with dog or fox fur. This odd-looking garment was as warm as a caribou parka, though not as lasting. By fall, both ducks and people were moulting.

To take maximum advantage of game resources, the islanders (the population has fluctuated in the past hundred years between 150 and 200 people) lived in widely scattered camps: in winter in igloos warmed by *kudliks* (seal oil lamps), in summer in sealskin tents or low, hovel-like sod huts.

With so much water in between and all around their islands (and open, thanks to currents and storms, for about eight months of the year) the Belcher Islanders were to the kayak born. "Their daring as kayakers surpasses that of any other Eskimo of my acquaintance," wrote Flaherty.

Though game was plentiful, life was risky and hard. Hunting by kayak in these treacherous, storm-tossed waters took a heavy toll. When the American naturalist Arthur C. Twomey visited the islands in 1938, he found that "almost a third of the native women on the Belcher Islands are already widows."

In 1933, the Hudson's Bay Company had opened a trading post on Tukarak Island. The islanders trapped perhaps more assiduously than before, became more dependent on white man's goods, but on the whole, one gathers from Twomey in 1938, their patterns of life changed little. They lived at the edge of the world: they knew little about the rest of the world, and the world knew nothing of them.

Then, suddenly, horribly, the Belcher Islands and the Belcher Islanders were in the headlines.

From the *Toronto Star*, 1941: April 18—"Mystic Lures Six To Freeze Naked in Storm"; April 21—"Star Falling in Arctic Sky Is Signal for Nine Murders"; August 5—"Arctic Tent to Be Court for Arctic Murder Trial"; August 20—"Jury Acquits Two Eskimos of Murdering Girl 'Satan'"; August 22—"Congregation Gave Eskimo Bullet to Shoot 'Satan'"; August 29—"This Time Eskimos Realize Jail Is 'Many Sleeps' Away."

Perhaps the famous Canadian anthropologist Diamond Jenness had visions of the possibility of such a tragedy when he wrote in 1928, "Hysteria is peculiarly common around the Polar basin; the long winter darkness and the loneliness and silence of the hunter's life made the Arctic peoples more susceptible to this disorder than the rest of the human race. So religion and hysteria went closely hand in hand."

Religion and hysteria. Missionaries had been to the Belchers on a few occasions. They left behind Bibles and prayer books in syllabics, and some murky notions of Christianity that became muddled in the Inuit mind with their ancient shamanistic beliefs. One of these beliefs was that spirits could become corporeal. They could enter a man, and from that instant he

Until mapped by the explorer and film maker Robert Flaherty in 1910, the Belcher Islands in Hudson Bay and their native people were nearly unknown to the outside world.

ceased to be himself, and became the spirit incarnate. From this belief to the idea that Christ in His Second Coming would be incarnated in an Inuk was but one step, and our own history is replete with examples that a messianic message believed by some and unbelieved by others can lead to murder, and to war.

The winter of 1940–1941 was hard on the Belcher Islands. Autumn had been stormier than usual and the men had not been able to hunt. Seals were scarce. The spectre of famine stalked the land. In their igloos, poorly heated because they lacked seal oil for the stone lamps, the men had plenty of time to brood. Keytowieack, the forty-seven-year-old catechist, read sections from the New Testament.

The coming of Christ. The idea fascinated twenty-seven-year-old Charlie Ouyerack. Christ, all-powerful, the man of miracles.

When Ouyerack was a boy, his father had been murdered. As he grew into a man, his need for self-assertion and power led him to seek command over spirits while in a state of trance. Now he brooded about Christ.

One night, while Keytowieack was reading from the Bible, the revelation came. "I am Jesus!" Ouyerack shouted. He rushed out of the igloo into the star-glittering night, the horizon aglow with the silent flames of northern lights. "I am Jesus!" Ouyerack shouted again. "His spirit has entered into me!" In that instant, as he raised his hands in glorious ecstasy toward heaven, a meteor streaked through the sky, trailing fire.

"It is a sign!" the people muttered in solemn awe.

When Peter Sala returned to camp next morning from a long hunt, he found his people in an advanced stage of mystic hysteria. Sala was one of the islands' best hunters, a strong, resourceful, courageous man. He had been guide to the American naturalist Arthur Twomey in 1938. When caught in a storm and deadly cross-currents, Sala steered the boat and the white men relied "on Peter like trusting children.... Few admirations I ever had equal my regard for Peter Sala as I saw him in those moments," Twomey wrote.

Now Sala was tired and hungry. The sudden wave of hysteria engulfed him.

"You are God!" Ouyerack shouted.

"You are God!" the people beseeched.

Sala hesitated, confused and frightened. But to him, too, revelation came. "Yes, I am God!" he said, and the people believed and were happy. They chanted and prayed.

One person did not believe. Sarah, a thirteen-year-old girl, and she said so.

Abruptly happy hysteria changed into hideous hate. "She is Satan!" Ouyerack screamed and they kicked her and beat her.

"I do believe! I do believe!" the poor girl whimpered. But it was too late. Two women dragged her out of the igloo and bludgeoned her to death.

"We have killed the devil!" Ouyerack exulted.

The catechist, Keytowieack, too, did not believe in earthly gods, but he believed in his own imminent death. Fatalistically he went to his igloo and waited.

Next day, Sala broke the ice window and threw his harpoon at Keytowieack. It pierced his sleeve.

"Look at me!" Sala commanded. "I am God! Say that I am God!"

The old man sat motionless. He did not answer.

"I am God!" Sala screamed in fury, turned to Adlaykok standing near him and commanded, "Shoot him! He is Satan!"

The bullet ripped through Keytowieack's shoulder. He reeled but remained silent. "I have no more bullets," Adlaykok said.

"Jesus will give you one," said Sala, and Adlaykok went to Ouyerack, got a bullet, and shot Kaytowieack through the head.

A month later, in February at another camp, Quarack, a famous hunter, fell under Ouyerack's spell and, at his command, shot another unbeliever, his son-in-law, Alec Keytowieack, son of the killed catechist.

Word of the murders reached Ernest Riddell, Hudson's Bay Company manager on the Belcher Islands. On March 13, he sent the wireless message that informed his head office and via them, the RCMP.

But before the police could take action, tragedy reached its climax on the Belchers.

Sala was away. Quarack was hunting. Ouyerack was at another camp. Mina, Sala's sister, a thirty-year-old, powerful, brooding woman had lived with Ouyerack after he became Jesus. Now he had left her. On March 29, her repressed fury broke forth in screaming hysteria.

"Jesus is coming!" Mina yelled. "Jesus is coming. We must go on the ice to meet him." She pushed and pulled the women and children of the camp far out onto the sea ice to await His coming. "Take your clothes off!" she commanded. "We cannot meet Jesus with our clothes on!" It was terribly cold. The other women hesitated. Mina, in a frenzy, ripped and clawed the clothes off the women and children. The children cried in fear and pain and Mina, now raving in madness and ecstasy, ran around the naked group, screaming: "Jesus is coming! Jesus is coming!"

When Sala returned, he found his two sons had frozen to death, also his mother, another woman, and two more children.

The trial was held in mid-August 1941. The RCMP had set up a marquee, as big as a carnival tent. Above the judge's bench, a table covered with a flag, hung the portraits of the King and Queen. Mr. Justice C.P. Plaxton in wig and gown presided, flanked by black-gowned lawyers from Ottawa and RCMP officers in scarlet tunics. On benches and on the floor sat the more than fifty Inuit witnesses, in eider duck parkas, like great man-birds, perturbed and puzzled by this weird panoply of white man's power.

> JUDGE: Charlie, why did you believe you were Jesus Christ?
> OUYERACK: It came to me that I was that. Also the Holy Ghost.
> JUDGE: What is the Holy Ghost?
> OUYERACK: Some friend of Jesus; they are not the same and he is not like a man.
> JUDGE: Where did you first hear of the Holy Ghost?
> OUYERACK: From the missionary.
> JUDGE: That was sixteen years ago?
> OUYERACK: Yes.
> JUDGE: Are you sure your memory is right?
> OUYERACK: One cannot forget a thing like that.
> JUDGE: But now you know you are not Jesus?
> OUYERACK: Yes.
> JUDGE: Why?
> OUYERACK: He is like me, but brighter than the sun. That is not me.
> JUDGE: But you knew this before?
> OUYERACK: Yes. But I did not remember. I was too happy at being Jesus.

The jury, composed entirely of white men, mainly prospectors brought over from the mainland, found the persons who had killed the thirteen-year-old girl Sarah "not guilty, on account of temporary insanity."

Mina, who had to be carried into the court on a stretcher, was declared insane.

Quarack received a suspended sentence with the proviso that he must provide Peter Sala's family with food until Sala was freed.

Sala, Ouyerack and Adlaykok were each sentenced to two years hard labour, to be served at the RCMP station at Moose Factory. And they were exiled, in perpetuity, from the Belcher Islands.

Ouyerack, the man who briefly thought of himself as the incarnation of Christ, died in less than a year after having been moved to Moose Factory. Silent and sullen, he wasted away. The official reason was tuberculosis. But the tests were negative. The Inuit on the Belcher Islands believed the man who had once, in frenzied fervour, felt that he was Jesus, had now, with his glory and power gone, willed himself to die.

In the fall of 1954, I talked myself onto the Catholic mission boat leaving Moosonee, the northern railroad terminal on the Moose River. It carried mail and supplies to the then still very isolated settlements on the east coast of James Bay.

On the return trip, we stopped at Cape Hope Island in James Bay. There, at the latitude of London, England, was Canada's southernmost Inuit settlement and I met its founder and patriarch, ninety-four-year-old George Wetaltuk, a wizened but wiry man, with an unruly shock of white hair and the wisdom of a nearly century-long life shining from his twinkling, alert eyes.

We drank large mugs of tea and Wetaltuk talked of long-vanished worlds. He had been born on the Belcher Islands. As a young man he had hunted polar bears armed only with an ivory-tipped spear. He had harpooned mighty walruses from his kayak. He had lived the ancient life of Inuit hunters before the outside world touched them.

But he had been curious about that alien world. In the late 1880s, he travelled with his wife and three children by dog team from the Belcher Islands across the short-lived, dangerous winter ice-bridge to the mainland and worked for the Hudson's Bay Company. In time, he became the company's chief pilot, guiding the great sailing ships from England through the poorly known waters of Hudson Bay and James Bay to Charlton Island in southern James Bay with its great, fortress-like warehouses (which I later visited), a major hub of European trade with the natives of the north.

It was on Charlton Island in 1910 that George Wetaltuk, then already known as Old Man Wetaltuk, met Robert Flaherty. He told Flaherty about the Belcher Islands, drew for him, from memory, after a more than twenty-year absence, that amazingly accurate map of the complex, convoluted islands. That map, reproduced in the 1918 *Geographical Review*, helped Flaherty to "discover" and explore the hitherto virtually unknown Belcher Islands.

I visited the Belcher Islands fourteen years after meeting Wetaltuk, near the end of a six-month, four-thousand-mile trip around Labrador and Ungava, travelling from settlement to settlement, often by canoe.

The chartered aircraft from Great Whale River brought a new world to the Belcher Islands, mechanics, electricians, carpenters, and me, still hitching rides whenever possible. New houses were being built on the Belcher Islands.

One house at North Camp (now the islands' only settlement Sanikiluaq) was the home of Charlie Crow. I spent a lot of time with Charlie. He made a big pot of tea, produced some bannock he had baked and I contributed jam. We sat in his kitchen and talked. Charlie had a phenomenal knowledge of the islands and their people. But he had never seen them. Charlie was totally blind.

Charlie had grown up on the Belcher Islands, where his father had been the Hudson's Bay Company store manager, and in the south, at schools for the blind. Now he lived on the islands where he felt most at home.

"It's different now," he said. "There's mostly young people here. There was a bad famine in 1952. People then lived in small camps. Far away. The weather was bad. The men couldn't hunt and many old people died. Starved to death. And then, in 1961, there was an epidemic of German measles. A lot of people died. Some children. But mostly old people. So now we

In 1959, all but two Inuit hunters on the Belcher Islands owned and used kayaks. A decade later, modern times and motor-driven canoes had replaced nearly all traditional kayaks.

have few old people. The past has sort of died with them. The old ways are dying out."

In 1953, when Charlie was a boy, all Inuit on the Belchers lived in winter in igloos, in summer in sealskin tents.

Two years later, all lived in canvas tents. And now, all lived in newly built houses. In 1960, all island hunters, except two, used kayaks.

Eight years later, all used canoes with outboard motors. There were lots of kayak skeletons near the old camp sites. But only three covered kayaks remained, probably the last Inuit kayaks in Canada. They were used in winter to retrieve seals shot at the floe edge, the limit of landfast ice.

In a few years, the people of these remote islands had been yanked from an ancient, unchanging past into a drastically different and constantly changing present. A sad collision of ancient and introduced beliefs had caused the tragedy of that fateful winter of 1940–1941.

"Do you think Mina and Peter Sala will return to the Belchers?" I asked Charlie Crow.

"No," he said firmly. "The people do not want that. They would bring back too many horrible memories."

He was right. Mina died on the mainland and so did her brother, Peter Sala, the man who, during one tragic arctic winter, had believed that he was God.

George Wetaltuk, who drew the first map of the Belcher Islands, and after whom a major bay on the islands is named, died in 1957. He was ninety-eight years old.

Chapter 16

EASTER ISLAND, CHILE
Remote Pacific Island Edged with Giant Statues

IMAGINE THIS: a long time ago, fate placed about a hundred people on a small, remote, uninhabited island and severed their contact with the rest of the world.

A thousand years later, fate returned to see what had happened.

It was not good. Fear and famine ruled the island.

It had begun well. The people were few. The island was rich. Wise kings ruled. A great culture evolved.

The population increased and split into rival clans.

They felled the island forests. They killed the island animals. They ravaged the sea near the island. The population kept growing and famine began to haunt the island.

A few were wealthy. Most were poor. The army of the poor increased ever faster and one day they rose in revolt.

They killed the rich. They killed the priests. They torched the temples. They destroyed the island's magnificent art.

They split into warring gangs. They fought and robbed and killed, and the victors ate the vanquished for there was not much else to eat.

This is more or less what happened on Easter Island in the Pacific, the world's most remote inhabited island. Some see in its tragic fate, as through a glass, darkly, the possible or probable future and fate of our entire world.

This island of tragedy and mystery has fascinated Western man since its

"discovery" on Easter Sunday in 1722. "There exists in the midst of the great ocean, in a region where nobody goes, a mysterious and isolated island," wrote the nineteenth-century French traveller and novelist Pierre Loti. "This island is planted with monstrous great statues, the work of I don't know what race, today degenerate or vanished; its great remains an enigma."

It all began thousands of years ago with the Polynesian expansion to the islands of the Pacific Ocean. "The greatest feat of maritime colonization in human history," a Pacific historian has called it.

These master mariners reached the Marquesas about 300 CE and settled this island group. Some travelled on to find new worlds: Tahiti, and then New Zealand (about 900 CE) in the south; Hawaii (about 800 CE) in the north; and Easter Island (about 400 CE), far to the east.

Easter Island is remote and lonely. It was formed, more than a million years ago, by three volcanoes that rose above the sea in fire and fury from the South East Pacific Plateau. The roughly triangular island is 22 kilometres (14 miles) long, about 11 kilometres (7 miles) wide and covers 165 square kilometres (64 square miles). It is about the size of Staten Island in New York Bay.

The nearest now inhabited land is tiny Pitcairn Island of *Mutiny on the Bounty* fame, 2,027 kilometres (1,260 miles) to the west. To the east, 3,266 kilometres (2,300 miles) away, is South America. And to the south, the ocean rolls on, vast and without land, all the 5,954 kilometres (3,700 miles) to Antarctica. Easter Island is a tiny, solitary dot on an empty ocean.

Sixty-eight generations ago, say the island's genealogical legends (about 400 CE, say today's scientists), a great chieftain, Hotu Matu'a, set forth, probably from the Marquesas, to settle new land. His high priest, Hau Maka, in a shamanistic vision-dream had flown far across the sea and had seen Rapa Nui, the promised land.

Like all great Polynesian voyages of exploration and settlement, this one was carefully planned. They loaded two great, double-hulled canoes with water, food, the plant cuttings and seeds of their main agricultural crops, sugarcane, bananas, yams, taro, and one domestic animal, the chicken. Several small Polynesian rats came along as stowaways.

The statues at Anakene and several other sites wear huge reddish scoria topknots. Each topknot, weighing as much as two elephants, was somehow hoisted up and placed on the head of a 3-metre (10-foot) statue.

Hotu Matu'a commanded one canoe. With him, legends say, were his wife, six sons, relatives, and retainers. His brother-in-law was in charge of the second canoe.

They sailed south and east for two months until birds told them they were nearing land. Easter Island, untouched, without a single mammal or raptor, had then probably the greatest seabird colonies in the entire Pacific. These birds roamed far in quest of food, some species 160 kilometres (100 miles) and more, and they guided the seafarers to their island.

The great canoes circled the island, the very island, Hau Maka said, that he had seen in his dream. They landed on the north shore, at Anakena, the only large beach on Easter Island, a place, then and still now, of exquisite beauty: a broad curve of pale pink sand merging with the turquoise sea. They called their island Rapa Nui or Te Pito o Te Henua (the Navel and Centre of the World).

Scientists now know that the colonists had arrived in a beautiful world. Few islands have been as intensively studied as Easter Island. Its aura of mystery and enigma is as irresistible to scientists as catnip is to cats. Two branches of science tell us a great deal about what the island was like when the settlers arrived and what they did and ate after they arrived: palynology, the analysis of pollen, reveals past vegetation; and the study of middens, ancient garbage dumps, informs us about long-ago meals.

Much of Easter Island then was densely forested, with many different types of trees, including some excellent hardwood species and a mammoth palm with a basal trunk diameter of more than 2 metres (7 feet).

Initially, the millions of seabirds, as on the predator-free Galapagos Islands, were probably tame and easy to kill. The colonists had no pigs, but they hunted pig-sized and pig-fat porpoises in the surrounding sea. They began to clear the forest and the rich volcanic earth was good for agriculture. The rats that had come along for the ride, went ashore, multiplied, and rat stew, the middens show, was a popular dish.

Centuries passed. The population grew and, over time, split into about twelve clans that divided Easter Island like a giant pie into territorial slices. About 800 CE, they began to build *ahus*, great ceremonial stone platforms and on some of them they erected *moai*, the giant stone statues that have made Easter Island so famous.

The *moai*, legends insist, were not gods but revered clan ancestors. They stood upon the *ahu* and looked inland, to the village, with magic, mesmeric eyes, the pupils of polished red rock or dark-glowing obsidian surrounded by white coral, guardians and protectors of the clan.

There is, today, little argument about how the statues were made. At the great quarry on the upper slopes of the volcano Rano Raraku there are, after all, about three hundred statues in every stage of production: from a tentative outline upon rock to the finished product ready for transport to its *ahu*.

The carvers worked with crude-looking basalt picks called *toki*. Many of these simple tools still lie near half-finished statues. To make a sculpture took hard work, persistence, time, and the skill of generations of master craftsmen. Chip, chip, chip, from dawn to dusk, brawny men in loincloths hacked away at the grainy, yellowish volcanic lapilli tuff from which nearly all the roughly one thousand Easter Island *moai* were carved.

Slowly the supine statue took form. Kneeling in narrow trenches on either side of it, the carvers sculpted the entire massive form, leaving only a supporting stone keel attached to the matrix.

Finally, after weeks or perhaps months of labour, the sculpture was nearly finished. The keel was cut, the freed statue was levered up and slid slowly, gently down the volcano slope into a hole. There sculptors finished the now upright statue, adding those symbols and details that gave the statue symbolic life and identity. Only the magic, glowing eyes were missing. They would be inserted, in the presence of priests, chiefs, and the worshiping people once the statue stood on its *ahu*.

The first statues were squat and fairly small, weighing a modest 5 to 6 tons. Decades passed and centuries and the statues became larger and larger. Rival clans and carvers, it seems, became obsessed with a "bigger is better" one-upmanship.

Gripped by monolithic megalomania, they produced legions of colossi; 10 tons, 20 tons, and finally, near the climax of this lithic apotheosis, the ultimate giants of Easter Island: a statue called Paro, 9 metres (32 feet) tall and weighing 72 tons; and a slightly shorter but broader statue weighing 87 tons that stands today on Ahu Tongariki.

Even that was not enough. Carvers started on the ultimate statue, the statue to dwarf all other statues, the statue that would fill its clan with pride and show its power and would humble all the other clans and fill them with envy. The statue is 21 metres (70 feet) long and weighs 270 tons, much taller and heavier than the Statue of Liberty. It lies in situ. It was never finished.

The last *moai* were crowned. At another quarry, carvers fashioned cylindrical topknots called *pukao* out of dark blood-red scoria rock. Then, in another amazing feat, they lifted the up-to-12-ton *pukao* and placed it upon the statue's head.

All this is daunting but comprehensible. But how did the islanders transport the giant statues from the quarry to the *ahus*, some of them 14 kilometres (nine miles) away? Theories abound, from the practical and possible to the preposterous ideas of the Swiss writer Erich von Däniken, who earnestly suggested the simple natives were assisted by an army of helpers from outer space.

The most widely accepted hypothesis is that they built corduroy roads with logs and lashed the precious statue firmly to a mighty wooden sled. About one hundred to 150 men, using plant fibre hawsers hauled sled and load cautiously to its final destination.

All this required an army of workers and extensive agriculture to feed them, the farmers, and the upper classes. The islanders also needed wood. Lots of wood. Wood to transport statues. Wood to build houses and cook their food. Wood to burn their dead in large crematoria. Wood to build new boats.

The forests fell. Rats ate the seeds of the few remaining trees. Dry winds, unchecked by trees, swept across the island. Crops withered and died. Lacking wood, canoes were small and frail. They no longer hunted fat porpoises. The population kept increasing, some claim to thirty thousand, though fifteen thousand to twenty thousand seems more likely. More than the island could support at the best of times. And now came the worst of times. With the protective forest gone, soil erosion destroyed hills and fields.

As famine ravaged the common people, the upper classes lost first prestige and then power. In about 1680, warriors rose in revolt. Gangs formed. Marauding killers wiped out rulers, killed priests. They turned upon each other and the killers became cannibals. Survivors fled and cowered in remote caves.

Armed mobs roamed the island. They killed the living and ate the dead. They also destroyed the symbols of past rulers. In iconoclastic fury, they toppled *moai*. They broke many statues and ripped out the eyes to destroy their sacred *mana*, their mystic power.

In his brilliant book *Collapse*, University of California professor Jared Diamond, points out that "Easter's isolation makes it the clearest example of a society that destroyed itself by overexploiting its own resources."

When, on April 5, 1722 the Dutch admiral Jacob Roggeveen saw Easter Island from his ship, *De Afrikaansche Galei*, the internecine wars had already killed most of the islanders. Only an estimated four thousand were left. It was Easter Sunday and Roggeveen called the just-discovered place Paasch Eyland (Easter Island).

He was not impressed. There were no trees and the island's "wasted appearance could give no other impression than of singular poverty and barrenness." The boats of the once-great mariners were now small, "bad and frail...and very leaky."

After more than a thousand years of total isolation, the islanders met other humans and it was terrible and terrifying. One hundred and thirty-four sailors went ashore, armed with muskets and cutlasses. When the fascinated islanders crowded close, an officer shouted in Dutch, "Go back!" They did not understand. They advanced. The sailors retreated, then shot. Many people were wounded. Twelve lay dead. The outside world had come to Rapa Nui.

Two Spanish ships commanded by Don Felipe Gonzalez y Haedo stopped briefly. He gave the naked, tatooed islanders biscuits, shirts and trousers. He took formal possession of their island for the king of Spain and sailed away again.

Four years later, in 1774, came the legendary English mariner Captain James Cook, observant and astute. Aboard his ship was a Tahitian who, speaking his own lan-

Monolithic stone statue and one of Easter Island's feral horses. Carved with stone tools from hard tuff, this giant head stands near the statue quarry of Rano Raraku.

guage, could converse with the Easter Islanders. "In colour, features and language, they bear such affinity to the people of the more western islands, that no one will doubt that they have had the same origin," wrote Cook.

He was appalled by the poverty of the island and its people. "Nature has been exceedingly sparing in her favors to this spot.... There is no wood or fuel." The island, wrote his naturalist Johann Reinhold Foster, was parched and "unfertile, hard earth, burned by the sun" inhabited by "lean, starved men and delicate women."

Looking at these war-ravaged people, he described as timid, starving and miserable, Cook, who had seen a few of the still standing *moai*, wrote in amazement, "We could hardly conceive how these islanders, wholly unacquainted with any mechanical power, could raise such stupendous figures."

The nineteenth century brought to the isolated island the vice and viciousness of the "modern world." Wrote the French ethnologist Alfred Metraux: "In 1822 the skipper of an American whaling ship paused at Easter Island long enough to kidnap a group of girls who were thrown overboard the following day and obliged to swim back to the island. One of the officers, simply to amuse himself, shot a native with his gun."

The bestial blackbirders came to the island, the cruel slavers of the Pacific. They lured the islanders with garish gifts to the beach, overpowered them, threw them into the fetid holds of their ships, and sold them for one hundred to two hundred U.S. dollars each on the slave markets of Peru. Among the 1,407 captives, about half the island's surviving population, were the last king of Easter Island and his son and the *tangata rongo-rongo*, the wise men who alone knew the secret of *rongo-rongo*, Easter Island's magic script.

In Peru, these pathetic slaves were quickly worked to death, mainly in the evil guano mines. A few hundred survived and were handed over, after international protests, to the French chargé d'affaires Edmond de Lesseps: "Human skeletons dried up with hunger, illness, running sores and abuse and scarcely alive."

On the ship that returned the retrieved slaves to their home, they succumbed to smallpox. Only fifteen survived. They arrived with the lethal disease and death raced across Easter Island. When the epidemic ended in 1877, only 111 Easter Islanders were left.

Missionaries came and told the last islanders about goodness and God. They protected their little flock but they destroyed much of the remaining "idolatrous" art: their magic wooden carvings, and the sacred *rongo-rongo* tablets incised with the unique pictographic reversed boustrophedon script of Easter Island, in which every alternate line of symbols is upside down, and which no one has been able to decipher. Only twenty-five of these tablets exist in the museums of the world. There is not a single one on Easter Island.

In 1888, Chile, in a burst of imperial ambition, annexed Easter Island and then didn't quite know what to do with it. It rented it to Scottish businessmen. They herded the remaining islanders into one village, Hanga Roa, and turned nearly all of Easter Island into one large sheep ranch.

Eventually the poor-paying sheep were exchanged for better-paying tourists. An airstrip was constructed in 1967. In 1966, Easter Island became a province of Chile. UNESCO proclaimed it a World Heritage Site. Giant planes filled with tourists arrive from Chile and Tahiti.

Life appears pleasant. The tragic past remains. Wrote the Pacific history expert Sir Peter Buck, "No native population has been subjected to such a succession of atrocities and disintegrating influences as the people of Easter Island."

The novelist and travel writer Paul Theroux called Easter Island "this lost island of damaged souls."

The five young men cutting the totora reeds that rim the Rano Raraku crater lake seemed like fairly happy souls. It was two weeks before a festival and they needed reeds to build a traditional Easter Island boat. It would carry the festival queen.

They chopped the tall, bright green reeds with machetes, made neat bundles, and loaded them onto their Toyota pickup truck. They were lean, well-muscled and wore only ragged shorts. It was hot in the sheltered crater. They worked hard, were sweat-soaked, mud-smeared, and had long, dark, wildly tousled hair.

"May I take pictures?" I asked in Spanish.

"Sure," they said, indifferent, and went on cutting reeds.

They stopped for lunch. They built a small fire with dry reeds and roots and pieces of eucalyptus wood and heated a large sooty kettle full of mutton chunks cooked with herbs.

"You want to eat?" they asked.

They had large leaves along as plates. We ate the mutton with pieces of bread, drank the broth, and lounged on the ground next to the fire.

"Where you from?" asked one of them.

"Canada."

"You speak French?"

"Yes," I said.

He promptly switched to fluent French.

"Where did you learn French?" I asked.

"We went to school in Tahiti," he explained. "We like Tahiti. We're not South Americans. We're Polynesians. We live on Rapa Nui. We are Rapa Nui. We speak Rapa Nui. Those people on Tahiti, they are like us. They are like our people."

Fifteen giant statues stand on the raised stone platform called Ahu Tongariki. The largest island statues weigh more than a hundred tons.

A group of French tourists drifted toward us. Most were women "*d'un certain âge*," as the French say, with the time and money for extensive and expensive tours to

"romantic destinations."

They eyed us with interest and took pictures.

"*Ils ont quand-même l'air sauvage,*" (They look rather savage) one woman said, her loud voice hovering between disdain and excitement.

"*Oui,*" a companion agreed. "*Mais le vieux, il pourrait être européen,*" (Yes. But the old one looks nearly European.)

They clicked more pictures and moved on.

My new friends laughed. "Welcome to the world of savages!" But the laughter was tinged with bitterness. We finished lunch and they went back to cutting reeds.

Those reeds had been exhibit A in Easter Island's most famous anthropological row.

Most anthropologists agree with Captain Cook that since the islanders look Polynesian, speak Polynesian, and consider themselves Polynesian, it is reasonable to assume that they are of Polynesian descent.

Not so, said Thor Heyerdal, famous for having crossed the Pacific on the balsa raft *Kon-Tiki*. The plebs, he conceded, may have come from Polynesia, but the upper classes and the master artisans came by reed boat from South America. Looking at the great *moai*, Heyerdal remarked with hauteur, "One thing is certain: This was not the work of a canoeload of Polynesian wood carvers." The presence of totora reeds, Heyerdal proclaimed, was proof that they arrived together with the master race from South America.

Remarks like that raised a lot of scientific hackles and anthropologists of the Polynesia versus South America origin camps fought a not-always civil war. Those believing in the Polynesian genesis of the Easter Islands appear, at present, to be winning. The reeds, they proved by pollen analysis, have existed on Easter Island for at least thirty thousand years. And all new evidence confirms that a Polynesian people were able to make, transport and erect those mighty *moai*.

In the destructive frenzy of their drawn-out wars, the islanders toppled all *moai*, the last one in the 1860s. Since then, some have been repaired and re-erected on *ahus*. The most extensive work was sponsored by a Japanese company, manufacturers of powerful cranes.

The Japanese arrived: a small army of engineers and experts, together with giant machines. They rebuilt the long Ahu Tongariki. A huge crane lifted fourteen *moai* and placed them on the platform. But the soaring machine and all the engineers were stymied by the last statue, the 87-ton colossus. The crane could not lift it. Auxiliary machines were brought in and finally the ancient stone statue was inched up onto the *ahu*.

It was humbling to think that all this had been done before by prehistoric islanders with their bare hands, with plant fibre ropes, ingenuity, and the very clever use of levers and leverage. These men had been disciples in spirit of Archimedes who said more than two thousand years ago, "Give me a lever and a place to stand and I will move the world."

Easter Island today is not very attractive. Its trees are gone. Its endemic birds are all extinct. Even seabirds are rare. The roads are dusty. The rolling grassy land looks dun and sere. Small herds of semi-wild horses roam the island.

Yet there are few places on earth that carry, despite the ravages of time and man, such a concentration of human endeavour and achievement.

It is most eerily apparent at the ancient Rano Raraku quarry. Here, for seven hundred years or so, artisans carved giant statues from the rock. And then one day, as if a whistle blew, they all downed tools and left, never to return. About three hundred unfinished, nearly finished, and finished statues lie or stand; and near many lie the basalt picks that were once used to create them. All are mute witness to a culture that rose, peaked and finally destroyed first its environment and then itself.

Chapter 17

AUCKLAND ISLANDS, NEW ZEALAND

The Eden Islands of the Subantarctic

W HAT A PARADISE!" exulted the British ornithologist Edward Wilson in 1904 when, after the Antarctic expedition with Robert Falcon Scott, he stopped for two weeks at the New Zealand-owned Auckland Islands.

Seventy-six years later, I spent part of an austral summer on these rarely visited subantarctic islands and they were paradise still, home to an amazing multitude of birds and seals.

Huge albatrosses nest on the Auckland Islands, and tiny cream and black tomtits. Stately penguins waddle across lawn-smooth coastal meadows past flocks of brilliant parakeets. New Zealand fur seals snooze on beds of shimmering bronze kelp. And the broad yellow crescent of Sandy Beach near our expedition hut, was covered with Hooker's sea lions, rarest of the world's five sea lion species. Nearly all breed on these remote islands and nowhere else in the world.

The islands were paradise until they were discovered. Then followed the familiar pattern of death and despoliation: the slaughter of island animals; settlement by humans; release of domestic animals that turned feral and destroyed the islands' native animals and plants. Another paradise is lost. It nearly happened on the Auckland Islands.

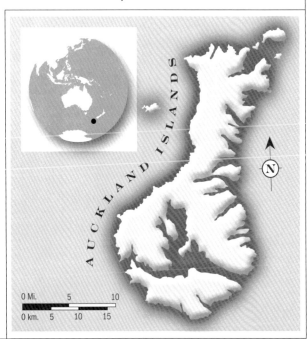

AUCKLAND ISLANDS

0 Mi. 5 10
0 km. 5 10 15

N

It seems strange today, but Australia, New Zealand and their islands were initially prized by Britain and America for the seal herds on their beaches and the whale herds in their seas.

"Australia was given to the enlightened world by the whaleman," Herman Melville said in *Moby Dick*. "The whale-ship is the true mother of that now mighty colony." Britain's prime minister, William Pitt, agreed. Whaling in the southern seas, he said in 1790, was for Britain a much-needed "source of immense treasure." When Charles Darwin visited Australia in 1836, he noted that the continent's "two main exports are wool and whale-oil."

Rare yellow-eyed penguins: an elegant parent with its massive, downy chick. These penguins breed in the forests of the Auckland Islands.

Sealing began shortly after England's most famous

navigator, Captain James Cook, explored and mapped the coasts of New Zealand and Australia in 1769 and 1770. By 1807, wrote the New Zealand historian Fergus B. McLaren, "the sealing trade was the most profitable of all ventures in the South Seas." It brought hardship and death to many and wealth to a fortunate few who wisely never went sealing. The sealers were a rough lot. Lord George Campbell of Britain's *Challenger* expedition met a shipload of them and remarked dryly, "Most of the crew looked as if they had left their country for their country's good." Where these men landed, seals and sealing were short-lived.

It was a captain of the famous English whaling-sealing house of Enderby & Sons ("a house which in my poor whaleman's opinion, comes not far behind the united royal houses of Tudors and Bourbons, in point of real historical interest," said Melville in *Moby Dick*) who discovered the Auckland Islands.

In 1806, Abraham Bristow, sailing a ship fully laden with whale oil from Australia to England, spotted the main island and named it Lord Auckland's Island, after a family friend, William Eden, first Baron Auckland, an economist who established the Bank of Ireland. Bristow did not stop, but noted hopefully in his journal, "This place, I should suppose, abounds with seals."

He returned in 1807, took official possession of the islands for Great Britain, killed droves of fur seals and sea lions on these pristine islands, and released pigs and rabbits as provender for future trips. Soon sealers from many nations joined the fray. Some returned with cargoes of fifty thousand fur seal skins and great barrels full of rendered seal oil.

It was all over in twenty rapacious years. When Captain Benjamin Morrell of the American Merchant Service made a detailed survey of the Auckland Islands in 1830, he found only twenty sea lions and not a single fur seal. On these islands which "once abounded with numerous herds of fur and hair seals [sea lions]" wrote Morrell, the sealers "have made clean work of it."

After the sealers came the settlers. With the introduction of the musket, the efficient killer, New Zealand's intertribal wars, always bad, became genocidal. One group of seventy Maoris, fearing for their lives, chartered a sealing vessel to start a new life on the uninhabited Aucklands, 482 kilometres (300 miles) south of New Zealand.

They found peace and not much else. The Auckland Islands lie in the path of terrible gale-force winds, the sea region known to sailors as the Furious Fifties. Winters were cold. The peaty, acid soil was unsuitable for farming. The

Maoris killed the trusting albatrosses and the more elusive feral pigs, and survived in chilly, often famished misery.

Their fate should have warned Charles Enderby, scion of the whaling firm. He, however, had visions of a prosperous and lucrative British colony on these remote islands and he formed a chartered company. He leased the entire Auckland archipelago, 55 kilometres (34 miles) north to south, 35 kilometres (21 miles) east to west, with a total land area of 62,000 hectares (153,208 acres), considerably bigger than the principality of Liechtenstein, for thirty years from the British government, at a "pepper-corn rate of lease for the first two years" and at the rate of one thousand pounds sterling for each ensuing year.

Enderby was an imperial dreamer and a good promoter. Queen Victoria named him lieutenant-governor of the Auckland Islands. He gave a splendid public dinner in London to celebrate the founding (on paper!) of the Auckland Island colony. Famous men attended, among them Sir John Pelly, governor of the Hudson's Bay Company.

With fame came funds, and volunteers for this venture, a whole bevy of benighted colonists, many of them young married couples. They set out in three ships, settlers, livestock and supplies, all they thought was needed to survive and thrive on a subantarctic island.

They arrived on December 4, 1849 in the deep, sheltered inlet of northeast Auckland Island, known as Sarah's Bosom (later renamed Port Ross) and were greeted on shore by the chilled, down-at-luck Maori settlers "all naked except for a seal loin cloth."

Undaunted, the colonists, being brave and British, unloaded the ships and began to build a town. They called it Hardwicke, in honour of the Earl of Hardwicke, governor of their company who, wisely, had remained in England.

The ships had brought the nucleus of a European society: a lieutenant-governor in Enderby, a doctor, clerks, surveyors, storekeepers, boatmen, bricklayers, carpenters, and labourers—306 people in all, including sixteen women and fourteen children. They constructed an administrative "government house," barracks to house the single men, eighteen dwellings for married couples, and a jail. They had three horses, forty-five cattle, 258 sheep plus fifty-one lambs, and a multitude of pigs.

The brave beginning soon came to a bitter end. The colonists plowed the spongy, peaty, acid earth. They sowed European grains, but little grew. In lovingly tended gardens, they planted on this subantarctic island the vegetables and berries of far-away England: turnips, cabbages, mustard, cress, radishes, raspberries and strawberries, and the gooseberry and red currant bushes they had brought from home. The plants died.

They tried small-boat coastal whaling. But they were English city folk and farmers, poorly suited to pursue giant whales in storm-tossed subantarctic seas. The Auckland Island colony of Hardwicke fell quickly on hard times.

In 1852, a ship brought news of the Australian gold rush, of men making quick fortunes at Ballarat and other just-discovered Australian gold fields. The hard-pressed colonists succumbed immediately to the siren call of gold and warmth. On August 5, 1852, after less than three years, the settlers left their nascent town and meagre fields upon the Auckland Islands.

That ended the ill-fated attempts to settle the rugged islands. But they claimed other victims. The Auckland Islands lay athwart the famous "circle route" taken by sailing ships from Australia, bound for Europe or America via Cape Horn. Driven by powerful westerlies, the ships sailed fast and some shattered upon the Aucklands' fog-hidden cliffs.

To succour survivors, the New Zealand government built huts on several islands and stocked them with provisions. They also released more pigs, as well as rabbits, goats, and cattle as food for castaways.

The voracious, normally hardy, and prolific goats, the bane of so many islands where they had been released, couldn't hack the Aucklands and for a very curious reason: the soft island earth did not abrade their hoofs. They grew and grew into weirdly-shaped clumsy cloven clogs, and the goats died out on all the islands.

Of all the introduced animals, pigs and cats did the worst damage. The pigs uprooted and devoured the islands' magnificent flowers, ate eggs and chicks of ground-nesting birds, and dug up the breeding burrows of petrels and prions. The feral cats took care of the lovely Auckland Island merganser. It is extinct; the last one was seen in 1905.

Since then, conditions have improved. The introduction of steam ships and the 1914 opening of the Panama Canal eliminated the southern sailing route. The islands, once again, were truly remote and isolated. Attempts were made to eliminate the most noxious of the alien feral animals.

In 1934, the islands became a reserve for the protection of fauna and flora, and they are now administered by New Zealand's Department of Lands and Survey. Slowly, thanks to protection and isolation, the Auckland Islands

Home to penguins and parakeets, the uninhabited subantarctic Auckland Islands are marvellously rich in birds and seals. A red-crowned parakeet collects seeds on Enderby Island.

became again what they had been before they were discovered: the Eden islands of the southern seas.

I spent the early winter of 1980 like a far-north stylite, living in a tiny hut atop a 13-metre- (45-foot-) high tower, its base surrounded by polar bears. A friend and I were there to photograph polar bears and study their behaviour. The polar bears were gathered at Cape Churchill on the west coast of Hudson Bay, awaiting the freeze-up of the bay so they could hunt seals on ice again. In the meantime, they slept or idly watched our behaviour.

This was our third season with the polar bears and many were acquaintances, bears we had observed in previous years. We recognized them by distinctive markings and behavioural traits that changed little from year to year.

We had no radio, no phone, no contact with the outside world. There were only we and the bears, watching each other. Some days I sat on a low rung of the tower and talked at length with one of the bears.

After three weeks, our chartered plane came from Churchill and buzzed the tower several times. Our entourage of bears got up and left. The plane landed on an esker near the tower.

"Your wife phoned," said the pilot. "All is well, but please call her immediately."

"Martin Cawthorn called from New Zealand," Maud said. "The Auckland Island expedition is on. You're a member. I have ordered your plane tickets to New Zealand. You have eleven days to catch the expedition ship."

Two weeks later, I landed on Enderby, northernmost of the Auckland Islands, and changed from studying polar bear behaviour in the Subarctic to sea lion behaviour on a weird and wonderful subantarctic island.

Our expedition was small: three men from New Zealand Television who, in the coming months, made several award-winning films; the sea-mammal expert, Martin Cawthorn, leader of the expedition; Simon Mitchell, his assistant; and I, naturalist, writer, photographer, assistant's assistant, hewer of wood and drawer of water.

Hewing wood on Enderby, I quickly discovered, was not so easy. There were lots of dead rata trees at the forest edge near our camp. But when I struck a tree, the axe bounced back with a wrist-wrenching jolt. This was ironwood. The brittle, fine-grained, blood-red wood could be flaked and splintered, but not cut. In the coming weeks, I became adept at chipping ironwood, a rarely needed skill.

The plant life of our island, and all the other Auckland Islands, was moulded by frequent and terrible storms. A third of the island was covered by massive rata trees that grovelled and twisted along the ground in an eerie fairy-tale forest straight out of the Brothers Grimm. From these writhing trunks, gaunt limbs reached high to heaven and to light, their long, leathery, lanceolate leaves forming a dense, rounded deep-green canopy, now, in the austral summer, spangled with myriad crimson blossoms.

Fleshy liverworts padded the moist peat-black forest floor. Deep green cushions of moss covered the prostrate rata trunks. Pepper-coloured lichens drooped from gnarled limbs. Olive-green bellbirds flitted through the forest's greenish gloom and filled the air with lilting, chime-like notes. Thickets of ferns, their fronds an ethereal green, bordered rills and bourns snaking through the forest.

A week after we arrived, the wind, nearly always strong, increased to a furious gale. I walked through the sheltering forest toward the west side of the 8-kilometre– (5-mile-) wide island. The wind screamed over the rata roof and there was the distant thunder of giant waves crashing against the island's 40-metre- (131-foot-) high coast of columnar basalt.

Beyond the forest, the gale knocked me down like a puppet. I crawled to a rise and watched in awe as immense waves hit the coast and exploded hundred metres into the air in walls of water, spray and spume. Above this primal chaos, albatrosses soared serenely, swooped down to pick up bits of food, and rushed up again, their long slender wings riding the wind. For these master aerialists of the world, it was fine flying weather. Some were wandering albatrosses that breed on the Auckland Islands. With a wingspan nearly 4 metres (12 feet) long, they are the largest seabirds in the world.

On the high moors of Enderby, above the rata forest, was a small colony of royal albatrosses. Sealers had wiped them out on this island in the nineteenth century. A few had returned in the 1940s and now twenty-five pairs bred on our island. Standing or sitting, the stately white birds had a certain Victorian dowager dignity. I visited them often and sat near one of the birds. Its huge, flesh-coloured beak seemed powerful enough to sever a finger with a snap. But when I gently stroked the satin-smooth breast of the brooding bird, she nibbled softly at my hand and looked at me with shining, black-brown eyes.

Royal albatross mating, at the age of nine, is preceded by several years of ardent wooing. Not far from the breeding adults, teenage albatrosses practised courting, with steps and movements as formal and stylized as a medieval dance. A couple faced each other, bowed and brayed, clappered bills like castanets, spread the long, narrow wings, raised their heads toward heaven and neighed in mutual ecstasy.

The main purpose of our expedition was to study the little-known Hooker's sea lions, rarest, and most mild-mannered of all sea lions (seal scientists refer to them fondly as "the gentle Hookers"). The dark-maned, 362-kilogram (800-pound) males had arrived before us and had fought their battles. The winners had established their territories on the half-mile-long Sandy Bay breeding beach near our camp. For the next month they all were males-in-waiting, each one jealously guarding his circle of sand.

The first female arrived in early December and the lucky bull on whose territory she settled soon acquired an additional fifty wives. Bulls and territory seemed to exert little allure; females were attracted by the presence of females and, as a result, while some males had females galore, most had none.

On December 10, the first of 392 pups was born. The dark, glistening newborn pup slid onto the sand and lay quietly for a few moments. Arching backwards, the mother sniffed her pup, picked it up gently, and held it for a moment. The pup cried, a tremulous, lamblike bleat. From that moment on, the female would recognize her pup by smell and voice among all the pups on the beach.

The mother placed the pup on the sand, it raised itself a little on its foreflippers, shook its head, and toppled forward. The mother swept the pup close to her body with a flipper. It sniffled and snuffled eagerly and made little sucking sounds. Finally, it found one of the four teats and began to nurse greedily. Droplets of milk trickled from the corner of its dark muzzle. About twelve minutes had elapsed since its birth.

For the next two months, Martin, Simon, and I immersed ourselves in the lives of "our" sea lions. Most adults ignored us. The pups, big-flippered, glossy-furred, with droopy whiskers and dark shiny eyes were curious and adorable. Only the immature males were a nuisance. One hundred thirty-six kilograms (300 pounds) of pep and bravado, but afraid to tackle the big bad bulls, these restless ruffians invented a game called "chase a biologist." The moment I appeared on the beach, a young male attacked, racing along with flapping flippers. If I ran, he was delighted. At last there was someone who was scared of him. But if I stood and stared at him he galloped slower and slower and came to a halt about 1 metre (3 feet) from me. He reared up and roared, trying to look impressive and dangerous. When that didn't work, he sort of shrank, looked embarrassed and slunk away.

In the late afternoon, I watched the penguin parade. I sat on a tussock near a penguin trail. A gabby flock of red-crowned parakeets landed near me. The emerald birds traipsed about on tiny feet, snipping and plucking grasses. A yellow-crowned penguin approached, one of the world's rarest penguins but common on the Auckland Islands. It walked past the flock of parakeets and headed for the forest to spell a brooding mate on their nest.

The pear-shaped penguin waddled toward me on stout, stubby legs and pink, sharp-clawed feet, pensive and slightly stooped, like an elderly professor with worries. His back and sides were slate blue, chest and belly glistening white, the pate and temples yellowish, hemmed by a gold-coloured circlet.

At 1 metre (4 feet) he spotted me and stopped, utterly nonplussed. He bowed and peered, recoiled, advanced, shuffled back and forth, dithered and worried, a little Hamlet with a problem. Other penguins came up from the sea. They, too, stopped. Then those in the rear pecked those in front. They argued, forgot about me, suddenly remembered their waiting mates, and rushed toward the forest, their plump bottoms swaying and bobbing.

In January, a research ship arrived to take us to other islands and a rare miracle happened: four days with hardly any wind. We landed on Adams Island, in the very south of the archipelago, one of only two islands that had always been free of alien animals. We came ashore on a narrow boulder beach, crept upwards through thickets of sharp-leaved grass trees and wind-twisted hebe bushes whose white blossoms smelled as sweet as honeysuckle.

The Hooker's sea lion is the rarest and least known of the world's five sea lion species. Most breed on the Auckland Islands. While their mothers are away at sea catching fish, two pups explore their island realm.

Suddenly, we emerged into a breathtaking garden: Fairchild's Garden, called by the ninetenth-century botanist F.R. Chapman, "One of the most wonderful nat-

ural gardens the extra-tropical world can show." We were among the very few people who have ever seen this place of exquisite beauty. Yellow and mauve, purple and delicate pink, the mass of flowers with deep-green succulent leaves rose up the mountain slope, and near the top nested wandering albatrosses. This is the way it once was on all the islands before those greedy pigs munched up their flowery glory.

We landed on Disappointment Island. It is aptly named. Many have tried to land on it, few have ever succeeded. Huge waves crash nearly ceaselessly against its steep-cliffed coast. We were lucky. It was just possible to get ashore. From afar, the dark-green island slopes looked strangely speckled. The specks were sixty thousand pairs of white-capped albatrosses, sitting solemnly on half-metre- (2-foot-) high pedestal nests amid a glorious sea of flowers. More than 90 per cent of all these albatrosses in the world breed on this one small island.

In February, the female sea lions started to take their pups to sea. The fat, pampered pups, some weighing 27 kilograms (60 pounds), had serious misgivings about this move from land to sea. The mothers patiently coaxed and called. A pup advanced timidly, recoiled, was caught by a wave and, bawling and splashing, was carried out into deep water. The mother surfaced near it, nuzzled the pup and turned. The pup followed, head held high and together they swam out to sea.

Our ship arrived and, after three months, we reluctantly left our paradise island.

Chapter 18

HERSCHEL ISLAND, CANADA
The Wild Island of Arctic Whalers

ERSCHEL IS A small, uninhabited arctic island in the Beaufort Sea, off the Yukon coast and west of the Mackenzie River delta. It is about 12 kilometres (8 miles) long and 8 kilometres (5 miles) wide, rising gently to a height of nearly 182 metres (600 feet). In summer, it is an island of rolling meadows, of flowers and birds, quiet and serene. It is the Yukon's first Territorial Park.

A century ago, Herschel was a very different place. It was, according to whom you wish to believe, "An outpost of civilization," (Vilhjalmur Stefansson) or "The Sodom of the Arctic...[inhabited by] "demons of debauchery and cruelty" (Nome, Alaska, newspaper, 1905). It was a "thriving arctic metropolis" (Captain Henry Larsen). But "the scenes of riotous drunkenness and lust which this island has witnessed have probably never been surpassed" (Reverend C.E. Whittaker).

It was a place where rather staid New England ladies attended opera performances and minstrel shows, and their husbands, who tended to be "corpulent and their hair thin" (Roald Amundsen) played whist and drank port.

"It was the only time and place in western Canadian history that complete and unbridled lawlessness ran amok" (R.C. Coutts).

There were Chinese on the island and Russians, Portuguese-speaking

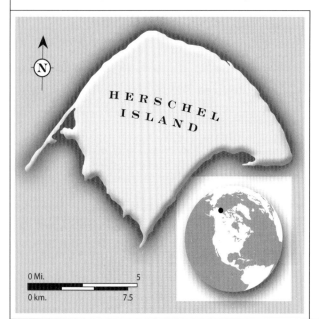

HERSCHEL ISLAND

0 Mi.   5
0 km.   7.5

Africans from the Cape Verde Islands, Hawaiians and men from Samoa, Arabs and Jews, Scandinavians and at least one German count who "aside from getting obnoxiously drunk...was a splendid steward" (Captain Bodfish).

And to a nine-year-old Inuit boy who saw it for the first time, it was: "Herschel! The great big town!" (Nuligak).

Whatever the views, it is hard to argue with the Reverend I.O. Stringer, later bishop of the Yukon, that this was "a community like none other that ever existed in Canada."

For a decade, from 1894 to 1905, Herschel Island was the whaling centre of the Western Arctic and, when whaling declined, it became the hub of the extensive fur trade of this region.

The island was discovered in 1826. John Franklin and his men descended the Mackenzie River in two open boats, then turned west to explore the unknown coast. Franklin reached the island on July 17 and named it after Sir William Herschel who had discovered the planet Uranus and became Astronomer-Royal to King George III.

Many Inuit lived then on Herschel Island. "It abounds with deer [caribou]," Franklin wrote, "and its surrounding waters afford plenty of fish." The explorer Vilhjalmur Stefansson described its harbour, the only one along this coast, as "one of the finest harbors in all the Arctic." Most important, the explorers saw near Herschel Island "a great many black whales [bowhead whales]."

Whaling was an ancient and immense industry. In 1846, 735 American vessels were engaged in whaling. The whaling industry employed between forty thousand and seventy thousand people. In 1852, 278 ships from New England were hunting whales in the northernmost Pacific and adjacent seas.

Their summer hunting season was short, their New England home ports more than 32,186 kilometres (20,000 miles) away. So in the "tween season" they sailed to the Polynesian Islands, or along the coasts of Africa and China, whaling and trading. Thousands of men deserted on exotic islands (among them Herman Melville). Some were adopted. Some eventually returned aboard other ships. And quite a few were eaten. In their stead, whaling masters hired on, or often impressed, a vast assortment of natives from the entire Pacific region and the coasts of Africa.

The bowhead of the Arctic was the whalers' favourite prey. It was colossal, slow, timid, and so fat it floated after being killed. It was swathed in blubber nearly a metre (2 feet) thick, yielding one hundred barrels of oil, used for street lights, lubricants, tanning, and steel tempering, and worth, in 1902, fifteen U.S. dollars a barrel.

From the top of the whale's cavernous mouth, larger than the average living room, hung six hundred to eight hundred triangular baleen plates, some as long as 4 metres (13 feet), weighing a total of a ton or more, and worth, at the end of the nineteenth century, nearly six dollars a pound.

Consisting of a keratinous substance akin to horn, baleen, the tough, pliable, and resilient precursor of plastics, had many uses. Bristles of hair brushes were made from it and the springs of the first typewriters, umbrella ribs and fishing rods, shoe horns, tongue scrapers, and buggy whips. Its principal use was for corsets, stays, bustles, and busks to keep the ladies of the day in the desired shape.

Around 1900, an average bowhead was worth ten thousand dollars and a large one up to fifteen thousand dollars and that at a time when a United States factory worker earned a dollar a day and a senior merchant marine captain one hundred fifty dollars a month.

In 1888, the North Pacific whalers sent an exploratory

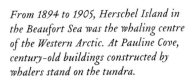

From 1894 to 1905, Herschel Island in the Beaufort Sea was the whaling centre of the Western Arctic. At Pauline Cove, century-old buildings constructed by whalers stand on the tundra.

mission from Point Barrow, Alaska, east, a whaleboat commanded by Joseph Tuckfield. He wintered with Inuit near the Mackenzie Delta and returned the following year after a 1,609-kilometre (1,000-mile) voyage in an open boat to report that whales in the Beaufort Sea "are as thick as bees."

This was electrifying news. The American revenue cutter *Thetis* promptly left to see whether Herschel Island were not by any chance in United States waters. It surveyed the island, sounded its harbour, named it Pauline Cove and reported, a bit regretfully, that Herschel was well within Canadian territory.

In the summer of 1890, two small steamers, the *Mary D. Hume* and the *Grampus* squeezed through the narrow lane of open water between the polar pack and the Alaska coast to spend the winter at Herschel. In July, the ice released the ships and from the last day of July on, they caught whales "as fast as we could handle them."

Laden with a fortune in baleen, the *Grampus* sailed home. The *Mary D. Hume* prepared to spend a second winter at Herschel. She took a total of thirty-seven whales and returned to San Francisco with a cargo worth four hundred thousand dollars.

That did it. The rush for the Beaufort Sea was on. Soon so many whalers wintered at Herschel that, one of the captains observed, their "crews formed a colony that was larger than many a town in the United States." Herschel, really an American exclave, was then also one of the largest towns in Western Canada. In 1894, the *Balaena* returned with sixty-seven whales, and the *Narwhal* with sixty-nine, each cargo worth about five hundred thousand dollars or roughly ten million dollars in today's terms.

The ships usually left San Francisco in spring and reached Herschel Island (8,046 kilometres [5,000 miles] from San Francisco) in August. They hurriedly unloaded a portion of their supplies into large warehouses that had been built ashore, and continued east to hunt whales. In September, before freeze-up, they returned to Herschel.

They collected the abundant driftwood, at least one hundred cords per ship. They cut fresh-water ice in a lake 3 kilometres (2 miles) from Pauline Cove as their winter water supply. Once the ships were frozen in, they housed them over with lumber and canvas, covered this with a layer of sod and, later, banked the ships with 3 to 4 metres (10 to 12 feet) of snow so that, with stoves blazing, it was warm on deck as well as below. They then settled down for the long winter until the ice released the ships again around mid-July.

In 1894–1895, fifteen ships wintered at Herschel Island with about one thousand whalers and one thousand Inuit. As told by the captains, several of whom had their families along, the season passed pleasantly. On October 16, the officers and ladies attended an elaborate birthday party given by Captain and Mrs. Sherman for their son Bertie, aged three.

The *Beluga* was "specially fitted for entertainments" with stage and auditorium, and officers and crew enjoyed performances by the "Original Christy Minstrels of Herschel Island." The ladies gave *soirées musicales* aboard their ships. The captains frequently played whist and drank port in the comfort of their cabins, or billiards in the living room of the large community building ashore (built in 1893), which the crews were also permitted to use "one or two evenings a week."

Elaborately scripted invitations were sent from ship to ship nearly each week "for supper and dance aboard some of the vessels," or for a fancy-dress ball. Ladies, admittedly, were in short supply. "For a partner in the Virginia Reel I had Miss Dorothy Porter aged 5 years," Captain John McInnis recalled.

At Christmas, a magnificent party was held and gifts were exchanged, the ladies "being the recipients of many useful articles." One week later, "they danced the old year out and the new year in" aboard the *Beluga* and on New Year's Day attended "an entertainment by Fay's celebrated opera." Outside it was −35° C. One badly frost-bitten sailor died.

In spring, Mrs. Sherman gave birth to a daughter and "the American ensign was displayed from the peaks of all vessels in honor of the event." The baby was baptized Helen Herschel. As the days grew longer and the weather warmer, tobogganing and skiing became favourite diversions. Often more than one hundred ladies, officers, and men slid down the glistening slopes "amidst great merriment."

The odd sour note does creep into these pleasing accounts of winter life on Herschel. Captain Weeks of the *Thrasher* fell into the hold and died. He was kept during winter in one of the ice cellars. In summer, the body was pickled in brine and shipped home. The blacksmith of the *Navarch* died of consumption. On January 20, in the midst of a "surprise party" aboard the *Beluga*, just as everyone was sitting down to a "substantial supper," an Inuk burst in to report that seven crewmen had deserted, taking with them dogs, sleds, guns, and provisions.

These were minor disturbances in a life that otherwise sounds pleasant, proper, and rather genteel. It certainly does not evoke visions of a "Sodom of the Arctic" where, according to one lurid account, "Rum flowed like water" in one long "Bacchanalian orgy" and "fighting, drinking and debauchery were the order of the day." Nor does it fit the description of "many whaling skippers" by the eminent naval historian Samuel Eliot Morison, as "coldblooded, heartless fiends."

Just what went on at Herschel while the captains dined and danced is a bit hard to determine because of a compact made by the officers to "keep their mouths shut when they went South." Even visitors to Herschel often kept mum. They were usually treated with the utmost kindness and courtesy by the whaling captains and felt indebted to them. Wrote Roald Amundsen, the Norwegian explorer during the first crossing of the Northwest Passage, "I prefer not to mention the many and queer tales I heard during my sojourn" at Herschel Island (1905–1906).

The captains and their chief officers were, as a rule, New Englanders; the mates often Scandinavians; subordinate officers, usually Cape Verde Islanders; the crews, from all over the world. The captains may have been middle-aged, balding, portly, and fond of port, but they were also tough, courageous, and determined, and they came prepared for trouble. Ship's stores included about forty pairs of handcuffs. On Herschel Island, said the Reverend C.E. Whittaker, the Anglican missionary, "their word was law, without any court of appeal."

The basic problem with the crews on Herschel Island was the combination of an eight-month winter, idleness, and liquor. The men chopped wood and hauled ice. The officers encouraged sports, "which helped to keep them from worse." But mid-winter weather discouraged outdoor fun. Once, while a group of whalers was playing baseball, one of Herschel's notoriously violent blizzards burst upon them. Only two managed to reach the safety of the ships. The others got lost and died.

That left liquor and women as the main forms of recreation. "There were drinking bouts almost every day," the Inuk Nuligak recalled in his wonderfully detailed memoirs. Henry Larsen, the famous captain of the RCMP ship *St. Roch*, who spent years in that region, said many whalers "moved in with Eskimo women, and a period of wenching and home-brewing followed that is still remembered in the north." Drunken parties often ended in brawls, occasionally in murder.

Perhaps the fairest assessment was made by Captain Larsen: "One should not judge these people too harshly.... To the Eskimos, this was an entirely new world opening up and the whalers themselves were often simple people who were unaware of the lasting damage they were causing."

That damage was catastrophic. Until the whalers came, the Inuit, as the explorer David Hanbury observed, enjoyed the "best of health." The whalers brought diseases to which the hitherto isolated Inuit had no immunity. Syphilis and consumption, two common sailors' afflictions, spread with devastating speed. In 1902, measles broke out and on Herschel, said Reverend Whittaker, "funerals followed day after day." Within two decades, 90 per cent of the region's Inuit were dead.

To convert the Inuit and mitigate, if possible, the corrupting influence of the whalers, the Anglican missionary I.O. Stringer came to Herschel in 1893. Seven ships were wintering in Pauline Cove. He was amazed by the number of buildings and people: "One can hardly realize that this is the Arctic Ocean." Stringer was a tall man, forthright and devout. Even the trader Charlie Klengenberg, who had little use for missionaries, liked him: "He was a fighter who put the fear of the Lord into several who were the better for it." It was an uphill battle. The Inuit knew the term "God" only as a frequently used swear word. Stringer preached his first simple sermons, helped by an Inuit interpreter named David Copperfield.

Herschel Island, then, was really an American colony. The United States flag flew from buildings and ships. American captains ruled whalers and Inuit alike. Their word was Herschel's only law and this fact irked Ottawa. To assert its sovereignty, Ottawa sent a detachment of North West Mounted Police to Herschel Island in 1903.

When the American whaling fleet arrived in August, two scarlet-coated officers, Sergeant F.J. Fitzgerald and Constable F.D. Sutherland, greeted the whalers on Herschel's beach and politely informed them that, henceforth, they were the law. The change did not sit too well with the autocratic captains, but they bowed to the inevitable with reasonably good grace, paid duty on imported goods and told their crews to behave.

Eight years later, while carrying the winter mail to Dawson by dog team, Fitzgerald and three companions were pinned down by a blizzard so terrible and prolonged, they starved to death.

By 1905, whaling was on the wane. "The whales, from being hunted so hard, were shy and hard to approach," noted Captain Bodfish. Petroleum replaced whale oil. Featherbone and the newly invented spring steel supplanted baleen.

Within three years its price dropped from five dollars per pound to forty cents. In 1908–1909, not a single ship wintered at Herschel. Most natives were dead or had left. Suddenly Herschel Island had become, according to Fitzgerald, "one of the most lonesome places in the north."

But then fur prices soared and Herschel, in the new guise of a trading centre, got a new lease on life. In the 1920s, arctic fox fur rose from two dollars fifty cents per pelt to a top price of sixty three dollars per pelt. Stefansson found Herschel "a busy place. Perhaps twenty-five or more Eskimo whale-boats and a dozen two-masted Mackenzie-built schooners were assembled here to trade with incoming ships." Herschel the Wild became Herschel the Tame, settled and sedate. "The place is getting too damn civilized," Inspector J.W. Phillips complained to Stefansson.

It was, Nuligak recalled in his memoirs, a good time and a happy, friendly place. "From Christmas to New

A cache of 170-litre (45-gallon) drums with aviation gas near the century-old warehouse of a whaling company. In the winter of 1894–1895, about one thousand whalers and one thousand natives lived on Herschel Island.

Year's the dancing drums never stopped." There were parties and feasts. "On Christmas Day we were all invited by the minister to dinner. On New Year's it was the HBC's [Hudson's Bay Company] turn to entertain us with all kinds of good things to eat. The RCMP also gave us a day, in between these two. We had all kinds of games and we returned home only when we felt like it." In an unofficial way, Herschel had become the capital of the Western Arctic.

Fur prices remained high throughout the 1920s. Some trappers earned as much as ten thousand dollars per year, then a fortune. When Nuligak visited the island in 1926, the harbour was packed with "a whole fleet of little schooners." Attracted by this wealth, Herschel became "a Mecca for itinerant dentists" eager to sell dentures and gold teeth.

In the early 1930s, fur prices dropped sharply. The police left the island. The traders left. The Inuit left. When Henry Larsen on the return trip through the Northwest Passage in 1944 stopped at Herschel, the place which he had known as a young man "as a thriving Arctic metropolis," was "completely deserted...not a soul was to be seen."

I was lucky. I lived on Herschel during one of its "abandoned" periods. In the early 1970s, before my stay, in view of the oil discoveries in the Beaufort Sea and along its shores, the idea was considered to build a deep-water marine oil terminal at Herschel. Pauline Cove would become a sort of Saudi harbour of the Arctic. A plethora of scientists from different disciplines descended on the island, made deep studies and wrote long reports. Then the idea was abandoned, the scientists left, their reports were shelved, and Herschel lapsed again into obscurity.

In the late 1980s, after my stay, Herschel became a Territorial Park, a fascinating park but, like all parks, hemmed by needed rules and regulations.

I spent the summer of 1978 counting white whales, together with Wyb Hoek of the Fishereis Research Board of Canada. In late April and early May, the about ten thousand white whales, or belugas, that winter in the Bering Sea begin their annual 3,218-kilometre (2,000–mile) migration through ice-choked seas, along the Alaska coast and past Herschel Island to spend the summer in the relatively warm waters of the Mackenzie River delta region.

It was a magic summer. From our helicopter high above the Beaufort Sea, we watched the pure white whales, sometimes as many as one hundred in a pod, surge smoothly through the dark sea, their heart-shaped flukes rising and falling in smooth cadence.

Once or twice a week, with a thrill of recognition, we spotted far below the last of the bowhead whales: bulbous black shapes of enormous size, the whalers' favourite prey. Twin fountains of exhaled breath hung like plumes in the cool air above the slowly swimming giant whales. Once—before the whalers came—an estimated thirty thousand bowhead whales lived in the Western Arctic. Now only a few thousand remain.

In late summer, Wyb left me, my gear, and food for more than a month at Pauline Cove on Herschel Island, which I shared with one resident family: Bob MacKenzie, trapper, trader, traveller, his wife, Liz, and their children.

I moved into the old RCMP home, built in 1893, a large, cool, comfortable structure. From the rafters of the house next door, murderers, sentenced to death, had been hanged in former days.

Bob invited me for supper. "We'll have char," he said. "There's lots of fish around Herschel. We freeze a year's supply in the ice cellars the whalers cut deep into the permafrost a century ago."

Bob's home was not your typical trapper's cabin. A large chalet, beautifully built of the abundant driftwood logs, it housed his family and his pets: tropical finches and tropical fish. To the left, past the entrance, was a spacious aviary, achirp with busy, jewel-bright finches. On the right there were large tanks with shimmering little fishes. Tall shelves along the wall were full of books.

A research vessel under charter to an oil company stopped for a day at Pauline Cove. A crew member, Jimmy Morton, had grown up on Herschel Island. As we walked together past the ancient wooden buildings, Jimmy recalled his childhood on Herschel.

"We lived in driftwood and sod houses then," Jimmy said. We walked past the former Inuit "village". Now only grass-grown mounds remained. "That's where we lived just fifty years ago."

He was eight years old when an influenza epidemic reached Herschel Island. "Most people died in a few days," Jimmy recalled. "I woke up one morning. My parents were very quiet. I shook them. They didn't move. They were dead."

Herschel was a place of memories, full with the ghosts of ages past. Rusting machinery from the whaling days lay scattered near Pauline Cove. The great community building where the whaling captains played billiard or drank after-dinner port, still stood, in amazingly good condition. The large warehouses that once held trade goods and baleen, were empty now. One carried a century-old sign: NORTHERN WHALING & TRADING CO.

The old Anglican mission, where Mrs. Stringer had given shorthand courses to whalers dreaming of soft clerical jobs, was nearly in ruins, but sort of inhabited. Within the double-roof of the building lived some forty black guillemots. It was their only known nesting site in the entire Western Arctic.

My stay on Herschel coincided with a top lemming year. Their numbers wax and wane in four- to five-year cycles, from rare to superabundant. They look like chubby, plush-furred mice with tiny tails and Herschel was aswarm with them. In consequence, this was also a peak year for arctic owls. Lemmings are their main food.

Bob's eight-year-old daughter, Mary Margaret, caught many lemmings and kept them as "pets" in a large box. It was a poor idea. Lemmings, at the best of times, are high-strung, irascible creatures. Crowded together in the box, they squeaked and fought and died of stress.

Wooden headboards mark graves of the many whalers who died and were buried on Herschel Island. Their work was hard and dangerous. Winters lasted eight months. Liquor and women provided recreation.

"Can I have your dead lemmings?" I asked Mary Margaret.

"What you want dead lemmings for?"

"I eat them," I said seriously.

"Oagh!" She grimaced in disgust, then, curious, asked, "What do they taste like?"

"Oh, delicious! Just delicious. But you know, they're really not for me. I want them for the baby owls."

The owlets had left their nests. They pressed themselves into the tundra grass when I approached, worried little mounds of brown-grey down, or clicked their beaks and tried to look fierce. There were dozens of them on Herschel Island, more than Bob had ever seen before.

I offered a dead lemming to an owlet. It grabbed it, swallowed it with a few energetic gulps, stood up, and got another lemming. It was a lovely creature: wrapped in fluffy-soft down, with densely feathered feet, a round head and shiny black beak, it stared solemnly at me with large, round, golden-yellow eyes.

Herschel was an island of life. Rough-legged hawks had their nests on valley slopes. Jaegers hovered above the tundra catching lemmings. Sandpipers probed the muck at the edge of tundra ponds, leaving a filigree of three-toed tracks. Snow buntings nested in the old whalers' buildings.

And Herschel was an island of the dead. Returning from my daily walks across the tundra I passed the many massive wooden boards that marked the whalers' graves. The inscriptions on some of them, burned in or set in leaden letters, were still legible:

> Henry Cruiz, died 1895, aged 29;
> Henry Williams, died 1896, aged 20;
> John Wilke, died 1894, aged 20;
> Edwin Isler, died 1897, aged 21;
> Joseph P. White, died 1894, aged 19;
> George Sorenson, native of Denmark, died 1897, aged 32;
> George Kealoha, died 1895, aged 18;
> George, infant son of George Edson, born Feb. 22nd, 1897,
>   died February 12th, 1898.

Chapter 19

SOUTH GEORGIA ISLAND, SUBANTARCTIC
Island of Whalers and Explorers

IT WAS ON SOUTH GEORGIA that the most famous and most heroic of all Antarctic expeditions started. It was on South Georgia that the expedition ended and on this rugged island he loved so much, the expedition leader, Sir Ernest Shackleton, was buried.

And from South Georgia, in 1904, began the hunt for the greatest animal that ever lived on earth. The majestic blue whales were killed with the newly invented grenade harpoon that exploded in their bodies. Their mighty carcasses were hauled to South Georgia Island to be turned into soap, fertilizer, margarine, and money.

The ruthless killing went on and on for three-quarters of a century "and not until it was too late did anyone recognize that the whalers were methodically eliminating the grandest animal that ever lived," wrote the famous American marine artist and author Richard Ellis in 1991 in his superb and tragic book, *Men and Whales*.

Between 1904 and 1978, 331,142 blue whales were killed. Protection was granted when too few whales were left to make the hunt profitable. By then the blue whale was on the verge of extinction.

"The greatest creature in the history of our planet may become extinct in our lifetime," wrote Ellis. "After slaughtering so many of them, we now find our efforts to protect these magnificent animals have probably come too late."

It all began with England's greatest mariner, Captain James Cook. During the second of his famous voyages of exploration, from 1772 to 1775, he circumnavigated Antarctica and became the first man to cross the Antarctic Circle. But he did not see the southern continent.

On January 17, 1775, he landed on a 170-kilometre– (105-mile-) long subantarctic island that later became the gateway to Antarctica. He named it Isle of Georgia after King George III and claimed the island for England.

Cook named the island, claimed the island, but he did not like it. He called it "Savage and horrible...the wild rocks raised their lofty summits until they were lost in the clouds and the valleys lay covered with everlasting snow. Not a tree was there to be seen nor a shrub even big enough to make a tooth-pick."

Apart from knocking the just acquired real estate, Cook made one fateful remark. On South Georgia, he said, and on the other subantarctic islands he had discovered "seals are pretty numerous."

Sealers responded instantly and brought death to the crowded rookeries. Many beaches of South Georgia were covered with a layer of fur seals. "It was impossible to haul up a boat without first killing your way," wrote the British sealer Robert Fides. The sealers could massacre the graceful Antarctic fur seals with ease, for, as Fides noted, "they were quite harmless."

James Weddell, the British sealer after whom both the Weddell seal and the Weddell Sea are named, noted in 1825 that "the number of [fur seal] skins brought off Georgia [South Georgia Island] cannot be estimated at fewer than 1,200,000." By the 1880s, the Antarctic fur seal was considered extinct.

This is one of those rare animal stories with a (so far) happy ending. In 1915, thirty-five years after its obituary was published, a single young male Antarctic fur seal was seen on South Georgia Island. A more thorough search found a few small colonies of survivors. With total protection, the fur seal population soared. They reached hundreds of thousands by the 1980s. Now more than a million of these elegant fur seals live again on South Georgia, the adored darlings, together with penguins, of tourists arriving with Antarctic cruise ships.

These fur seals eat some fish and squid. But their main food is krill, the shrimp-like crustaceans that swarm the far-southern seas in shoals so dense they once fed millions of giant whales. Now most of these whales are rare, and the fur seals are surrounded by a surfeit of food.

For the whalers of the world, the seas were inhabited by two types of whales. The right whales, like the arctic bowhead, were slow, fat, timid, fairly easy to kill and, when killed, floated.

Then there were the other whales, the giants of the family—the blue, the fin, and the humpback whales—that were too large, too powerful, too fast to be pursued and killed by men with rowing boats and hand harpoons. Even if they did succeed in killing such a whale, in death it sank and, weighing eighty times as much as boat and crew, would, unless cut loose, haul its killers down into the sea.

It was the blue whale, above all others, that inspired both awe and greed. This is the "leviathan" of John Milton's *Paradise Lost*:

> Hugest of living creatures, on the deep
> Stretch'd like a promontory sleeps, or swims
> And seems a moving land, and at his gills
> Draws in, and at his trunk spouts out the sea.

This was the whale of which Herman Melville said, "Prodigies are told of him."

In the austral summer of 1911–1912, a female blue whale was killed by a catcher ship and winched ashore onto the flensing deck at Grytviken, the whaling town on South Georgia. This whale was 33.5 metres (110 feet 2.5 inches) long. Her weight was estimated at 195 tons, the equivalent of thirty-five adult bull elephants, the size and four times the weight of a 128-passenger Boeing 737. She was the largest blue whale ever recorded, the largest animal that ever lived on our earth.

Everything about the blue whale is awesome. It feeds primarily on *Euphausia superba*, the reddish, shrimp-like creatures whalers call krill, that exist in schools so vast, they cover square miles of ocean and turn the sea a deep blood red.

Expanding its cavernous gular pouch, the blue whale sucks in 60 to 70 tons of water and krill. Its 4-ton, car-sized tongue moves up, expels the water through its baleen plates as through a sieve, and the whale swallows the immense mass of retained shrimp, tons and tons of it each day.

A blue whale baby weighs 4 tons at birth, suckles avidly its mother's fat-rich milk, and gains about 90 kilograms (200 pounds) each day.

These whales of wonder also produce the loudest sound of any living creature—yet we humans cannot hear it! Says the *Guinness Book of Records*, "The low frequency pulses made by blue whales when communicating with each other have been measured at up to 188 decibels, making them the loudest sounds emitted by any living source. They have been detected 850 kilometres (530 miles) away." These deep, dark moans and groans that travel great distances in water are of

such extreme ultra-low frequency that they are inaudible to humans.

Humpback whale surfaces and spouts near South Georgia. At the whaling town of Grytviken on South Georgia, 175,250 killed whales were processed. The remaining whales of this region are now protected.

Until 1900, blue whales numbered about 225,000 and, as Melville said, "The whole world was the whale's...for [the blue whale] is never chased by whalers." The fate of these superb, sentient animals of great power and beauty, was sealed when the Norwegian Svend Foyn invented the harpoon cannon firing a deadly explosive-filled projectile into the whale, and when, in 1904, his fellow Norwegian Carl Anton Larsen set up the first antarctic whaling station at Grytviken on South Georgia. "Then commenced the murder of these gentle, 30-metre (100-foot) giants," Ellis noted sadly.

About 600 BCE, the Phoenicians invented a process known as saponification that converted goat fat into soap.

In the late 1850s, Napoleon III, emperor of France, sponsored a contest to find a butter substitute. It was won by the chemist Hippolyte Mège-Mouries. His new product was called margarine. Initially, it was made primarily with beef fat.

To whalers, the great whales of the southern seas were a God-given bounty of blubber that, properly saponified and hydrogenated (a process developed by the German chemist Wilhelm Normann in 1903) could be made into soap and margarine.

By 1900, being clean had become classy, and even the hitherto unwashed masses tried to wash at least once a week (usually on Saturday evening). The demand for soap soared and so did the demand for margarine, the cheap "butter" for the common man. These factors, plus Foyn's timely invention of the grenade harpoon and the presence of South Georgia doomed the great whales.

"God," wrote Foyn piously, "had let the whale inhabit [the sea] for the benefit and blessing of mankind, and consequently I consider it my vocation to promote these fisheries."

This sentiment, which mixed so nicely piety with profit, was shared by many Norwegians, the master whalers of the twentieth century. Foremost among them was the whaling captain Carl Anton Larsen. Backed at first by Argentine capital, he arrived on November 16, 1904 in South Georgia with three ships, sailed into the superbly sheltered Cumberland Bay and established at its head the first Antarctic shore station. He called it Grytviken (cauldron or pot cove), for on shore lay the try-pots once used by sealers to render fur seal fat and elephant seal blubber into oil.

Five weeks later, Larsen's catcher boat brought in the first whale to Grytviken. It was winched onto the shore flensing deck, its thick blubber layer was removed and rendered into oil, and the *skrott* (the remaining carcass) was dumped into the sea. Another 182 whales were brought to Grytviken that first season.

It became a huge industry. By 1909, Grytviken alone had a population of 720 men and four women. Another thousand men worked at the seven other shore stations built on South Georgia.

During the next sixty-two years, dozens of powerful, cannon-equipped catcher boats killed the great whales, an average of more than three thousand each year, and hauled their carcasses to South Georgia for processing.

It was hard, filthy work. R.B. Robertson, doctor aboard a British whale factory ship, visited Grytviken in 1950 and wrote scathingly that it was "the worst-administered place in the colonial possessions of Great Britain, the most sordid, unsanitary habitation of white men to be found the whole world over, and the most nauseating example of what commercial greed can do at the expense of human dignity. I think that, if Captain Cook were to see it today, he would probably burst into tears."

Grytviken, with its miasmic smell of rotting whale guts, may have been the pits, but it was also the springboard for many Antarctic expeditions, including the failed yet perhaps most admirable and heroic of all Antarctic ventures, the 1914–1916 *Endurance* expedition of Sir Ernest Shackleton. Comparing him to other expedition leaders, the British explorer Apsley Cherry-Garrard, author of *The Worst Journey in the World*, wrote, "If I am in the devil of a hole and want to get out of it, give me Shackleton any time."

The family motto of this tall, burly Anglo-Irishman was *"Fortitudine vincimus"* (By endurance we conquer), and few humans endured and conquered as much as Shackleton did.

He found his mission and his mettle as a member of Robert Falcon Scott's 1902 *Discovery* expedition.

In 1908, Shackleton led his own expedition to Antarctica. The goal: the South Pole. Shackleton and three companions nearly made it. After enduring terrible hardships, they reached 88° 23' S, less than 160 kilometres (100 miles) from the pole and victory and fame. There, Shackleton turned back. He would not risk the lives of his men in a final and possibly fatal dash for glory.

He left England on his next expedition, to attempt "the first crossing of the last continent," with his ship *Endurance* on August 1, 1914. On August 4, 1914, Britain declared war on Germany. Shackleton immediately offered the *Endurance*, himself and his crew for service. The Admiralty responded with a one-word telegram: "Proceed!"

They reached Grytviken on November 5, 1914. The ice, the whalers warned, was much worse and more extensive than in other years. They were right. After a month on South Georgia, planning, training, hoping the ice might shift, Shackleton left on December 5, 1914. Three days later, the *Endurance* was cautiously manoeuvring south through heavy pack ice.

The ice gripped the ship and held it. They drifted west and north with the ice during the long austral winter. The ice moved and twisted and crushed until the *Endurance* "was bending like a bow under titanic pressure.... Millions of tons of ice pressed inexorably upon the little ship," It groaned, cracked and crumpled, and then their ship was ground into the sea.

Shackleton and his men camped on the moving ice and drifted north until they reached the edge of the pack, then rowed their three wooden lifeboats to the small, isolated Elephant Island. They reached the bleak island of bare rock and ice on April 19, 1916. They had been adrift on the Antarctic pack ice for more than five months.

To save his men, Shackleton decided to sail to South Georgia. It was a desperate venture: perhaps the most difficult and daring small-boat voyage ever made. Shackleton knew it. In a final letter, left with his men on Elephant Island, he wrote, "In the event of my not surviving the boat journey to South Georgia...you can convey my love to my people and say I tried my best."

Their boat, the *James Caird*, was 6 metres (19 feet) long. It was autumn, the season of vicious Antarctic storms. Shackleton and five companions sailed 1,287 kilometres (800 miles), hammered by gale-force winds, towering waves, constantly drenched by ice-cold water. The heavy seas began to destroy their small wooden boat. They sailed like that for seventeen days.

They landed at King Haakon Bay on South Georgia's uninhabited southwest coast. To get help, they had to cross the mountainous, glacier-covered island. No- one had ever crossed South Georgia. On maps, the interior of the island was a blank. The whalers "regarded the country as inaccessible."

Grytviken, once the whaling capital of the subantarctic regions. Founded in 1904, the town was abandoned in 1966. At the far right is the whalers' church.

Shackleton set out together with two men. They had no crampons, no climbing gear. Three men in ragged

clothing, torn boots, exhausted from their terrible boat trip, they walked and crawled and clawed over steep rock and soaring glaciers, non-stop for thirty-six hours, then staggered into the Stromness whaling station.

"We had suffered, starved and triumphed," Shackleton wrote later. "We had reached the naked soul of man." He had achieved the impossible and he saved all his men on Elephant Island.

Shackleton returned to South Georgia in January 1922, the first stage of another expedition. He was busy in Grytviken, that "strange and curious place...[where] the old familiar smell of dead whales permeates everything," when a massive heart attack killed him. He was forty-seven years old.

Shackleton might have been buried in Westminster Abbey. But Lady Shackleton felt that burial on South Georgia was more appropriate to the spirit of her husband. And there, at the edge of the whalers' cemetery, his crew buried him while one of the men played "Brahm's Lullaby" on his banjo.

Whaling, in the meantime, had grown into an immense business. "Some twelve thousand men go down to the Southern Ocean each year to hunt the whales," wrote the whale ship's surgeon R.B. Robertson in 1950. In addition to the shore stations on South Georgia, there were now huge factory ships, enormous floating slaughterhouses, that processed all the killed whales brought to them by their fleets of fast, cannon-equipped catcher ships. In 1958, they killed 64,075 whales. In 1961, their peak year, they killed 66,090 whales.

The capital invested was enormous. It had to be amortized. To find the last whales and make a final profit, sonar, spotter planes and helicopters were used. The whales did not have a chance and when nearly all were dead, whaling suddenly ceased.

On South Georgia, the shore stations were abandoned. Grytviken was briefly leased to the Japanese, but even they could not find enough surviving whales to make it pay and, in 1966, Grytviken was closed. After nearly two hundred years of slaughter, first of seals and then of whales, South Georgia became a sanctuary.

There are moments or hours in life that one never forgets. Even years later, an inner vision of the event remains, as crystal-clear as when it happened. Our ship, the Russian icebreaker *Akademik Ioffe*, an ex-Soviet research ship changed into a dollar-earning tourist liner, was far into antarctic waters when two humpback whales joined us.

The day was superb, one of the best I have experienced in all my trips to Antarctica: not a breath of wind, the sun intense and warm, the sky a deep, soft blue, the sea as smooth as glass. The humpbacks surfaced near our ship and for the next two hours we watched entranced the water ballet of two 40-ton whales, immense power in smooth, fluid, gliding motion.

They rose through the greenish, pellucid water, rolled and turned with sensuous grace, slid past each other, rubbed softly against the side of our ship, then suddenly, as upon command, splashed the sea into foam with their long, triangular, white-edged flippers and humped smoothly forward. For one moment their giant flukes rose house-high into the air and then the two great whales slid smoothly into the deep.

We waited, rushed from starboard to port, and suddenly there was a yell: "Left! Left! They're coming!" Our two great whales surged up with a gleaming wake of bubbles and foam, spouted high and for a moment covered us with their moist, misty, smelly breath (and photographers cupped their lenses) and began again their gliding, sliding water dance.

It was beautiful and to me, and I think to many of the others, deeply touching. For nearly a century the humpback and the other great whales of these seas had been ruthlessly hunted and brutally killed. Grenades were fired into them to explode in their bodies and they died in agony. Once there had been one hundred thousand humpback whales in the seas of the world. Now only six thousand were left. Our two whales, so beautiful and trusting, were probably the first generation of post-whaling whales, the first ones to live and play and pair again in peace.

We were vividly reminded of those whaling days when we sailed into South Georgia's Cumberland Bay. It was 6 a.m. Our ship eased cautiously through the luminous fog into King Edward Cove. The anchor rattled down. The fog lifted slowly, and between the dark sea and the still fog-wrapped soaring mountains lay the rust-red ghost town of Grytviken, where more than 120,000 whales had been "processed" between 1904 and 1966.

The whaling museum, replete with history, had white walls and a bright red roof. The white whalers' church was built in Norway, taken apart, shipped, reassembled on Grytviken and consecrated on Christmas Day 1913. It was used for regular services, for three marriages, thirteen baptisms, and often for funerals. More than a hundred whalers lie buried in the large cemetery south of the dead town. At the whaling museum, my guidebook informed me,

"American dollars, British pounds, and German deutsche marks are accepted, but credit cards are not."

I walked slowly through the former whaling town, past the boiler house, the blubber cookery, the bone cookery, the meat cookery where thousands of whales had been converted into soap, margarine, bone meal, and fertilizer. Fur seals slept in the shade of the great whale oil tanks. Penguins waddled sedately on the rutted, sedge-covered streets of long ago.

A simple, rough-granite stone marks the grave of "ERNEST HENRY SHACKLETON, EXPLORER."

Chiselled into the reverse of the stone is Shackleton's favourite quotation from the poet Robert Browning: "I hold that a man should strive to the uttermost for his life's set prize." Beyond the grave rise the jagged black mountains and coruscating glaciers that Shackleton crossed to save his men.

I was working at the time on a book, published in 2002 as *Glimpses of Paradise: The Marvel of Massed Animals*. I had observed and photographed a small colony of king penguins during the months I lived on the Falkland Islands. Now I wanted massed king penguins and South Georgia, with two of the world's largest king penguin colonies, was the place to go.

We sailed into the Bay of Isles, past Albatross Island with its tens of thousands of fur seals near shore and thousands of albatrosses near the top of the island. Zodiac boats brought us ashore at Salisbury Plain. I always find it touching the way homesick Brits name remote spots in the world after loved places at home. If there is one place on earth that does not resemble Salisbury Plain in Wiltshire, England, with its megalithic Stonehenge, it's Salisbury Plain in South Georgia, where two hundred thousand king penguins stand shoulder to shoulder against a backdrop of shimmering glaciers.

For people who like animals, South Georgia on a summer day can be paradise. Most animals are not shy and there are few places on earth with such a profusion of sea birds and sea mammals: a million fur seals, 360,000 elephant seals, hundreds of thousands of king penguins, six million gold-tasselled, perky macaroni penguins, tens of thousands of albatrosses, and millions of petrels and prions. Non-native, and shyest of all, are about two thousand reindeer, now feral, whose ancestors were imported from Lapland and released long ago by Norwegian whalers as a source of sport and fresh meat.

South Georgia weather can change abruptly from sublime to vicious. We went ashore at 6 a.m. at Saint Andrews Bay to visit another, even larger colony of king penguins. It was drizzly, grey, and dreary. Most tourists trudged obediently toward the distant penguin colony, while I, warned by more than thirty years spent in arctic and subantarctic regions, headed for a weathered but sturdy hut built long ago for biologists.

At 8 a.m., the wind picked up sharply. I rushed to shore and caught the last Zodiac to the ship. The shore party crowded into the hut.

On board, we stared in awe at the mounting waves. The wind rose to gale force, with gusts that exceeded 160 kilometres (100 miles) per hour, sheared off the tops of waves and filled the air with flying spume. Our great ship, anchored in a sheltered bay, heeled over nearly twenty degrees. No boat, we felt, could survive the few-hundred-metre trip between ship and shore.

It was a very humbling thought, that Shackleton and his five companions had sailed their 6-metre-(19-foot-) long wooden boat through wind and waves much worse than this in icy autumn weather across 1,287 kilometres (800 miles) of open sea to seek help for their friends marooned on Elephant Island. "By endurance, we conquer" was Shackleton's family motto. On South Georgia, he and his men endured and conquered. And on South Georgia, years later, he died.

Grave of the famous explorer Sir Ernest Shackleton. To rescue the crew of his doomed ship Endurance, *Shackleton crossed glacier-covered South Georgia. "We suffered, starved and triumphed," wrote Shackleton. He died in 1922.*

Chapter 20

THE DRY TORTUGAS, FLORIDA, U.S.A.
The Fortress Island

THE FLORIDA KEYS are beautiful. Some are crowded today, the real estate prices sky-high. Others are amazingly untouched, edged with dense mangrove forests, home to small, elegant key deer. At the southwestern tip of this 321-kilometre- (200-mile-) long arc of islands lies Key West. (The first Spaniards to land upon it found human bones and called it Caya Hueso [Bone Island], later anglicized to Key West). Inhabited today by some of the oddest and some of the nicest people in the United States, Key West was once the home of Audubon and Hemingway, and the part-time home of U.S. president Harry S. Truman.

Key West, despite what many people think and say, is not the end. The keys and the United States continue westward into the Gulf of Mexico.

You can go there from Key West by daily ferry. Or by floatplane. The first time, if you can afford it, go by plane. You fly above some of America's best-preserved coral reefs. The sea is cobalt blue and turquoise in the shallows. Remnants of a wreck (more than two hundred ships, some laden with treasure, sank in this area) rest upon a shoal. A single mangrove tree grows upon the wreck. It may be the beginning of a new island.

Thirty-two kilometres (20 miles) out of Key West you pass the uninhabited, tree-covered Marquesas Keys, home to turtles and seabirds.

You fly another 80 kilometres (50 miles) toward the west and there, just north of the Tropic of Cancer, on the latitude of southern Egypt and central India, something strange appears: a mighty fortress in the sea, covering an entire 6-hectare (16-acre) island, massive, squat, hexagonal, its 15-metre- (50-foot-) high walls the mellow red of ancient bricks. It looks as strange and out of place in the empty, shimmering sea as a dinosaur browsing in a suburban garden.

This is Fort Jefferson, the "Gibraltar of America," the largest brick fortress in the Western Hemisphere, designed to protect the soft southern underbelly of the new United States from incursions by European powers, Britain, France and Spain, reluctant to relinquish their hegemony over the vast New World territories they once "owned."

The fortress has embrasures for 450 cannon that once included the then state-of-the-art bulging Rodmans that could lob a 136-kilogram (300-pound) shell into a ship 4 kilometres (3 miles) away.

They could, but they never did. Fort Jefferson took decades to build and by the time it was nearly finished, both naval guns and Weltpolitik (international politics) had changed, and the mighty fortress was obsolete.

The fiasco fortress that never saw action, became a nasty, top-security military prison. Its most famous and most tragic inmate was Samuel A. Mudd, the country doctor from southern Maryland who, on April 15, 1865, set the broken leg of the famous actor John Wilkes Booth who, at 10 p.m. the previous evening, had shot and killed the president of the United States.

Your plane is now near the immense fortress, shielded from the sea and invaders by a seawall and a moat. You ask your pilot to circle the amazing structure. "Only once," he says. "We must not scare the birds."

Fort Jefferson on Garden Key and six other small, nearby keys, plus the sea around them form now the 259-square-kilometre (100-square-mile) Dry Tortugas National Park, a bird and sea turtle sanctuary, a favourite goal of history buffs and of tourists who love to snorkel near Fort Jefferson in the glass-clear, fish-rich sea.

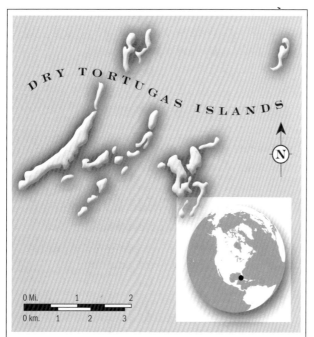

In 1513, the Spanish explorer Juan Ponce de León, once a shipmate of Columbus, sailed north and west from Puerto Rico, searching for the fabled "fountain of youth," that could rejuvenate all who drank from it. He did not find it (but, to judge by TV ads, many Floridians are still searching for the elusive elixir).

Ponce de León discovered land at Easter time, the season called "*Pascua Florida*" in Spanish, the Easter Festival of Flowers, and he called the new land Florida.

On the return voyage, Ponce de León passed seven sandy keys. They were teeming with turtles and he named them Cayos las Tortugas, (the Turtle Islands). There was no water on these keys, and they became known as the Dry Tortugas.

Florida changed hands repeatedly. The Spanish owned it. The British got it. The French tried to settle it. Then it belonged to Spain again and Spain finally ceded Florida to the United States in 1821.

The U.S. felt vulnerable. To protect its southern lands and the vital shipping lanes from the Gulf of Mexico into the Atlantic, the government decided to build a colossal fortress on 6-hectare (16-acre) Garden Key.

It was to be the latest thing in fortress engineering: the most daring, most impregnable, the biggest. It was all that, but, unfortunately, it was not to be the best.

Digging deep, keeping the sea at bay with caissons and with cofferdams, they built on the coral base a massive foundation, 4 metres (14 feet) wide and more than half a metre (2 feet) thick.

Upon this rose the fortress, its walls 2 metres (8 feet) thick, forming a hexagon with two thousand massive brick arches that supported the three tiers of gun emplacements for 450 cannon.

Slaves built the immense structure, using more than sixteen million bricks shipped south from Pensacola, 804 kilometres (500 miles) away. Cement and stone came from New York, 2,413 kilometres (1,500 miles) to the north.

Then came the extras: casemates for a 1,500-man garrison; 109 cisterns to collect and store rain water, with a total capacity of 5.6 million litres (1.5 million gallons); powder magazines; an oval "hot shot" furnace to heat cannonballs and heave them, red-hot, into the holds of enemy ships and set them on fire; officers' quarters; a large parade ground.

Work began in 1846. By the time it neared completion in 1875, Fort Jefferson was obsolete, a monstrous mass of bricks that, in case of conflict, the recently invented rifled naval guns could have quickly reduced to rubble.

This fort that never fought cost 3.5 million dollars to build, an enormous sum at a time when a U.S. factory worker earned less than a dollar a day and when most of the slaves that built it were not paid at all.

During the Civil War, Fort Jefferson nearly fought. It was manned by Union soldiers. Early in the war, a Confederate fleet approached and demanded surrender. In answer, the fort commander threatened to blow their entire fleet right out of the water. The Confederates looked at all those glowering gun ports and sailed away. The fort commander probably heaved a sigh of relief. His threat had been bluff. The fort was undermanned and the famous 450 gun emplacements held only one single gun that worked.

Near the end of the Civil War, a young man in Washington planned to kill Abraham Lincoln, president of the United States. John Wilkes Booth was a member of a family of famous actors: his father, Junius Brutus Booth, was considered the greatest Shakespearean actor of his generation; his older brother, Edwin Thomas, was now nearly equally famous; John Wilkes Booth, twenty-seven, was also a well-known actor, but, envious of his more famous brother, handsome, vain, temperamental, yearning for an immortal role. He was an ardent supporter of the southern cause, favoured slavery, and hated Lincoln with a passion.

In December 1864, Booth, reconnoitring a post-assassination escape route, stopped at the house of Samuel Mudd, a tall, red-haired, prematurely balding country doctor in his early thirties living on a 202-hectare (500-acre) farm, 40 kilometres (25 miles) southeast of Washington. With southern hospitality, Mudd invited the young actor for supper and Booth spent the night at the doctor's home.

Key to the Gulf of Mexico, Fort Jefferson on 6.5 hectares (16 acres) of Garden Key was the largest fortress in the U.S. seacoast defence system.

On April 9, 1865, Confederate general Robert E. Lee

surrendered to Union general Ulysses S. Grant at Appomattox. The Civil War was over.

Five days later, on the morning of April 14, Booth heard Lincoln would attend that evening a performance of the comedy *Our American Cousin* at Washington's Ford's Theater.

At 6 p.m., Booth entered the deserted theatre. He fixed the door to the presidential box so it could not be locked.

Shortly before 8 p.m., President and Mrs. Lincoln and their guests arrived at the theatre. Booth was having a drink at a nearby tavern.

At 10 p.m., during the third act of the play, Booth walked into the theatre. The president and his guests were not guarded. Booth opened the door of the presidential box, drew a derringer-type pistol, and shot the president through the back of the head.

Booth swung himself over the balustrade, shouting: "*Sic semper tyrannis!* The South is avenged!" (Thus always to tyrants!), the words Brutus is supposed to have uttered when he stabbed Caesar to death.

As Booth jumped onto the stage below, the spur of his boot snagged in the American flag draped over the edge of the presidential box. Off balance, he dropped heavily and snapped the tibia of his left leg just above the ankle.

He hobbled out, got onto a horse held by a stagehand and fled Washington together with another conspirator.

The broken leg foiled their plans. At 4 a.m., in great pain, Booth remembered Mudd. His home was near. Booth and his companion stopped. Booth, disguised, knocked and told the doctor he had fallen off the horse and broken his leg.

Mudd cut off the high riding boot. He wrapped the injured leg in cotton, splinted it, and helped Booth to go to bed upstairs. The fugitives spent the day at Mudd's home and left next night.

Lincoln was dead. America was awash in rumour, hysteria, sorrow, and hate. A few days later, soldiers found the cut boot, carrying inside the name J. Wilkes, in Mudd's house. The doctor was arrested.

Other conspirators and alleged conspirators were arrested. Edwin H. Stanton, the secretary of war, said publicly he wanted them all tried, convicted, and hanged before Lincoln's funeral.

At the trial, Mudd insisted that when he treated Booth he had not recognized him and that at the time he had had no knowledge of the president's death. It did not help him.

Booth was cornered in a barn and shot. Four of the alleged conspirators, including one woman who, most historians today agree, was not guilty, were sentenced to death and hanged. Four others, tried by military court, received life sentences of hard labour. One of them was Dr. Mudd.

The four prisoners were shipped to remote and isolated Fort Jefferson, now a military maximum-security prison. "That fatal isle, the Dry Tortugas...a perfect hell," one of the condemned men, Samuel Arnold, wrote later.

Above the entrance to Mudd's cell someone had written, "Whoso entereth here leaveth all hope behind," an American version of Dante's famous inscription above the gates of hell: "All hope abandon, ye who enter here."

The cell was small, dark, and dank. In summer, it was stifling hot. The "wether allkillen warm," wrote one of the guards, Sergeant Harrison Herrick, in his diary. Spelling was not his forte, but his observations were astute, revealing, and sometimes funny.

Bored to distraction, some men caught the cat of Mrs. Devendorf, wife of one of the officers. On Sunday, March 19, 1865, Sergeant Herrick wrote in his diary: "After retreat Doctor Holder & old Frost had a cat thron in the Break Water for the Shark, but he didnot seam to like cat meat...& som of the prisners haled her up on an old shirt that they had fast to aline. Mrs. Devendorf was mighty mad about it."

Life was hard at the grim, lonely fortress in the sea. Ships came infrequently. The water in cracked cisterns was brackish and bitter. Stored rain water became filthy and foul. Bread and flour crawled with weevils. Meat on the hot island became so rotten, even dogs would not eat it.

Mudd tried to escape in the base of a coal ship. He was caught and henceforth manacled.

Two years passed. In August 1867, disaster hit Fort Jefferson. Of its three hundred residents, guards and prisoners, 270 were struck by yellow fever, an often fatal, terribly painful, mosquito-borne disease. The prison doctor died. Mudd volunteered his services.

For prisoners and guards alike, he was an excellent, devoted and kind doctor, treating the dreadful disease, with patients, in agony, vomiting, in the final stages, the feared "coffee grounds," black, coagulated blood, the result of severe internal hemorrhaging. The usual yellow-fever death rate was 80 per cent of all infected. Yet Mudd saved most. Only thirty-eight of his patients died.

The officers at Fort Jefferson signed a petition asking President Andrew

Jackson, in view of the doctor's devotion, to pardon Mudd.

That petition never reached the president. But others spoke up and in 1869, after four years' incarceration at Fort Jefferson the "conspirators" were amnestied and released. One had died in the yellow-fever epidemic. Edman (Ned) Spangler, the hapless stagehand at Ford's Theater, whose only sin had been to hold John Wilkes Booth's horse on that fateful night when the president was killed, was suffering from tuberculosis. Mudd took him to his home in Maryland and cared for him until Spangler's death.

The U.S. army was unhappy. Its once mighty model fortress, the "Gibraltar of the Gulf," was now a remote, obsolete, useless, costly mass of masonry. In 1874, the army abandoned it. For a while, the navy used the fort as a coaling station. Then the navy lost interest. The largest brick fortress in the Western Hemisphere, periodically racked by hurricanes, mouldered slowly under the searing sun.

In 1908, the Dry Tortugas were made into a wildlife refuge to protect the islands' large tern colonies. In 1935, by order of President Roosevelt, Fort Jefferson became a national monument, and in 1992 the seven keys, the sea around them, and the old and ailing Fort Jefferson became, by order of President George H. Bush, the Dry Tortugas National Park.

A just-discovered treasure of gold and silver took us for the first time in 1975 to Fort Jefferson. The treasure, part of a vast trove found by the famous Florida salvager Mel Fisher, was on display at Key West and our seven-year-old son, René, was fascinated.

A guide told the story. The Spanish treasure fleet had left Havana, Cuba, in early September 1622, great ships laden with gold and bars of silver, with bales of indigo and tobacco, including the 600-ton galleon *Nuestra Señora de Atocha*, and the galleons *Nuestra Señora del Rosario* and *Santa Margarita*.

Hit by a hurricane, the treasure fleet was driven onto the feared shoals and reefs between Key West and the Dry Tortugas. Towering waves destroyed the fleet, 550 persons drowned and treasure worth more than two hundred fifty million dollars sank with the ships. The *Rosario* struck the Dry Tortugas. There, a few survivors were rescued.

Now Mel Fisher and his crew of experts and divers had found part of the *Atocha* treasure. Maps showed the location. There were large pictures of the Dry Tortugas and of Fort Jefferson.

"Can we go there?" asked René.

I had just returned from a six-month expedition to the high Arctic. This was our first time together. We hired a small floatplane and took off for Fort Jefferson.

The pilot was nice; a tall, lanky, smiling man who liked kids. He folded himself into the pilot's seat. René sat next to him. It was his first flight in a small plane. The pilot flew low and talked. He spotted swimming turtles. We passed the *Atocha* wreck and several others, dark, dead shapes in the turquoise sea, and the pilot told the grisly stories of terrible shipwrecks and marvellous rescues that children love to hear.

He circled the great red fort, splashed down, and taxied gently to shore.

"You have four hours," he said.

That morning we were the only visitors. A friendly warden took us in tow. From the air, the mighty fortress had looked like a bastion, massive and inde-structible, a man-made Rock of Ages. Now, up close, the huge building appeared aged and cracked, shedding mortar and bricks.

"It's much too heavy for its base," our warden said. "It was built on soft coral. It sank. It crumbled and cracked. They had a very clever system of col-lecting rain water and storing it in cisterns. As the ground shifted, the cisterns cracked. Now most of them are full of salt water."

"Do you live here?" asked René.

The warden laughed. "Fort Jefferson now has a population of five. We live here. We have rooms, a desalination plant to make fresh water and generators for electricity."

He showed us Dr. Mudd's cell and told us his story. A small room, gloomy, with narrow slit windows, drafty and damp.

"Did he stay locked up in his room all the time?" asked René, awed by that thought.

"No," said the warden. "Prisoners worked on repairs, planted trees, cleaned out the cisterns. They did all sorts of work. Always watched by armed guards."

We made the rounds high on battlements that had never seen battle, a near-ly 1-kilometre (three-quarter-mile) walk. René straddled some of the black-painted cannons that had never been fired. Far beneath us in the moat a shark swam in the lime-green water.

"Can we go swimming?" asked René. There's just so much history a seven-

year-old wants to hear.

"Sure," said the warden. "Don't worry about the sharks. They're small and don't bother humans. But be careful. There can be quite an undertow."

Massive walls of Fort Jefferson were built with sixteen million bricks. The fort was never used in war, but for many years it was a military prison.

The floatplane roared up. We circled the fortress once more, a slave-built giant hexagon in the shimmering noonday sea. The plane droned eastward. The pilot stopped talking. René lolled limply in his seat. He was sound asleep.

That was thirty years ago. René is married now and has two children. When they visit Fort Jefferson, as one day, no doubt, they will, he will find a place both changed and changeless. The great fort is still crumbling, is still being repaired. It is no longer remote and lonely. Now the fortress that was never invaded is visited by about one hundred thousand tourists each year.

Chapter 21

Lembata Island, Indonesia
The Island of Sacred Boats

HE HUNTERS LAUNCHED their boat on a receding wave and rowed and paddled with all their strength to an ancient rhythmic chant: "*Hilabé, hilabé, héla, héla, hilabé, hilabé, héla, héla ....*"

They hoisted their golden-yellow palm-leaf sail, sailed out into the Savu Sea and their chant changed into a song, an ancient invocation of the spirits, with the recurrent theme: "We are the men from Lamalera, We are the hunters of the whale," sung in Lamaholot, the language of their island.

These were the sea hunters of Lamalera, an isolated village on the small island of Lembata, part of Indonesia's Solor Archipelago, 1,900 kilometres (1,180 miles) due east of Jakarta. Their boats are sacred and, they believe, immortal. Their prey is gigantic and dangerous. The crew is whipcord lean and tough, burned a deep mahogany brown by the searing tropical sun. Boats and the hunt, frozen in time, have changed little in seven hundred years.

I was very lucky. The spirits were kind to me. The boats are holy. The hunt is holy. A crew had very reluctantly agreed to take me along. "Only for one trip!" they insisted. They had taken a risk. A stranger may inadvertently break a taboo, offend the spirits, and become the Jonah of the fleet. Yet on my first trip, while all other boats returned empty, mine returned in triumph with a 1-ton manta ray and a huge whale shark. This, the hunters believed, showed that the spirits approved my presence and henceforth I was welcome in every one of their boats.

To the villagers of Lamalera, each one of their fifteen boats is a living being, a physical link to their ancestors and to their ancestral home. That home, their legends tell, was on an island to the north.

About seven hundred years ago, their island home was destroyed by a tidal wave. The survivors, in two boats, after long travel came to the harsh, dry, uninhabited volcanic coast of Lembata. They built their new village above a crescent beach facing the turbulent but life-rich Savu Sea and named it Lamalera (a place in the sun).

Other tribes inhabited the cloud-drenched, fertile highlands of Lembata. The coast was sun-burned, sere, and empty. Since they could not live off the dry, barren land, the people of Lamalera turned to the ocean. They became hunters of the largest animals of the sea, pursuing their giant, dangerous prey in sacred boats that never change.

One of the two boats that brought the people to Lembata seven hundred years ago was called *Kebako Pukà*. On our hunting trips in the Savu Sea, I often travelled in the *Kebako Pukà*. The magic image on its prow, a snake coiled around a mountain, symbolized the tidal wave that, long ago, had destroyed their ancestral home. Our boat, the crew assured me, was identical in every detail to the Urboat that brought the people to Lamalera. This is probably true, for in a never-ending cycle of death and resurrection, each boat is a precise copy of its predecessor.

When a boat dies, of old age, in a storm, or is smashed by an enraged 40-ton whale, the village observes two months of mourning. During this time, the new boat is built by craftsmen of great skill and steeped in the ancient magical lore of Lamalera's boat-building clans. They are called *ata mola* (priests), for their work deals with spirits, with the life, the death, and the rebirth of a boat, a sacred boat of Lamalera.

It takes eighteen trees to build a boat. Each plank is carefully adzed to boat curvature. No plank is ever bent, for that would offend its spirit. The root end of each tree is at the stern, with its life force flowing forward to the "head" of the boat.

The planks are caulked with palm fibre oakum mixed with a milky-white tree resin. The entire boat is doweled, each hand-carved hardwood peg is driven in with a stone hammer. The crosspieces are carved to fit the boat

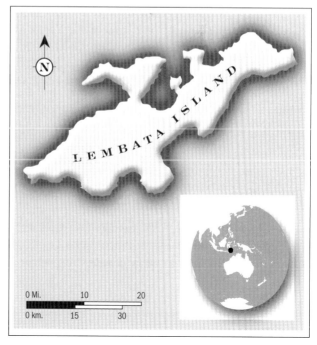

and lashed to it with rattan. No nail, or screws, or anything metal may be used in the construction of the vessel.

When the boat is completed, its sacred symbol is painted on the prow, often magic eyes that look unceasingly for prey. The boat is "fed." Its planks are rubbed with the brains of a manta ray, to give the boat's spirit the power of the mighty fish.

The new boat receives the same name as its predecessors through countless boat generations. In solemn rites on the beach, the boat is blessed and aspersed, formerly with chicken blood, today with holy water. The dead boat is reborn and in Lamalera mourning turns to joyous celebration.

The finished *peledang* (as such a boat is called in Bahasa Indonesia, the national language) is a heavy, sturdy, 9-metre- (30-foot-) long craft, nearly 2 metres (6 feet) wide in the beam, tapered at bow and stern, with a false keel of soft wood, often damaged in rough landings and then replaced. The boat is given great stability by two sturdy outriggers. Beyond the bow juts out a narrow, 1.5-metre- (5-foot-) long bamboo and plank platform, the harpooner's precarious stand.

The huge square sails of the boats, glowing golden in the morning sun, are woven from the leaves of the gebang palm and are suspended from 7-metre- (25-foot-) high bipod bamboo masts. Each boat carries from seven to nine *kafe*, single-flued harpoons of ancient and unique design, and a rack-full of 3-metre (10-foot) bamboo harpoon poles.

The hunt is the life of Lamalera, a hunt both sacred and sacrificial, a primal sea animal hunt that in this mystic form has survived nowhere else on earth.

That survival is due, in part, to Lembata's isolation. The Solor Archipelago north of Timor was briefly visited and described by the Portuguese in 1620 and was then again forgotten by the outside world for nearly three hundred years until, early in the twentieth century, Jesuit missionaries began to visit the islands. In 1913, Catholic missionaries from Germany established a permanent mission at Lamalera. The faith of Lamalera now is a syncretic mixture of devout Catholicism with animistic beliefs in the sanctity of hunted animals and their spirituality.

Village life is regulated mainly by *adat*, the ancient oral code of custom and conduct. At the beginning of each *lefa*, the hunting season during the time of the south-east monsoon, from early April until late November, the priest blesses

the fleet. But prayers are also said to Kotekema, the spirit of the sperm whale.

The sperm whale, *ikan paus* (the great fish), is their most feared, most respected, most sought-after game. Catches peaked in 1969, when they took fifty-six whales, and declined sharply thereafter. The whales' spirits had been offended, said the villagers. Tourists from a passing ship bought one of the sacred sperm whale skulls that line the beach. The spirits were angry. The boats returned empty. The village suffered. For many years they took less than ten whales a year. Finally, in the 1990s, repeated prayers appeased the spirits, catches improved and life became easier for the two thousand people of Lamalera.

They take primarily young male sperm whales, 6 to 12 metres (20 to 40 feet) long, because they are most common in the deep, squid-rich Savu Sea, and also because crews are leery of the rare, large (up to 18 metres [60 feet] long, weighing 60 tons) sperm whale bull with its immense power.

In March 1974, two boats from Lamalera sank after being towed for more than 80 kilometres(50 miles) by a big male sperm whale. A third Lamalera boat picked up the swimming crews. All drifted for many days, until they were rescued by a passing ship.

Apart from dolphins that are too fast and baleen whales that are taboo, the Lamalera hunters take all animals of the Savu Sea: manta rays, their most common and important prey; several species of shark, including the great white, but most often the large, lethargic whale shark, known in Lamalera as *ikan iyo bodo* (the stupid fish); small toothed whales; sunfish; marlin; and dorado.

The hunt is hard. The men slave all day beneath that relentlessly burning sun and 70 per cent of the time they return with nothing. They do not eat all day and very rarely drink. Their suffering, they believe, appeases the spirits of their prey. I shared, for weeks, their suffering, the torpid boredom of days adrift upon an empty, sun-soaked sea, the wild, frenzied excitement of the hunt.

Travelling east from Bali, it took us eight days to reach Lamalera, from island to island by crowded ferries, across islands in crowded buses. Maud grew up in Indonesia, speaks the language, is charming, and we managed.

The ship for Lembata and other Solor Islands left at midnight. It was a heavy-timbered, round-hulled coaster, a relic of Dutch colonial times, allowed to carry, said a tarnished plaque in Dutch, 64 tons of cargo and sixty-four passengers.

It carried hundreds, their bags and bundles and boxes, their screaming, hog-tied pigs and squawking chickens. A tip got us a bit of deck space, wedged in between a girl with eczema and a black pig with diarrhea. The sea trip to Lamalera was supposed to take four hours. We ran into a storm and it took ten. The ship heaved and yawed and rolled. People cried. Some prayed. Our eczema girl was seasick and vomited all over Maud. Our poor pig was seasick at both ends.

The ship hove to far off Lamalera. Great waves crashed in white breakers on the distant beach. Small boats, paddled by young men, crested the coastal surf, bounced near our ship, rose on a wave, were loaded in an instant, fell away and rushed toward shore. One carried Maud and half of our possessions. The next one carried me, my boxes with camera equipment, and a waterproof, whitewater bag with our passports, tickets and a lot of cash in small-denomination bills.

Maud hit the beach, soaked but safe, and instantly impressed upon some young men that she would pay well if, on the next arriving boat, they would save the camera boxes, the bag with cash, and, if there was time, her husband.

My boat rolled and slipped on the sea-side of the surf, shot ashore on the largest wave, five young men pounced, grabbed everything and me and made dry sand before the next wave hit. We had arrived.

It was a world remote and different from most other worlds we knew: a pre-money barter society. The village nurse, the teachers, and the priests received salaries. Everyone else lived by barter. The village carpenter made chairs and tables and was paid by clients in food, clothing, or services. Lamalera was a one-industry village. The men hunted sea animals. A portion of meat, blood and fat was used in our village. The rest was traded to other villages for the agricultural foods Lamalera lacked.

We paid for everything we needed in cash, always the exact amount agreed upon. Since no one had money, no one had change.

We rented the so-called White House, a fairly white house on a rock ridge above the north end of the beach. It belonged to an absentee Lamaleran, the captain of an Indonesian ship. Two of his sisters looked after the house. They also cooked for us. Nearly every meal they prepared was made with slightly rancid whale oil or slightly rancid shark liver oil. Both are nutritious and perhaps delicious when one grows up with them. We found them vile. Maud procured plant oil and henceforth cooked herself the Indonesian meals we love. Thanks to her, we quickly became part of the village and I became the non-hunting member of a boat crew.

Weather permitting, the fleet left every day (except Sunday) at dawn. The ten-man crew slid the heavy boat from its palm-leaf-thatched shelter at the back of the beach on a slipway of hardwood logs to the sea edge and the roaring, thundering surf. I was told to get into the boat, sit down, and hang on.

It looked deadly. But the men stood calmly beside the boat and waited for the highest wave. A shout, a mighty shove, the crazily tilting, bucking boat rode out upon the receding wave, and the men slid aboard, otter-smooth. They poled the boat beyond the breakers, settled upon the thwarts and began to row and paddle.

A mile or two from shore, they stopped. The *belawai*, (the harpooner), honed his harpoons on an ancient, time-smoothed stone. With that ritual the hunt became holy. The men took off their hats and prayed: first a communal paternoster in Lamaholot and then a final plea: "Lord bless our hunt and let us return alive."

They raised the mast, the great golden sail unfurled, and we sailed straight out with the morning off-shore breeze, 12 to 19 kilometres (8 to 12 miles) into the Savu Sea. At that distance, they tacked and jibed, back and forth, the crew alert for the telltale spout of a distant whale, the curved tip of a manta ray's wing, the sheen of a shark near the surface.

Toward noon, the wind often fell and I learned what it means to be becalmed beneath the equatorial sun. "As idle as a painted ship upon a painted ocean," said Samuel Taylor Coleridge in *The Rime of the Ancient Mariner*: the lazy roll of oily swells; the dull creaking of the boat; the faint flapping of the sail; the terrible, burning glare of the sun.

The crew, lean men and tough, sat quietly and endured. They did not eat. They did not drink (nor did I, but I learned to fill up, camel-like, with water every morning before we left). They lolled on the thwarts, limp in the shimmering heat, heads shielded by woven lontar-leaf helmets, smoking thin, palm-leaf-rolled cigarettes, passing lighted cigarettes back and forth in the boat, for most were too poor to buy matches.

Suddenly one man yelled, "*Ikan pari!*" (a manta ray), and in an instant the heat-torpid crew swung into frantic action. They shed their sarongs and, now nearly naked, straining with every fibre of their lean, hard bodies, dark

The sea hunters of Lamalera, a village on isolated Lembata Island, leave at dawn with palm-leaf sails unfurled.

skins gleaming with rivulets of sweat, they rowed and paddled to the rapid, rhythmic cadence of an ancient song.

The harpooner stood at the tip of his narrow bow-stand, a dark, deadly figurehead to our racing boat. As the boat was nearly upon the ray, the great fish, alarmed, began to dive. The harpooner tensed and in a great arching leap flung himself upon the prey and drove the harpoon in with all his skill and power. As the boat shot past, pulled by the wounded, frantic fish, he grabbed a racing outrigger and slid smoothly aboard.

This is another unique feature of the Lamalera hunt. The harpooner always jumps, like death-fated Ahab, upon the back of a great whale, upon a shark, upon a manta ray. It is extremely dangerous, but it greatly increases the harpooner's accuracy and killing power. That is important. Their boats, for all their sanctity and seeming strength, will not survive a prolonged struggle with the mighty sea creatures that are their prey.

The great manta ray dove swiftly and deep. The wrist-thick palm-fibre rope flew overboard in spinning loops, deadly to anyone caught in a coil. Finally, the rope went slack.

As the men strained with all their strength to haul up the struggling 1-ton fish, they sang a loud and ancient song. That song, they believe, follows the harpoon line and is heard by the spirit of the great ray. "We do not hunt for fun," they sang. "We desperately need your flesh to live, to feed our hungry children." Part magic incantation, part ardent plea, the song must appease the mighty manta ray's spirit, or else no one can kill it.

When the ray was near the surface, several men jumped overboard. It was their moment of greatest danger, for the thrashing wings of the powerful fish can break both men and boat. They dove beneath the ray and stabbed it with their *druries*, long-bladed, razor-sharp knives. The principal aim in the hunt of whale, or ray, or shark, is to kill quickly. They drove their blades into the manta ray's brain and the great fish died instantly.

After the wild excitement, the shouting, rushing, hauling, leaping overboard, there came a sudden silence. The men were totally quiet. Each man was praying, communing with the spirit of the fish he had just killed, speaking to it, thanking it, ending the hunt in deep respect and gratitude.

They cut up the manta ray, loaded the boat and began to row home. The wind picked up. Our square sail with its large, indigo-painted cross, filled, the men stopped rowing, and the heavily laden boat slid smoothly along. I dozed, lulled by the heat and the whispering sound of the sea.

The yell "*Ikan iyo!*" (a whale shark), shook me awake. The largest shark in the world, average length 10 metres (32 feet), average weight 10 tons, the record weight, reportedly, 45 tons, the weight of forty-five cars.

The huge form glided slowly through the sea, just beneath the surface, a dark, smooth bluish-green, dappled with cream-colored spots. It seemed unaware of danger and imminent death. The hunters called it "*ikan iyo bodo*" (the stupid fish).

The harpooner leapt onto the shark's back and drove the harpoon deep into the 10-ton fish. It dived but hardly fought. They hauled it up, men swam beneath it and stabbed it. It thrashed feebly and died.

They lashed the fish, as long and much heavier than our boat, fore and aft to outrigger and boat. The wind was strong now. It drove us home. The men had prayed fervently to the spirit of the fighting manta ray. The spirit of the poor lethargic shark, the "stupid fish," barely got a thank you.

To lighten the boat most of us jumped out in the surf and rushed up onto the beach. That beach was the centre of Lamalera life. There naked, nut-brown children frolicked in the surf and old men sat in the shade and smoked their thin palm-leaf cigarettes. They talked of long-ago hunts, wove new sails, or braided new rope.

All came to help haul our boat ashore, from tiny tots to ancient men. It was unloaded, cleaned, and dragged into its thatched shelter.

The prey was quickly and expertly cut up and divided among all the members of my boat clan: the hunters, the sail makers, the boat builders, the shares determined by ancient custom. The largest portion went to the harpooner upon whose skill and daring depended the success of the hunt and the life of the village. His share was called *lei maké*, (the wages of his feet), in tribute to his superb balance upon the narrow harpooner's stand.

The meat was sun-dried on racks. Oil rendered from whale blubber and the vitamin A–rich shark-liver oil, was drained into bamboo containers, to be used for cooking and for the lamps of Lamalera. The village had no electricity, no TV, no radio, no newspapers, no roads, and no cars. Every part of the prey, including blood for soups, was utilized. To waste anything was considered a grave sin, for it would offend the ever-present spirit of the prey.

Every Saturday at dawn, the women and girls of Lamalera walked 8 kilo-metres (5 miles) to Wulandoni, the ancient, neutral inter-tribal market, carrying heavy basins with meat, fat, and oil on their heads. They walked smoothly and straight-backed along a path used by untold generations. Many twirled the *lelu,* (distaff and stone whorl), spinning cotton thread while they walked and talked.

At the market, tribal women from the mountain villages spread their agricultural produce in the shade of a huge and ancient tree. The Lamalera women sat apart. All paid, in kind, a tiny tribute to the market clan, a whistle shrilled and bartering began. There was little or no haggling. Every item had a traditional barter value. A piece of dried whale meat, for example, two fingers wide and a hand-length long was worth twelve bananas.

In the afternoon, the women returned, their basins filled with maize, rice, yams, with bananas, cassava, and many other fruits and vegetables. They reached Lamalera by evening in time for a festive meal.

On Sunday we went to the 6:30 a.m. mass in the large church of Lamalera, high on the hill above the sea. Above the altar were paintings: our crescent beach with many people walking toward a central, shining figure of Christ, one of the men carrying the typical broad-bladed Lamalera paddle.

Of the service we understood nothing, for it was no longer in Latin but in the local Lamaholot. But the singing was superb: choir and congregation in antiphonal chant, ending with the Bach-Gounod version of "Ave Maria," sublimely spiritual and deeply moving: "Pray for us sinners now and at the hour of our death."

Thanks to the success of the boat that had taken me along on my first trip, showing the spirits' approval of my presence, I was *persona grata* on all future trips. A few were successful. Most were not. We sailed out into the Savu Sea and tacked, searching an empty ocean for prey. Days of nothing. The torrid heat beneath that searing sun. Other boats in the distance, weirdly distorted by loom, swaying, elongated, dream-like in the shimmering sea. Five hours. Six hours. We returned with the evening breeze. "*Tida ada,*" said the men, resigned. "Nothing."

Between long days of nothing, sometimes for the entire fleet of fifteen boats, came the moments of excitement: the spotting of prey, the chase, the intense wish-prayer "Don't dive! Don't dive!" the harpooner taut, deadly, directing the boat with shouts, lean bodies drenched in sweat, chanting, praying, the soaring leap of the harpooner, the kill. Usually manta rays, sometimes sharks, once a *temu bola* (a pilot whale).

Weeks passed and on a perfect day for whaling, the great whales came. If the waves are high, the tossing boat makes the hunt impossible. If the sea is satin smooth, the whales usually dive and flee as the boat approaches. This day the waves were short and sharp and choppy. It was a small-boat whaler's sea.

Two blue whales surfaced near us. The men did not move. These whales were far too large. They were also taboo. *Adat* forbids their hunt. The whales swam slowly, majestically past us, dwarfing our boat, the largest animal that ever lived on earth.

Soon after, another whale surfaced a hundred yards ahead of us, an *ikan paus* (a sperm whale), with its immense bulky head and distinctive bushy, forward-angled spout. It was a large male, about 15 metres (50 feet) long and weighing about 45 tons. It was far too large and powerful a whale to be tackled by our sacred but relatively frail boat.

After a whale has been butchered on the Lamalera beach, women carry basins of fat and meat to their homes. The hunt of large sea animals, little changed in seven hundred years, provides the village with food and barter goods.

My boat had not caught anything for more than a week. The helmsman said something and the crew responded with an eager shout, gripped by that strange fervour that makes men ride joyfully into battle and death. They bent to the oars and rowed and rowed like men possessed. Upon his wildly yawing narrow platform beyond the prow, the harpooner swayed in perfect balance with the boat.

I knew the awesome power of that whale. Thirty-eight years before, I had been on sperm whale hunts with the men of Lajes on the Azores island of Pico, men whose grandfathers had sailed with Yankee whalers, who used large, strong American whaleboats, and still spoke American whaling lingo. I had seen such boats smashed by harpooned and enraged sperm whale bulls, had seen men crippled in such attacks, and heard of others that had been killed.

My crew knew all that. But in the manic frenzy of the hunt all fear vanished. They rowed and chanted and cried in the wild, shrill ecstasy of men facing great danger. Anticipating disaster, probably the loss of our boat, I switched from Nikon to Nikonos, a waterproof underwater camera.

The whale had dived deep. Now it swam leisurely at the surface, spouting regularly. It made a few shallow dives, but kept travelling northeast, breathing at regular intervals, mighty, unconcerned.

Fifty yards. Forty. Twenty. The lean, hard bodies gleamed with sweat and spray. Their chant became wilder and wilder, a scream to the spirits, violent and primal. The harpooner held the long harpoon straight up, tense, ready.

At fifteen yards the whale dived. Not alarmed. Just ready for another dive, another meal of squid in the deep. The great male rolled smoothly forward, his giant, twin-lobed fluke rose high in front of us and he slid down into the sea.

The crew stopped, slumped, the tension draining out of them. The spirits had decided. In calm acceptance, they hoisted the sail and we returned to Lamalera, not successful but at least alive.

Chapter 22

LORD HOWE ISLAND, AUSTRALIA
The Island Paradise

IT IS PLEASANT TO LIVE without enemies. Safe. No fear. No need to flee. No need to hide. No need to fight. No need for flight.

And so, on a few remote islands free of enemies, some birds gave up flying. Long ago, their ancestors flew. They must have flown to reach the islands. As the catchy French chanson sings, "*Si tu étais à Tahiti, tu n'étais pas là à pied!*" (If you were in Tahiti, you didn't get there on foot.)

Once established on a safe island, some birds walked more and more and flew less and less. Flying may appear sublime, the very essence of soaring joy and freedom, but flying for birds (and most humans) is expensive. Flight demands a lot of energy, consumes a lot of calories, requires a lot of fuel (for birds in the form of food), needs powerful flight muscles, and a keeled sternum.

Flight accounts for about 25 per cent of a flying bird's musculature and, in most birds, for more than 50 per cent of their daily food-energy need. Walking is less glamorous, but it is also less energy-demanding. On some safe islands birds followed a "why-fly" evolution and became down-to-earth pedestrians.

I met such a bird on the subantarctic Auckland Islands, south of New Zealand: the Auckland Island snipe. It can still fly, but it prefers to walk. Considered by some scientists to be "a living fossil," this brown-grey snipe survived because of "freedom from ground predators." It scurries mouse-quick through sedges and grasses and only *in extremis*, when pursued, does it fly up on short, whirry wings in a low parabolic curve, comes down, and runs on. Given a few thousand more years of peace, this bird will probably become a flightless snipe.

Peace ended for island birds with the arrival of hungry humans and their rapacious minions: cats, dogs, pigs, goats and cattle, plus rats, their fellow travellers. They killed the trusting birds, ate their eggs and chicks, and destroyed their habitat. The road to extinction is paved with the names of island animals.

"Throughout the past four hundred years," wrote the biologist David Quammen in his excellent but sad book *The Song Of The Dodo*, "as humanity achieved ubiquity and dominance on Earth, the extinction of species has been largely an island phenomenon."

Since 1600, 171 species and subspecies of birds are known to have gone extinct. Of that total 155 species, or more than 90 per cent, lived and died on islands.

The first and most famous victim was the dodo, a fat and friendly, 18-kilogram (40-pound), turkey-sized, flightless pigeon that had lived for countless millennia in peace and plenty on predator-free Mauritius Island in the Indian Ocean. Until 1505. That year the Portuguese discovered Mauritius and the huge plump pigeon. It was trusting, tame, and flightless and they called it *doudo*, (fool or silly bird). Scientists later named it *Didus ineptus*.

A few, brought to European courts, were admired and painted by Dutch and German artists. The paintings survived. The dodos didn't. Humans, dogs, and pigs destroyed them. The last one was killed in 1681. It was the first extermination of an island bird by Europeans in historic times. Its very name became synonymous with extinction: "Dead as a dodo!"

As more islands were discovered, exploited, and settled, more island birds shared the fate of the dodo. Among them was a small, remote, solitary island east of Australia. Wrote Quammen, "Lord Howe Island, a lonesome little bump halfway between Australia and New Zealand, lost more species and subspecies of birds than the combined total lost in Africa, Asia and Europe."

It was a little paradise, situated, said the famous underwater photographer David Doubilet, "In a strange and empty corner of the sea."

Crescent-shaped Lord Howe Island, the tiny remnant of a once-vast shield volcano, is only 11 kilometres (6 miles) long and 2.8 kilometres (7 miles) at its widest. Covering 1,455 hectares (3,595 acres), it is about a quarter the size of Manhattan Island, a speck of land in an empty ocean, 770 kilometres (478 miles) northeast of Sydney, Australia.

Dazzlingly beautiful, the little island, just north of the cool Tasman

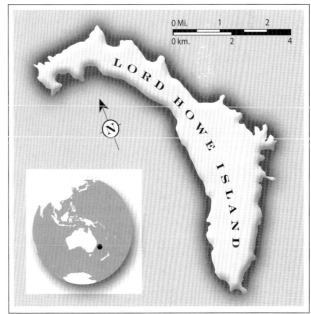

Sea, is bathed by warm equatorial currents and fringed by the world's south-ernmost coral reef. Its narrow waist is flat and lush, its beaches wide and shimmering, the reef encloses a shallow lagoon of the purest aquamarine, the island ends are mountainous and densely forested.

Before it was discovered and despoiled, Lord Howe Island was home to millions of seabirds and fifteen species of landbirds. Fourteen of them were endemic. They existed on Lord Howe Island and nowhere else in the world. Nine of them were exterminated by humans and by rats. Another native bird, the lovely flightless Lord Howe woodhen, was pursued to the edge of extinction. In the early 1980s, only three breeding pairs survived.

In a roundabout way, the American Revolution led to the discovery of Lord Howe Island. Until then, Britain sent most of its surplus convicts to America. The revolution stopped that. Jails and prison hulks in Britain became over-crowded. How about Australia, Lord Sydney asked King George III. It's far, empty and ours, and never mind the natives. The king agreed and in January 1788, the First Fleet of eleven ships arrived in Port Jackson, where Sydney now stands, and founded a penal colony.

Flightless Lord Howe Island woodhen is one of the world's rarest birds. Twenty years ago, less than one hundred survived. Now, with total protection, the rare rail is rallying.

Earlier, in 1744, Captain James Cook had discovered

Norfolk Island, 1,600 kilometres (994 miles) northeast of Sydney, and praised its tall trees and fertile soil. It might be a good place for another convict colony thought the commander of the First Fleet and sent the small navy tender HMS *Supply*, commanded by Lieutenant Henry Lidgbird Ball, to reconnoitre. On February 17, 1788, he passed a hitherto unknown island and named it Lord Howe, in honour of Richard, Lord Howe, First Lord of the Admiralty.

Nearly a month later, on March 13, on the return trip from Norfolk Island to Port Jackson, Lieutenant Ball sent "a boat to examine the island and found abundance of turtles."

Soon other ships of the First Fleet landed at Lord Howe and death came to this peaceable kingdom, which had never known predators. Wrote Thomas Gilbert, commander of HMS *Charlotte*, in May of 1788, "On landing a very agreeable scene presented itself." There were many "gannets, large and fat" and tamer "than geese in a farmyard."

The woods of Lord Howe were full of "large fat pigeons" so tame "as to be knocked down with little trouble." "Partridges" (woodhens) were every-where. "Five or six dozen" came so close to Gilbert that "I was able to take nearly the whole lot." He particularly admired a chicken-sized white bird. "The cock birds were very beautiful; their white feathers were tinged with azure blue." He killed six of them.

Their boat "deeply laden with birds, cocoanuts, cabbages, eggs, fish, etc." these first visitors to Lord Howe Island returned to their ship.

Paradise became a place of slaughter, a larder for passing British navy ships, for whalers, and for traders. Killing was so easy on this island of innocents. The ship's surgeon Arthur Bowes Smyth landed on Lord Howe in 1788 and noted in his journal, "Many hundreds [of birds]...were walking totally fearless & unconcern'd in all part around us, so that we had nothing more to do than stand still a moment or two & knock down as many as we pleas'd wt. a short stick."

The first settlers arrived in 1833, three white men from New Zealand and their Maori wives. They brought pigs, goats, and cats to the island.

By 1860, three of the island's land-bird species were extinct: the unique white gallinule Commander Gilbert had admired, its plumage "tinged with azure blue"; the Lord Howe pigeon, fat and fearless, a fatal combination; and the ruby-red and emerald-green Lord Howe parakeet, cute and trusting and, while it lasted, a favourite food of immigrant cats.

More settlers came, from New Zealand, Australia and whalers from New

England. More ships arrived. On June 14, 1918, the steamship *Makambo* ran onto rocks and, ripped and leaking, headed for shore. To lighten the ship and salvage cargo, the crew dumped bales and boxes into the sea. On them, leaving the sinking ship, hundreds of rats drifted ashore.

The rats loved Lord Howe Island. The climate was perfect, the living easy. Within a few years they multiplied to plague proportions, exterminated six more species of landbirds and drove others to the edge of extinction.

The rats also threatened Lord Howe's most important export crop, the seeds of its unique feather palms, named howea palms after their native island. That vital harvest, munched by ravenous rats, declined from seventeen million seeds a year before World War I to fewer than two million.

Lord Howe Island, once home to so many unique and beautiful birds that now have vanished forever, was, and still is, home to more than 180 species of flowering plants, one third of them endemic.

The little island's most impressive resident is a gigantic tree, the Lord Howe banyan, a megalomaniac fig. Some take up half a hectare (1 acre). The largest one, reputedly, covers 2 hectares (5 acres). From the branches of the main trunk, aerial roots descend into the earth, form subsidiary trunks, that grow more branches with more aerial roots that become sibling trunks, until the banyan stands majestically upon the land like a multi-pillared cathedral, larger than a football field, grander than Grand Central Station.

Most important to Lord Howe are the island's unique tall and slender howea palms. The first settlers called them thatch palms because they used the fronds to thatch their modest palm-log houses.

If you have a potted palm in your home, chances are it was born on Lord Howe Island, for the howeas of Lord Howe are the world's most popular ornamental indoor palms. The island now exports about three million seedlings a year.

It began with palm seeds in the late nineteenth century when conservatories with tropical plants were all the rage with Europe's nobility and wealthy bourgeoisie. (Meet me at the "Second palm tree to the left" goes a conservatory assignation in Oscar Wilde's play *An Ideal Husband*.) The great favourites were the howeas with their lovely feathery fronds.

Initially, all Lord Howe Island settlers were squatters, living on land owned by the Crown. The island belongs to Australia; it is a part of the State of New South Wales. The Lord Howe Island Act of 1953 gave the islanders tenure "in perpetuity" over the land they occupied. The rest of the land, about 75 per cent, became a national park in 1981.

In 1982, in recognition of its "exceptional natural beauty" and "the high proportion of rare and endemic animals, plants and invertebrates" it possesses, Lord Howe Island was placed on the UNESCO World Heritage List.

That accounts for all the land there is. Unless a leasehold comes free, which very rarely happens, no new settlers can come to the island. With three hundred inhabitants, this paradise is full. In addition, a maximum of 393 tourists may be on the island at any one time. Paradise, authorities have declared, should not be crowded.

The five-person Lord Howe Island Board consists of two government-appointed and three island-elected members. They have a palm-based budget. The board owns all the island palms, pays the "seeders" (as seed pickers are called), grows and sells the seedlings (primarily to Dutch wholesalers), and uses the profit (about a million U.S. dollars a year), to finance public works.

Lord Howe is tranquil now, remote and peaceful. All native animals are protected. The alien invaders that killed so many of the island birds and endangered native plants, have nearly all been exterminated. The hogs are gone, the goats have been killed. Lord Howe now is cat-free and nearly rat-free. Even domestic cats are not allowed and dogs are few and frowned upon. There is no place for pets in a paradise that once again is primarily for the birds.

"We don't lock doors," said Cheryl Williams. She smiled, a bit apologetically. "Our island is really a very quiet place." She had just picked us up at Lord Howe Island's airport and was showing us our cabin.

"During the holiday season," the travel agent in Sydney had told us, "the island is booked solid. With city people who want to get away from it all. And, you know, they only have beds for 393 visitors. That's the limit."

Now it was January and they had room for us on the island. The sixteen-seater Beechcraft was only three-quarters full. They weighed the luggage. They weighed us. Since I'm so thin, I felt I should be allowed some extra luggage. But that's not the way it works.

The plane droned east for two hours. Beneath us clouds, beneath the clouds an empty sea. I dozed. The pitch changed, the plane descended, banked sharply through the clouds, and we had a brief glimpse of Lord Howe Island, deep green, edged with white breakers and a turquoise sea. The plane roared to a stop on the 888-metre- (2,913-foot-) long runway.

Cheryl, friendly, organized, and energetic, picked us up with her car, one of 184 on the island. "We use them mainly to pick up guests and parcels," she said. "Most of the time we walk or use bicycles. There's only a few miles of road on the island."

It rained. The island looked lush and green and orderly—rural England with palms. Cheryl and her father Alan operate Somerset Lodge with twenty-five cottages. "Somerset, Massachusetts, that is" she said. "My mother's a Thompson. From Nathan Thompson, a whaler from Somerset near New Bedford. He settled here in 1853."

Genealogy is important on Lord Howe. Maud, thank God, is good at that. Within days she knew most of the islanders, their ancestry, the names of their children, and who was related to whom. She and I divide the world: people for her, birds for me.

Our cottage was lovely: living room, bedroom, bathroom, balcony. Surrounded by palm trees festooned with mosses and great clusters of staghorn ferns. It was very quiet, only the faint, distant murmur of the surf, the gentle cooing of emerald doves in the garden.

"What do you plan to do today?" Cheryl asked.

Relax. Rent bikes. Shop. Go swimming, we said.

"Neds Beach is close and good. Take bread. The fish expect that. By the way, tomorrow is Wednesday. There's lunch at the Shick's place. Kingfish, usually. It's very nice."

There was no one at Neds Beach. Only a large cabin with snorkelling gear, fins, masks, suits, a box on a table, and a list of rental rates on the wall with a request: "Please put the money in the box."

The fish were expecting us. The moment we stepped into the warmish, glass-clear sea, the water swirled and we were surrounded by a mob of eager fishes: green-and-silver wrasses, boldly barred damselfish, silver drummers, large trevallies and sea mullets, some more than half a metre (2 feet) long, all hoping for bread. They snatched up our gifts. A few nibbled gently at our legs. Feeding fish at Neds Beach is an island tradition.

Paddling slowly, we drifted above the milky-white reefs and marvelled at the multitude of jewel-bright fishes that swam in and out of coral caves.

We ate on the balcony. The air was

Clouds cling to Mounts Lidgbird and Gower on remote, 15-square-kilometre (5.9-square-mile) Lord Howe Island, 788 kilometres (490 miles) east of Australia in the South Pacific.

warm and humid, the night still, the pitter-patter of rain on palm leaves, the distant calling of shearwaters returning from the sea with food for their chicks. After dinner, we watched TV: *Attila* by Giuseppe Verdi, from the Teatro alla Scala in Milan, a superbly sung tale of a violent world very far from our peaceful island.

Lunch on Wednesday in the lovely garden of Judy and Ray Shick. Another island tradition. Charcoal-fried kingfish, home-baked bread, wonderful salads fresh from island gardens. Some thirty people arrived, mostly visitors plus some islanders.

We sat on benches and chairs on the carpet-smooth lawn, surrounded by sweet-smelling frangipani bushes, eating, talking, laughing. Two birds walked out of the bushes onto the lawn, small-chicken-sized, russet-brown, with long, strong, slightly decurved bills, and maroon-red, amber-speckled eyes. They walked casually among us, evidently expecting lunch.

"They eat mostly worms and grubs," said Judy. "But they come here on Wednesdays to get bits of fish."

They were Lord Howe woodhens, a flightless rail, amongst the rarest birds on earth. In the early 1980s, only seventeen were left. Their plight helped to save this island paradise, my island lunch neighbour explained.

In the early 1970s, an amply moneyed consortium had the bright idea to turn little Lord Howe Island into a glitzy-glamorous tourist resort with the works, including a super-airstrip for jumbo-jets.

The islanders, helped by Australian environmentalists, fought the plan. The endangered woodhen became their emblem. Paradise, so nearly lost, was saved and the woodhen was saved too.

Long ago, the woodhens were numerous. They divided the island into small territories and lived happily ever after until humans and rats arrived. The woodhens were tame and tasty, a fatal combination. Nine endemic Lord Howe Island bird species were exterminated by humans and rats. The woodhen nearly became the tenth. At the time of the tourist-resort furor, only a few survived in the dense, subtropical rainforest on the slopes of 875-metre (2,870-foot) high Mount Gower at the south end of the island.

Fearing imminent extinction, scientists captured most of the surviving birds and began a captive-breeding program. It was a wonderful success. Captive hens laid five to six clutches of eggs a year that were brooded in incubators.

Over the years, several hundred woodhens were released. "There are at least four hundred woodhens now on our island," my lunch neighbour said proudly. The two woodhens that had joined us for lunch, ate their share of kingfish and then walked back into the forest.

A pair of fairy terns was courting on a branch only a few metres from our balcony. This dainty bird is often called the Holy Ghost bird for it is a celestial vision: its silky plumage is pure white, its slender wings translucent, its large, black-rimmed eyes the deepest midnight blue.

They are also called love terns and the two near our balcony were delightfully in love. They sat close together on their branch and alternately preened the fine feathers on each other's faces, the "preenee" uttering soft, buzzing chirps of pleasure.

Unlike the half million sooty terns that nest on Lord Howe Island and adjacent islets and mate and lay eggs with synchronous precision, the lovely but erratic fairy terns make love whenever they feel like and as a result eggs are laid and chicks are born at any time of the year.

They also don't believe in housekeeping. They do not build a nest. Instead, the female, in a sort of reproductive high-wire act, balances her single, cream-colored egg any place that pleases her at the moment: a bare branch, swaying palm frond, the lintel of a shed, atop a piece of driftwood. One fairy tern was incubating her egg on a branch above the island's main road. Feathers fluffed over her egg, she watched with interest the cars and bicyclists that passed beneath her, calm and without any fear.

In the late evening, armed with flashlights, we bicycled toward Neds Beach. We heard the brouhaha from afar. The fleshy-footed shearwaters were returning to their nests in the palm forest. The ground was honeycombed with their metre-long burrows. One homing-calling shearwater is a very noisy bird. More than a million nest on Lord Howe and nearby islets, and the large colony near Neds Beach filled the night air with an eerie chorus of mewling and wailing.

We walked cautiously to the edge of the colony. Several birds were sitting near their burrow entrances. We knelt near them. They looked at us, dark eyes shining in the light, without any fear.

Their popular, ominous name is muttonbirds. Their fatty flesh reminded British colonists of nice, fat mutton. "Muttonbirding" was a profession. The muttonbirders went from burrow to burrow, reached far in, hauled out the plump, downy chicks and wrung their necks. Muttonbird chicks and muttonbird feathers for featherbeds were among Lord Howe Island's first exports in the nineteenth century. Now the shearwaters, like all other birds on Lord Howe Island, are protected. Their colonies have grown and are now among the most important in the world.

The red-tailed tropicbirds are not nearly as numerous. Few people have ever seen one. The few hundred pairs nesting on Lord Howe Island form the largest breeding colony in the entire world. It is a lovely bird: its white plumage tinged with a delicate apricot-pink flush, the bill bright red, the white tail ending in two carmine-red streamers longer than the entire bird.

The tropicbird's scientific name is Phaethon, after Phaëthon, the son of Helios, the sun god. He tried to drive his father's golden chariot and got zapped by Zeus with a thunderbolt.

Tropicbirds are among the master aerialists of the avian world. To see them fly is to witness perfection. I climbed up to Malabar Ridge at the northern end of the island, where a sheer cliff plunges 656 feet (200 metres) down to the sea. In niches on this inaccessible cliff were the nests of the tropicbirds. In each nest was an absolutely adorable chick: a tiny, fluffy creature wrapped in the purest, silkiest whitest down, with large dark eyes and tiny, pitch-black palmate feet.

I sat for hours at the edge of the cliff and watched, entranced, the flight of the tropicbirds. They rode the wind, followed its currents, soared in the updraft near the cliffs, twisted their wings, landed gently on the nests and fed their waiting chicks.

Our time was up. Like others, we left paradise reluctantly. A few days later we were in Tokyo where our son René was then a teacher. As we were pushed with hundreds of others into a jam-packed subway car, I thought with nostalgia of the peace we had known on Lord Howe Island.

Chapter 23

Zanzibar, Tanzania
Island of Slaves, Ivory, and Cloves

IN THE TENTH CENTURY BCE , when, the Old Testament's book of Kings says, "Solomon was king over all Israel...[he assembled] a navy of ships in Ezion-geber [today's Aqabah in Jordan]...on the shores of the Red sea." The ships were manned by Phoenicians, the master mariners of the time. They sailed far south and "came to Ophir, and fetched from thence gold...and silver, ivory and apes and peacocks...and precious stones." They made that journey "once in three years."

If, as some historians believe, Ophir, the land of gold and ivory, was on the coast of today's Zimbabwe, King Solomon's fleet, sailing along the coast of east Africa, certainly passed and may have stopped at the island of Zanzibar.

Most travellers to that region stopped in Zanzibar, already famous in antiquity as a place of trade and wealth. Fleets of ships came to it from Persia, from Arabia, from India, even from far-away China.

At its zenith, Zanzibar controlled a vast empire, a coastal strip of eastern Africa, from Somalia in the north to today's Mozambique in the south, plus an immense hinterland, in all nearly 10 per cent of sub-Saharan Africa, and its Arab rulers boasted, "When the pipes are played in Zanzibar, all Africa east of the lakes must dance."

Marco Polo never came close to Zanzibar. But he heard much about it from the Arab traders he met on his travels and reported in 1295, "Many trading ships visit the place, which barter their goods for elephants' teeth and ambergris, of which much is found on the coasts of the island in consequence of the sea abounding in whales."

This was the wealth of Zanzibar, the luxury goods the Orient craved: immense quantities of ivory, greatly prized in the Middle East and especially in China; ambergris, a waxy concretion expelled by sperm whales, that floats upon the sea, the most precious ingredient of oriental perfumes; the lovely tortoiseshell of hawksbill turtles that cabinet makers in the Middle East and India used for exquisite inlay work; cloves and other spices; and human beings.

On Zanzibar was the most famous, most infamous slave market in the world, where each year fifty thousand slaves were sold. In the early nineteenth century, Zanzibar was known as "the emporium of Africa."

Monsoon winds that changed direction with the seasons shuttled the trading fleets of many nations back and forth across the Indian Ocean. They arrived from Asia with the northeast monsoon that blows from October to April and returned, laden with the wealth of Africa, with the April to October southwest monsoon.

Persians and Arabs began the monsoon-driven journeys to east Africa nearly two thousand years ago, trading with African Bantu people who spoke Swahili, a word derived from the Arabic *sahil*, meaning coast. They called that coast "Zinj el Barr" (the land of black people), and this became the name of Zanzibar.

In 1421, the largest fleet that ever existed arrived in Zanzibar, 317 ships with twenty-seven thousand sailors. It was the fifth of seven expeditions, led by Admiral Cheng Ho during that brief Ming dynasty period when China was the greatest maritime power on earth.

Cheng Ho seemed a strange choice to be a Chinese admiral: by training he was a soldier, not a sailor, he was a commoner, a Muslim and a eunuch. But the Ming emperor Yongle respected him greatly and gave him the task to build a fleet of unprecedented power and splendour. It included sixty-two *baochuan* (super-ships), each one 123 metres (460 feet) long, 57 metres (190 feet) in the beam, with nine masts, acres of sails, and a crew of more than a thousand sailors. These were the largest sailing ships ever built.

For one brief moment in its history, China was exuberantly, extravagantly expansionist, and this mighty fleet was meant to vaunt its power, to intimidate

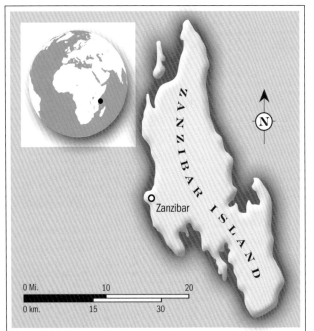

and impress. The first voyages were to India and Persia, exploring, trading, exacting tribute.

In 1421, the Chinese fleet sailed to Zanzibar. No record survives of its arrival. But one can try and imagine it: into the harbour of this tropical island which had never seen anything bigger than an Arab dhow, sailed a fleet of 317 ships, sixty-two of them half the size of the *Queen Elizabeth*. The anchors rattled down and Admiral Cheng Ho landed, surrounded by ten thousand Chinese dignitaries, soldiers, and sailors.

All that is left of that startling meeting of two disparate worlds, are shards of Ming pottery in Zanzibar and along the east African coast, and the record that the fleet returned to China with an immense amount of ivory and, as a special gift for the emperor, two zebras and one giraffe.

Admiral Cheng Ho died on his seventh and last great journey, which included a side trip to Mecca. Shortly after, a new emperor scrapped the fleet and China retreated once again into its xenophobic isolationist shell.

After the Chinese came the Portuguese. Europe awoke abruptly from its introspective medieval lethargy, keen to see the world, to explore, exploit, and conquer it.

The Portuguese led the way. In 1488, Bartolomeu Dias reached southern Africa, the Cape of Good Hope. Nine years later, in 1498, Vasco da Gama rounded Africa, and sailed north along its east coast. There he engaged an Arab pilot who guided him with the monsoon winds to India. On the return journey da Gama stopped in Zanzibar.

The Portuguese, better armed than the natives, conquered quickly. In 1503, they captured twenty dhows in Zanzibar harbour, and forced the island king to pay them tribute. They subdued in quick succession the wealthy cities of eastern Africa and the much wealthier cities of Arabia. In 1507, they captured Muscat, the capital city of Oman. By 1560, the Portuguese ruled Zanzibar. They built a church and, around it, the beginnings of today's Zanzibar Town.

It was all about wealth and profit, the immensely lucrative trade in spices, ivory, and slaves. For centuries the Arabs had controlled Zanzibar and the Indian Ocean trade. Now the Portuguese took over. Unfortunately for them, the British and Dutch were close behind.

In 1591, Sir James Lancaster, one of Queen Elizabeth's pet explorer-pirates, snuck into Zanzibar. He loved it. "This place for the goodness of the harbour and watering," he wrote, "and plentiful...fish...and sundry sort of fruit" was perfect. But Lancaster soon found that he had "to take good heed of the Portugals," and escaped only thanks to timely warnings "from the King of Zanzibar," who, though really a Portuguese puppet, had little love for his masters.

But little Portugal, with colonies, forts and settlements from Brazil to China, was badly overextended. Others usurped its monopolies. The British took India and much else, the Dutch southern Africa and the Spice Islands (now Indonesia) and the Omani sultans, first reconquered Muscat in 1650 and then, within decades, conquered Zanzibar and the east African coast.

By 1744, the sultans of Oman were also sultans of Zanzibar. Now slaves became the island's main export. The slave trade was ancient. On the eastern African coast it had been carried on for more than two thousand years. Its importance is reflected in the Arabian tales of *One Thousand and One Nights*, where every ruler of note, every merchant of wealth has a vast retinue of slaves: as labourers, as domestic servants, as concubines.

Chained stone slaves in a pit on Zanzibar. Near this spot was the infamous slave market where six hundred thousand humans were sold in forty three years to a fate of drudgery and death.

To the rich, slaves were both necessity and status symbol. As a rule, a manumitted slave's first ambition was to acquire wealth and slaves. Concubines, too, were for use and ostentation. King Solomon, says the Bible, had seven

hundred wives and three hundred concubines. Sultan Sayyid Said of Zanzibar, more modest, had only seventy-five concubines.

For the Middle East, Persia and India eastern Africa became the principal source of slaves. From the Zanzibar-controlled coastal strips, slavers raided villages in the interior. Their captives, men, women and children, yoked and chained, were marched to the coast, carrying loads of ivory. Most were taken to Zanzibar, 40 kilometres (25 miles) off the east coast of Africa, and sold on its famous market.

The slavers paid custom duty on all slaves landed on Zanzibar. This was the principal source of the sultan's wealth. "Zanzibar," wrote Charles Miller in his fascinating book, *The Lunatic Express*, "operated the Indian Ocean's largest and most smoothly functioning slave production machine."

In the late eighteenth century, with the immediate hinterland denuded of marketable humans and the demand for slaves rising sharply, the Arab slavers, heavily armed, began to penetrate deeper and deeper into unknown Africa. They encouraged intertribal wars and feuds, provided firearms and were paid in slaves.

The slaving caravans became enormous. Those of Zanzibar-based Hamed bin Mohamed, known as "Tippu Tib," whom Miller called "the Rockefeller-Croesus of the slave industry," consisted of two thousand porters (mostly slaves) and one thousand armed guards (mostly Arabs plus mercenary tribes-men from far-away Baluchistan). Efficient, ruthless, and cruel, they harvested humans in a region half the size of Europe and sold the survivors of the grue-some slave marches on Zanzibar's great market.

The unknown interior of Africa began to fascinate and lure Europeans. The era of exploration began and Zanzibar became the gateway to Africa.

In the second century CE, the Greek geographer Ptolemy, living in Alexandria, then a predominantly Greek city, prepared a cosmographic map of the world. It shows the Mediterranean lands with amazing accuracy. "Arabia Felix" and the Red Sea are presented in detail and Zanzibar is shown. In Africa, or "Ethiopia Interior" as Ptolemy called it, a few lakes are outlined, plus the "Mountains of the Moon," source of the river Nile. The rest of the entire continent is marked "*Terra Incognita*" (the unknown land).

In the early nineteenth century, more than 1,600 years after Ptolemy, nearly all Africa was still *Terra Incognita*, vast, nameless, white space on the maps of the world.

In 1806, Sayyid Said, a clever and ambitious youngster and son of the late Sultan bin Ahmed, killed his cousin Bedr bin Seif, regent of the realm, and became sultan of Oman and Zanzibar.

Sayyid Said liked power, wealth, and recognition. He imported cloves, once the monopoly of the East Indies. They thrived in Zanzibar. The island soon furnished 90 per cent of the world's cloves and became famous as the "Spice Island."

The sultan encouraged foreign trade. In 1839, America was the first foreign nation to open a consulate on Zanzibar, soon to be followed by the consulates of Britain, France, Germany, Italy and Belgium.

Bombay merchants sent their agents to set up stores in Zanzibar. American ships arrived with trade goods, especially a coarse, strong, cotton cloth known locally as *merkani*. It was all delightfully profitable. A bolt of *merkani* worth five U.S. dollars, bought a slave girl in interior Africa, who was sold for twenty-five dollars on the Zanzibar market and resold for one hundred dollars in Muscat.

Zanzibar became so wealthy and important that in 1840 Sultan Said shifted his capital and his court from Muscat, Oman to Zanzibar. It now became the centre of an empire. From his 1,657-square-kilometre (640-square-mile) island, about half the size of Belgium, Sultan Said ruled Oman, the east coast of Africa, and claimed a somewhat vaguely bordered hinterland roughly twenty times the size of England.

Zanzibar became, in fact, an Arab state with an Arab ruling class and an Arab and Indian mercantile class lording it over a native African population. Zanzibar Town had a population of about one hundred thousand, larger than the population of many European cities and much larger than Montreal or Toronto at that time (Montreal's population then was fifty thousand).

European missionaries and explorers arrived in the 1840s and 1850s. For Sultan Said they were a nuisance and a danger, pioneers of European imperialism, yet he treated nearly all of them with courtesy and kindness. Their motto was "explore and publish." They spread the fame of Zanzibar but also the infamy of its slave trade.

In the early morning of December 19, 1856, the ship carrying Richard Burton, famous soldier, explorer, and linguist (he reportedly was fluent in twenty-nine languages) came in "view of the mysterious island of Zanzibar." Burton gushed with romantic enchantment: "Earth, sea, and sky, all seemed wrapped in a soft and sensuous repose.... The sea of purest sapphire...lay basking under a blaze of sunshine." The air was rich with the sultry smell of cloves "and all was voluptuous...hazy and mellow."

A closer look was less romantic. "Corpses float at times upon the heavy water" of the harbour, Burton complained. "The shore is a cesspool."

The explorer-missionary David Livingstone, usually the kindest of men, was frankly appalled by the miasmic smell of Zanzibar: "The stench from the exposed sea-beach, which is the general depository of the filth of the town, is quite horrible. At night it is so gross and crass, one might cut a slice and manure a garden with it. It might be called 'Stinkibar' rather than Zanzibar." No one, Livingstone warned, "can truly enjoy good health here." Cholera outbreaks in 1858 and 1869 killed fifty thousand Zanzibaris.

If a pestiferous damp heat hung over Zanzibar Town, the slave trade was infinitely more evil. Many were killed in brutal raids. Then began the march of yoked captives to the coast. The ship's captain, A.J. Swann, met a slave caravan and spoke with the Arab headman: "I see women carrying not only a child on their backs, but, in addition, a tusk of ivory." When a woman becomes weak, he asked, who carries the ivory? "She does," replied the smiling headman. "We spear the child and make her burden lighter. Ivory first, child afterwards."

The caravan trail was strewn with corpses. Livingstone estimated that for every five slaves captured only one reached the coast alive.

Even then, their suffering did not end. Since the sultan demanded a tax for each slave landed, the "wretches were thrown overboard when sick, to prevent paying duty," wrote Richard Burton, "and the sea-beach before the town...presented horrible spectacles of dogs devouring human flesh."

For the market, the surviving unfortunates were primped and painted to fetch a better price. The men were smeared with oil to show strength and cover blemishes. The women were artfully painted with henna and kohl to enhance desirability.

These human wares were then paraded in Zanzibar's slave market where, wrote the Royal Navy captain Thomas Smee in 1811, "a process of examination ensues which for minuteness is unequalled in any cattle market in Europe." The girls, in particular, were "handled in the most indecent manner in the public market by their purchasers."

About one-third of the slaves was sold in Zanzibar. The rest were crammed into the holds of slave dhows, six hundred or more per ship, pressed tightly together in a dark hellhole, fetid and foul and swarming with rats and vermin.

The dead and dying were thrown overboard. The survivors were sold on the slave markets of Arabia, Persia, and India.

Publicity was bad for slavery. Abolitionists, enraged and empowered by the terrible tales of cruelty brought back from Africa by explorers, demanded action. In 1772, slavery was outlawed in Great Britain. In 1833, it became illegal in the entire British Empire and the slave trade was outlawed. Officially it ceased even in Zanzibar. Clandestinely it continued there into the twentieth century.

Between about 1840 and 1870, Europeans explored Africa. After 1870, the European powers divided Africa among themselves. It was all fairly amicable and gentlemanly. Diplomats met in London, Paris or Berlin, drew lines on maps and said, "You can have this, if you let me have that."

Fishing dhows anchored off Zanzibar. The boats are built on the island. Larger dhows once sailed with monsoon winds to India and back.

Germany wanted Uganda. It also had its eye on Zanzibar. In 1890, rival claims were hashed out at a conference in Berlin. It so happened that Germany had a row

with France and Russia at the time and needed Britain's good will. So the kaiser and his ministers said, in essence, to Great Britain, "We'll take Tanganyika [today's mainland Tanzania]. You can have East Africa [today's Kenya] and Uganda. And you can also have Zanzibar." The British, just to show that they, too, could be magnanimous gave Germany Heligoland, a 60-hectare (150-acre) sandstone islet off northwest Germany that England, long ago, had pinched from the Danes.

The sultan of Zanzibar's realm had been divided. He had not been consulted. He was merely informed. And, being, powerless, he acquiesced.

Zanzibar's days of glory were over. Oman had seceded and had again its own sultan. Europe had gobbled up its east African empire. Abolitionists had ruined the slave trade. The first plastics replaced ivory in piano keys and billiard balls. Zanzibar became a British protectorate. Its sole prize left was spices. It kept producing 90 per cent of the world's cloves.

Zanzibar, no longer important, drowsed on in languorous stagnation for decades except for one brief war in 1896, a row between pretender cousins who both wanted to be sultans. The war began at 3 p.m. local time. Shooting started at 3:02 p.m. It ended at 3:40 p.m. One cousin surrendered. The *Guinness Book of Records* lists it as "the shortest war in history."

After World War II, the British Empire crumbled. In 1963, Zanzibar declared itself an independent sultanate. It was short-lived. Zanzibar became a pawn in the East-West power play of the time. The Soviet Union reportedly fanned, fomented, and financed the long-simmering resentment of the poorer Africans against the upper classes.

The coup came on January 12,

1964. In one orgiastic night of murder, rape, and looting, seventeen thousand people were shot or hacked to death. Nearly all were Arabs and Indians. The last sultan escaped and went to live in southern England. Zanzibar became a people's republic.

Three months later it joined Tanganyika. The united country was called Tanzania, taking the "Tan" from Tanganyika and the "Zan" from Zanzibar.

Not all the revolutionaries lived happily ever after. In 1972, Zanzibar's president Abeid Amani Karume was assassinated and in the aftermath forty-three men were sentenced to death for high treason.

As largesse from the East began to dwindle in the late 1970s, Zanzibar turned slowly right. Cuban and East German "advisors" went home. Cloves and other spices remained the island's main export. Tourists discovered the island, its beautiful beaches, its coral reefs, its "romantic" history, the palaces of the sultans, the maze of narrow streets in Stone Town, the old part of Zanzibar Town. On the site of the once-famous slave market now stands the Anglican cathedral of Zanzibar.

An article in the September 2003 edition of *National Geographic* magazine states that there are still "27 million slaves in the world."

We took the slow, and cheap, morning ferry from Dar es Salaam (the Haven of Peace), capital of Tanzania, to Zanzibar. We ran the gauntlet of shouting touts and pushy porters and ended up in a corner of the ship's lounge with a large Zanzibari family. The head of the family, in long white robe and embroidered cap, sat next to me.

"We're coming home from a wedding," he said. "I'm sorry those people bothered you," he added a bit apologetically, "but you know, they are very poor. They try to make a living."

"Where are you staying on Zanzibar?" he asked.

"I don't know," I said. "We'll ask a taxi driver for a hotel."

"Stay at the Garden Lodge," my new friend advised. "It belongs to an uncle of mine. They're good people. Tell them Amin sent you. They will give you a good price."

The hotel was simple but good, cheap, and the people nice. We had a home, unpacked, and slept in lovely warmth. We had just left January-cold Montreal.

We ambled through town, exotic, tropic, strange, absorbing new sounds and smells and sights. We stopped to admire a large intricately carved wooden door studded with brass bosses.

"That was the house of Tippu Tib," a passerby explained. The most-notorious and the richest of the nineteenth-century Arab slavers. Now, we were told, "many families live in that house."

After too much plain fare on planes, we wanted a spicy meal and went into an Indian restaurant. It was early. We were the only guests. The proprietor, a young man whose family had long ago come from Goa in India, brought us the menu. We talked a bit. The meal was nice and hot, the beer deliciously cold. Life was good.

An African came into the restaurant. Very conservatively dressed, in a dark suit, white shirt, black shoes. He ordered beer, chatted with the proprietor in Swahili, then, seeing us alone, came to our table and asked politely: "May I join you?"

We assumed he was a tourist guide looking for clients. He had a round, dark, friendly face, greying hair and strong, rather elegant hands. About seventy years old, I guessed.

"Where do you come from?" he asked. He spoke a BBC-neutral, upper class English.

"From Canada," we said.

"Do you speak French?" he asked, and when we said yes, he continued in perfect Parisian French.

He had noticed my accent. "Where were you born?"

"In Latvia," I said. "I'm Baltic German."

"Do you speak Russian?" he asked and when I said yes, he switched into fluent Russian.

"Where did you learn so many languages," I wanted to know.

"Oh, that's a long story," he said with his warm gentle smile and steered the talk to other topics. He told us much about Zanzibar, about the sultans, about Princess Salme, the daughter of Sultan Said, who shocked her family to the core by eloping with Heinrich Ruete, a young Hamburg merchant. Our friend was charming, amusing, a brilliant raconteur.

After an hour he rose. "I must go," he said. We thanked him, shook hands, he talked for a moment with the Indian, paid for his beer, and left.

The Indian came over. "I hope he didn't bother you," he said.

"Oh no," Maud assured him. "Such a kind and charming man. Who is he?"

"That gentleman," said the young Indian with a sardonic smile, "is our most famous mass murderer."

And then he told us the man's story: "He was born on Zanzibar. His parents were very poor. His father loaded ships in the harbour. He went to a mission school. They found that the boy was extremely clever. Somehow they got him a scholarship to finish his schooling in England.

"I've heard he attended Oxford and then went to France and studied there. That's where he somehow got involved with some extreme-left student movement. He moved to Soviet Russia. To study." The Indian looked up. "I think they also trained him.

"He came back to Zanzibar and was one of the leaders of the revolt that overthrew the sultan's government and killed people. They say of all those killers he was the worst. He used guns and a very long knife and he just butchered people—men, women and children. All night."

He looked at us. "You know they killed seventeen thousand people in that one night. Mostly Arabs and Indians."

Zanzibar is famous for its spice plantations. Peach-sized nutmeg produces two valuable spices: nutmeg and, brilliant red around its kernel, mace. It is used as a condiment and also in medicines.

"Were members of your family killed?" Maud asked softly.

"My father had feared something like that might happen," said the Indian. "We had moved to Oman. That's where I grew up. But many, many of my relatives were killed."

"What happened to that man?" I asked.

"He got a job with the new government," said the Indian. "But that was not good enough. They say he became a member of an extreme-Maoist group that tried to change the government. The president was killed. Many people were arrested. Some were condemned to death. He was one of them.

"They took him out for execution. At the last moment they took him back into prison. Two weeks later, they took him out again to be executed. And at the last moment brought him back. That went on for years. In between, I've been told, he was tortured. He was in that prison for twelve years. Finally, some years ago, there was an amnesty and he was released."

"What does he do now?" we asked.

The Indian smiled. "He's become very religious. He does good work in the church. Helps people. He's got some sort of job because he speaks so many languages. But mostly he does church work. Teaches children. They say he is very nice with children. And from time to time he comes in here, drinks a beer, and we chat."

We walked slowly back to our hotel, pensive and a bit perturbed. History is so much simpler when you read about it in books.

We lived for weeks on Zanzibar. All day I studied the behaviour of the island's clever monkeys, masters of the arcane art of neutralizing poisons; or, led by an expert, photographed a great variety of spices at the spice plantations; or watched men whipsaw planks to build dhows, as they were built a thousand years ago; or joined some of the fifteen thousand island women tending their seaweed gardens in crystalline lagoons. In the evening, tired and content, we swam in the lambent sea.

We strolled through the maze of narrow alleys of Stone Town, the oldest part of Zanzibar Town. We ate in one of the many restaurants, often charcoal-fried fish, fresh from the sea. A couple of times we met our polyglot friend. He always greeted us with a lovely smile and exquisite courtesy. A charming man who, it was said, had once murdered many with horrid brutality.

Chapter 24

ROBBEN ISLAND, SOUTH AFRICA
On this Island, Nelson Mandela Was Imprisoned for Eighteen Years

T HE VIEW FROM Table Mountain, near the south tip of Africa, is superb. As you stand near the edge of the table-flat, 1,073-metre- (3,402-foot-) high plateau, the beautiful city of Cape Town with its magnificent harbour spreads out beneath you, from the lower slopes of the mountain down to the sea.

On your left, the Cape Peninsula, rich in Cape Mountain zebras, gazelles, monkeys, and sure-footed klipspringers, stretches like a curved finger to the south. It ends in steep, wave-battered cliffs, called Cape of Good Hope in 1488 by the Portuguese explorer Bartolomeu Dias. This, he hoped, was the route to India and, beyond it, the spice islands of the Far East.

Ten years later, another Portuguese explorer, Vasco da Gama, rounded the Cape, sailed on to east Africa and from there with the monsoon winds to India.

At the Cape, two oceans meet. In the west, on your right as you look down from Table Mountain, is the Atlantic. Just east of the Cape, the Atlantic ocean meets the Indian Ocean, often in titanic conflict. The Cape of Good Hope was also called the Cape of Storms.

Beyond Cape Town is Table Bay with a single small island in the hazy distance. It is only 11 kilometres (6 miles) southwest of Cape Town, yet it is a world away, a greenish oval in a lead-grey, wave-stippled, ice-cold sea.

This is Robben Island, once a leper colony, a place for exiled Xhosa chiefs and Malay princes, South Africa's most notorious maximum-security prison, and now a shrine, a place of pilgrimage, visited by more than three hundred thousand people a year. In 1999, UNESCO declared this little 575-hectare (1,420-acre) island a World Heritage site.

Once, a small rolling steamer took prisoners and their wardens to the island. Now fast, elegant ferries shuttle tourists between Cape Town and Robben Island.

It only takes half an hour. But not long ago, "journeying to Robben Island was like going to another country."

Those words were written by Nelson Mandela, Robben Island's most famous prisoner. He was a political prisoner for twenty-seven years, eighteen of them spent on Robben Island, at a time when, Mandela said, this small island "was without question the harshest, most iron-fisted outpost in the South African penal system."

In 1990, Mandela was released from prison. In 1993, he received the Nobel Peace Prize. In 1994, Nelson Mandela, the prisoner of Robben Island, was elected president of South Africa.

The last prisoners and their wardens left Robben Island in 1996. It is a museum now, a place of history, of memories, "a monument," wrote Ahmed Kathrada, a South African of Indian descent, to the "triumph of the human spirit against the forces of evil." He spent twenty-six years in the Robben Island prison.

Robben Island, once a grim prison, is now also a nature reserve. It is home to one of the most important, fastest-growing colonies of the elsewhere-endangered South African penguin. Near the north tip of Robben Island is a small colony of South African fur seals.

In the beginning, it was an island of seals and birds. Robben Island, or Robbeneiland, means "Seal Island" in Dutch. Europeans discovered fur seals and penguins in South Africa on February 3, 1488, four years before Columbus discovered America. "Within this bay," Bartolomeu Dias reported, "is an islet on which are many very large seals...and birds that cannot fly [and have] the voice of an ass braying." That was the jackass penguin, now usually called, more politely, the black-footed or South African penguin.

Ten years later, Vasco da Gama, en route to India, stopped at the same seal island, counted three thousand seals, and "for our amusement...fired among them with our bombards."

Vasco da Gama reached India, but

at a cost. More than half his crew died of scurvy. The food on most ships of the time was ample but awful: salt beef or salt pork, hardtack, gruel and duff, a stiff flour pudding boiled in a bag. British and Dutch sailors got plenty of beer, Portuguese and Spanish sailors received poor-quality wine. None of them got fruit or vegetables.

Cape Town, South Africa and, beyond it, feared Robben Island where apartheid-era governments held political prisoners in a maximum-security prison. Now Robben Island is a national shrine and favorite goal of tourists.

In medieval times, when most voyages were short, this did not matter. But with the long voyages to just-discovered America and the much longer voyages to the recently dis-covered Far East, scurvy became a major problem. Ships

sailing from Holland to the Spice Islands (Indonesia), a trip that took three months, and sometimes four and five, often lost half their crew to scurvy, the fatal disorder resulting from a near-total lack of the antiscorbutic vitamin C in their ship's diet.

Human lives were cheap at the time. Still, losing half his crew was a nuisance for any ship's captain. To diminish death by scurvy, captains often stocked islands on their sailing routes with goats, sheep and pigs, fresh meat for future voyages.

That became Robben Island's first role: a handy larder for European sailing ships, half-way to or from East India. The island's fur seal with their luxurious deep-pile, silky-soft pelts, were another attraction. Sealers came from Holland and France. In 1610 alone, they killed forty-five thousand fur seals on islands near the Cape of Good Hope, including Robben Island.

In addition to the usual island population of feral goats, pigs, and sheep, the Dutchman Joris van Spilbergen released, in 1601, two quick-breeding hyraxes from the nearby mainland on Robben Island, as future food for mariners.

Called dassies in South Africa, the hyraxes that look like grey-brown, dumpy rabbits are really ungulates, small relatives of the elephants. They are common in South Africa. You can see them any day loafing on the rocks of Table Mountain. On Robben Island, fat dassies fed generations of sailors and, after the 1650s, became the staple food for Robben Island's first prisoners.

For more than 150 years after its discovery by the Portuguese, southern Africa was of no interest to Europeans. Fleets of ships sailed past the Cape, laden with trade goods from Europe or spices from the Orient. They often stopped at Robben Island for fresh meat, feral animals, penguins, dassies. The mainland they ignored.

Despite that island meat supply, scurvy continued to be a major problem. To fight it, the mighty Dutch East India Company (founded in 1602) decided to establish a victualling station at the site of present-day Cape Town.

In April of 1652 (ten years after Montreal was founded), the Dutch ship's surgeon Jan Anton van Riebeeck sailed to the head of Table Bay and started there, on the site of present-day Cape Town, together with a small group of settlers, a sort of garden colony. Its main purpose was to supply East India Company ships with meat, fruit and vegetables. From this modest beginning, grew white rule over southern Africa.

The Cape colonists came often to Robben Island, to hunt, to collect penguin eggs and to mine the limestone used in the mortar of Cape Town's first buildings. Three centuries later, Robben Island prisoner number 466-64 (Nelson Mandela) mined limestone in the same quarry "and remained at the quarry for the next thirteen years."

As the Cape Colony grew and expanded and settlers spread farther and farther across southern Africa and the Dutch East India Company became a vast colonial empire, the governors at the Cape and the governors of the company found a new use for Robben Island. It became their dumping ground for undesirables and the first political prisoners: lepers, lunatics, criminals, rebellious slaves, African Xhosa chiefs, Malay and Ceylonese princes, Muslim priests, several kings of East Indian islands, and Thuintjie van Warden, the wife of a Cape Town burgher. She was found guilty in 1672 of "evil speaking" against other women of the colony and was sentenced to six weeks' banishment to Robben Island.

From the point of view of those who ordered banishment, Robben Island, like the famous prison-island Alcatraz in San Francisco Bay, was ideal. It was close to a city, yet a world away and nearly escape-proof. The Benguela Current, with water from Antarctica, rushes into Table Bay and is icy cold. The waves are grim; the currents vicious; the sharks, including great whites, are common and greedy. Over the centuries, many tried to escape from Robben Island. Only a few succeeded. Most drowned or were recaptured.

Robben Island's prison population mirrored to some extent the complex shifts and currents of power struggles in southern Africa. Losers were likely to end up on Robben Island.

First came the gradual agricultural expansion of the Dutch-descended Boers (farmers) into lands held by African tribes, with resultant wars and battles.

Then came the sudden growth of industry. In 1869, the vast diamond deposits near Kimberley were discovered. In 1886, near the Witwatersrand, usually called "the Rand," the world's richest gold-bearing reefs were discovered. Three years later, Johannesburg, the "City of Gold," was the largest town in South Africa. The entire region became suddenly immensely desirable. The result was the 1889–1902 Boer War. The Boers lost, the British won, and South Africa became part of the British Empire.

In World War II, Robben Island acquired strategic importance. Germans and Italians were bombing Allied ships in the Mediterranean. Rommel was alarmingly close to the Suez Canal. The old "Cape Route" to India was once again vital and Winston Churchill demanded that Robben Island be fortified.

Troops arrived on the island. Giant artillery guns were installed. Bunkers were built and hundreds of ships were degaussed to protect them from magnetic mines. Germany did not attack Robben Island, but U-boats did destroy several Allied ships near the Cape.

In the 1948 general election in which, as in past elections, only whites were allowed to vote, the Afrikaner-dominated National Party won. It promised apartheid (segregation) of blacks and whites, and claimed, with considerable sophistry, that this was a policy promoting the separate-but-equal advancement of both racial groups. In practice it meant the continued rule and dominance, economically and politically, of the white minority over the black majority. Even the most famous South African of the time, Jan Smuts, hero of the Boer War, field marshal in World War II, and prime minister of South Africa denounced apartheid as "a crazy concept, born of prejudice and fear."

For more than forty years, fear and prejudice ruled much of South Africa. Blacks demanded equal rights. There were protest marches, demonstrations, crippling strikes. From their bulwark of apartheid and power the whites retaliated with repression and arrests. Among those arrested was Nelson Mandela.

The son of a Xhosa chief, Mandela grew up in a traditional mud hut. He went to a mission school, the first member of his family to ever attend school, and received, in the spirit of the time, "a British education" and a British name: Nelson.

He studied law, became a lawyer, and joined the African National Congress

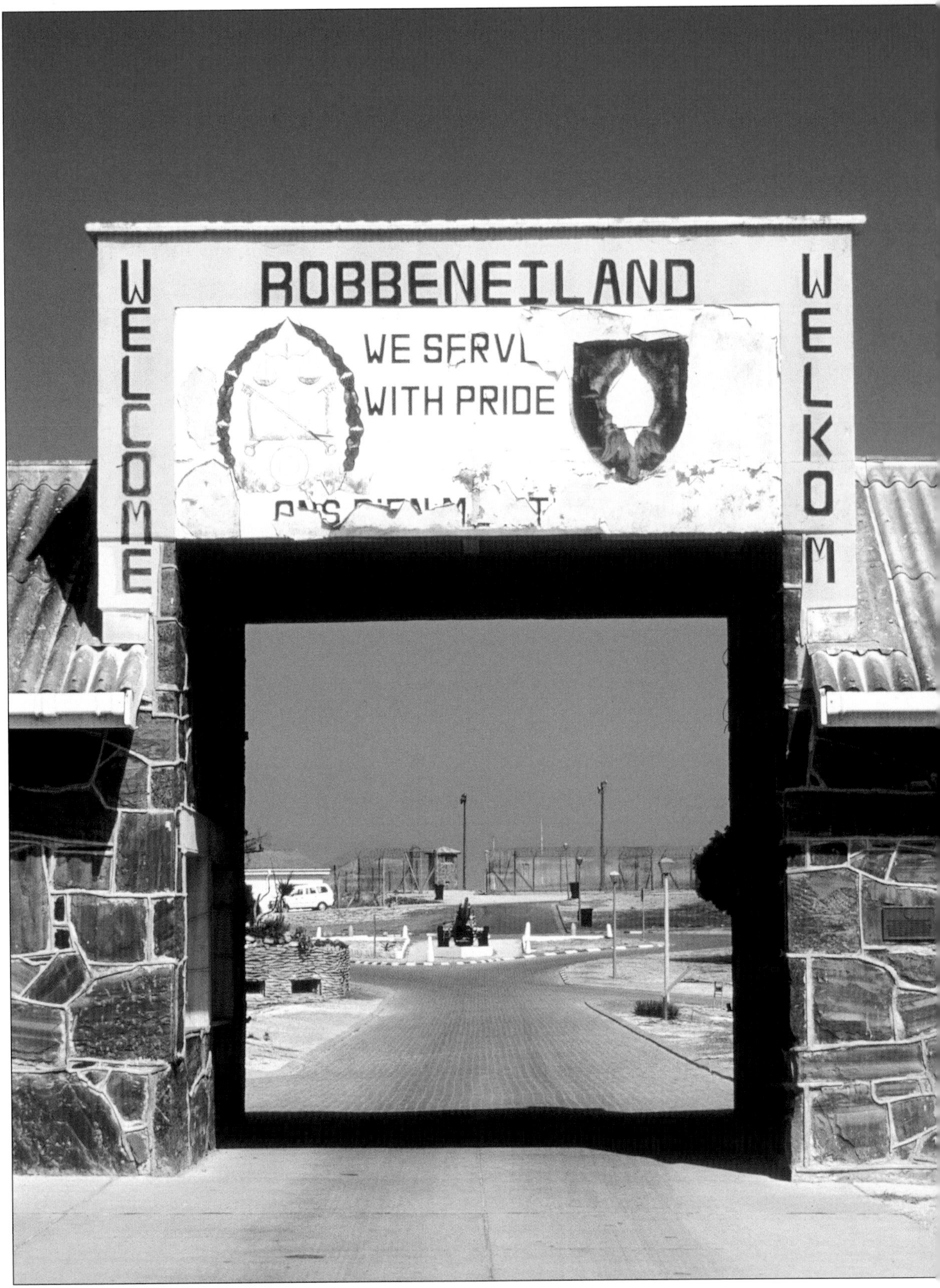
WELCOME
ROBBENEILAND
WELKOM
WE SERV
WITH PRIDE

(ANC), the black organization and later political party fighting most aggressively for equal rights. When, in 1960, the ANC was outlawed, Mandela became the leader of the underground ANC in South Africa. To most black South Africans he was a "freedom fighter." To most white South Africans he was a "terrorist." He was arrested, charged with advocating violent rebellion, and sentenced to life imprisonment.

After the war years as an island fortress, Robben Island remained under navy control until 1958. Then it became again a prison and, soon afterwards, South Africa's most notorious maximum-security prison. Mandela and other black activists were taken to the island in 1963. Burly white wardens greeted them in Afrikaans: "*Dis die Eiland! Hier gaan julle vrek!*" (This is the island. Here you will die.)

The recently constructed maximum-security section was a massive, fortress-like prison within the vast Robben Island–prison complex. The prison's corridors were long, the iron-barred, cage-like cells on either side were damp and small. Mandela's cell was about 2 metres (7 feet) long and 1.8 metres (6 feet) wide. There was no bed, only a sisal mat on the cold cement floor. The panes of the small, barred window were covered with whitish paint, so that the prisoner could not see the sky.

"I was forty-six years old, a political prisoner with a life sentence," Mandela wrote in his moving and inspiring memoir, *Long Walk To Freedom*, which I read while Maud and I lived on Robben Island.

Nelson Mandela survived twenty-seven years in prison with stoicism, patience, hope, and iron discipline. The work was hard, the food bad, the isolation from the outside world nearly total. While some wardens were strict but basically decent persons, others were brutal, primitive men who tried to humiliate and degrade the prisoners. "Prison is designed to break one's spirit and destroy one's resolve," wrote Mandela. Prison authorities did their utmost to stamp "out that spark that makes us human and each of us who we are."

Prisoners were allowed to send their families one five-hundred-word letter once every six months and receive one letter from them. But the letters were often severely censored and maliciously cut.

Ironic inscription on gateway from pier to prison island. "We Serve with Pride" does not refer to prisoners. It was the motto of the prison guards. The gate was built by political prisoners.

Mandela worked for thirteen years in the island's limestone quarry. The glare and dust damaged the prisoners' eyes and in later years Mandela had to wear dark glasses. There were brief moments of pleasure. Walking under armed guards to the quarry, "we could smell the eucalyptus blossoms, spot the occasional springbok or kudu grazing in the distance."

Years passed, "each day like the one before; each week like the one before it, so that the months and years blend into each other." While the prisoners lived in island-isolation and never-ending, never-changing routine, the world at large was changing, South Africa was changing.

Around the world "apartheid" had become an evil word, Robben Island a symbol of oppression. Trade sanctions imposed by many nations began to hurt South Africa. Rebellion smouldered and flashed. It became the sort of war neither side could win but that slowly destroyed the country both sides loved.

Improvement to prison life came with terrible slowness. Certain books were, after years, permitted. Some prisoners were allowed to continue university studies. In 1975, Mandela was allowed to briefly see his daughter Zindzi. He had seen her last when she was three years old. Now she was fifteen.

Robben Island became too famous, too notorious, too symbolic. In 1982, Mandela and other political prisoners were transferred to a mainland prison.

As the boat took him to Cape Town, Mandela looked back at the island and realized that "I had grown used to Robben Island. I had lived there for almost two decades."

Compared to Robben Island, the new prison was like "a five-star hotel." After sleeping for more than eighteen years on a cement floor, Mandela slept once again on a bed. But he did miss "the natural splendour of Robben Island."

Governments changed. Attitudes changed. In 1989, F.W. de Klerk became president of South Africa and began to dismantle the hated apartheid system. After forty years, the ANC became again a legal organization. On February 10, 1990, Nelson Mandela was released: "My ten thousand days of imprisonment were over." First imprisoned at forty-four, he was now seventy-one years old.

In 1993, Nelson Mandela and F.W. de Klerk were jointly awarded the Nobel Peace Prize.

On April 27, 1994, South Africa held its first non-racial, one-person-one-vote election. The ANC won.

On May 10, 1994, Nelson Mandela was sworn in as president of South Africa. Among the guests he had personally invited to his inauguration were three former prison wardens from Robben Island.

It was penguins that brought me to Robben Island. For some people, penguins become an addiction. I am one of them. Over the years I have studied and photographed most of the world's eighteen penguin species, from Antarctica and the subantarctic islands to the little Galapagos penguins that live nearly on the equator.

Robben Island is world-famous for its infamous prison where Nelson Mandela spent eighteen years. For a penguin lover, it's an ideal place to study and photograph the South African penguin. The colonies of this elsewhere-endangered penguin are large on Robben Island, well-protected and growing. Could I live on the island, I asked the South African embassy in Ottawa and showed them some of my books.

It may have been an unusual request, but the embassy staff was charming and arranged it all with the Robben Island directorate. And thus, during the austral summer of 2004, Maud and I were on the 9 a.m. tourist ferry speeding from Cape Town to Robben Island where, we had been promised, we would have a house, a staff car, meals with the staff, lots of peace and penguins, and visits to the prison early in the morning before the tourist rush.

A security officer picked us up at the island's Murray's Bay Harbour pier where prisoners once arrived. Ahead of us was the incredibly ironic archway that greeted prisoners :

ROBBENEILAND [Robben Island]
WELCOME—WELKOM
WE SERVE WITH PRIDE

The last line, the motto of the prison wardens, was flanked by the emblem of Robben Island (a lily), and the prison badge (the scales of justice, an open book, and two large, crossed keys).

Our simple white-painted house had been a warden's home. The garden, once probably lovingly cared for by the prison guard or his wife, was now rank with grasses and weeds. In the evening, gazelles often grazed in our garden. Mandela, after ten years of asking, was finally given permission to have a small garden in the prison courtyard. "The sense of being custodian of this small patch of earth," he wrote later, "offered a small taste of freedom."

Robben Island is small: 4 kilometres (2 miles) long and 2 kilometres (1 mile) wide. The perimeter road, well-paved with stones broken by prisoners, including Mandela, circles the island in 12 kilometres (7 miles).

We drove slowly past centuries of history: the tall, gleaming-white Anglican church; the small bank that was once a leper morgue; the elegant, red-roofed house of the prison governors, now used by visiting VIPs; the lime-stone quarry where Mandela worked for thirteen years; a broken ship, a Taiwanese fishing boat wrecked in 1975, one of more than thirty ships that have died on the rocks of Robben Island, and now a perch for rows of cormorants and other seabirds.

We passed the last house and were suddenly and amazingly alone on this lovely island, on our left the coastal rocks and, in the distance, Cape Town and on our right the summer-dry, tawny African veld with herds of gazelles and antelopes. Mandela and other prisoners worked here, collecting seaweed from the rocky beach for sale as fertilizer in Japan, with the view of Cape Town and "Table Mountain looming behind it, looking agonizingly close," he remembered.

In the late afternoon in a sheltered sandy bay, we watched the arrival of the penguins. They had been feeding all day, catching anchovies and pilchards in the cold, fish-rich sea.

They surfed ashore, took a few rapid, wobbly steps past the high-water line and stood, droplets of water gleaming on their tuxedo plumage. They glanced at us with benign indifference and proceeded with their evening toilet, cleaning and preening their shiny feathers.

They gathered in small groups, bowed, argued and suddenly, stridently hee-hawed, a crass braying to which the African penguin owes its other name: jackass penguin.

Corridor of the maximum-security prison on Robben Island. In a tiny cell on the right, Nelson Mandela lived for eighteen years. After his release, he was elected president of South Africa.

Young penguins court with a great deal of pomp and passion and then mate for life. Now they should really have gone to their island burrows and spelled their mates on the nests. But before assuming domestic duties, they liked to stand in chummy groups in the evening sunshine, meditating with eyes half closed, or having little gentlemanly tiffs with a pushy neighbour. Penguin watching is one of my life's great joys.

Most guides that escort tourist groups through the prison maze of Robben Island are former prisoners. Our guide was James, a powerfully built but very gentle man of about sixty, an ANC member who had spent twelve years on Robben Island.

"Don't you mind being back in prison?" I wondered.

He shrugged. "It's a job," he said, then smiled "and now I can go home at night."

"Do former wardens visit the island?"

"Not the really bad ones," James replied a bit grimly. "I guess they're sort of shy now. But many of the others do come. We talk. They have their memories. We have our memories."

James led us to Mandela's cell. We walked on and on, long corridors echoing the metallic clank of prison doors.

The cell was as it had been when Mandela lived in it: small, cold, austere, walls and cement floor a sickly prison-green, the window covered with dull white paint. A thin mat lay on the floor, two worn blankets, a small table, a chair. Here Nelson Mandela had lived for eighteen years. "I have found," he later wrote, "that one can bear the unbearable if one can keep one's spirit strong."

Chapter 25

St. Helena Island, South Atlantic Ocean

*The Remote Island Where Napoleon, Once Master of Europe,
Spent the Last Years of His Life*

APOLEON WAS BORN on August 15, 1769 on the island of Corsica in the northwestern Mediterranean, which King Louis XV of France had bought the previous year from the Italian city-state of Genoa.

Napoleon died on May 5, 1821 on St. Helena, a small, isolated island in the South Atlantic owned by the mighty East India Company and "lent" to Great Britain to imprison an emperor who, only a few years previously, had been the most powerful man in the world.

Between these dates, the world changed and Napoleon did much of the changing. Europe's ancient, agricultural-feudal world crumbled. With Napoleon, in many ways, our modern world began. He was the most famous man of his time. He was among the most famous men of all time.

He was a military genius. Over the years he led three million men into more than sixty battles with nearly all the great powers of Europe and the Mameluke armies of Egypt. He marched from victory to victory and he and the men he led exulted in *"la gloire,"* the glory and triumph of power and conquest. But more than a million men died in his wars and millions more were wounded. He won nearly all the battles, but he lost the last ones: the Battle of the Nations at Leipzig in 1813 and, finally, the Battle of Waterloo in 1815.

He had a vision: a united Europe, powerful, prosperous and at peace, with a common currency, a common law, bound by the liberal principles of *"liberté, égalité, fraternité,"* accepting gracefully and gratefully the wise and benevolent dominance of France and its glorious emperor, namely Napoleon.

That vision vanished at Waterloo. His archenemies, the British, that despised "nation of shopkeepers" on "this sceptered isle" he had not been able to invade and conquer, were about to cage the mighty eagle of France and dump him on a small, rocky island in the middle of nowhere. His rise had been brilliant and meteoric. His fall was abrupt and cataclysmic.

Napoleon was born in Ajaccio, Corsica, to Italian parents of modest means. He was baptized Napoleone Buonaparte.

At the age of nine he received a royal scholarship to study at the Royal Military School in Brienne, France.

At sixteen, he graduated from the École Militaire in Paris with the rank of lieutenant: shy, skinny, small, a bit gauche, speaking French with an Italian accent, remembered by his teachers as an ambitious loner who excelled in mathematics and who had an astounding ability to memorize and concentrate.

In 1789, a mob stormed the Bastille. The French Revolution began. Siding brilliantly and often ruthlessly with the winning factions, he routed the enemies of the young republic. At twenty-four, he was brigadier general.

Leading the Armée d'Italie, he annihilated the great armies of Austria. At twenty-seven, he was general.

To stymie Britain and threaten its eastern empire, Napoleon invaded Egypt, destroyed its Mameluke armies and carried the war into Syria. That glorious adventure ended on a sour note when Britain's Admiral Nelson sank the French fleet in the Bay of Aboukir.

Back in France, Napoleon took part in the machinations that overthrew the *régime* and was chosen First Consul. That made him sole ruler of France. He was thirty-one years old.

He transformed France into a modern, centralized state. Working twenty-hour days, he oversaw the creation of a new civil code of law for France, the Napoleonic Code, still the basis of civil law in France (and in the province of Quebec and the state of Louisiana). He instituted monetary reforms. The coin of the realm was now the "napoleon." He ordered the building of roads and canals; created the Bank of France; gave equal rights to Protestants and Jews; and organized a

0 Mi. 1   2   3   4
0 km.   2   4   6

SAINT HELENA ISLAND

N

modern national civil service. He chose as his personal emblems the soaring eagle and the busy bee.

Wedged into the base of a steep-walled valley is Jamestown, the capital of St. Helena Island. Once owned by the East India Company, the remote island became famous as the place of Napoleon's exile.

On December 2, 1804, he crowned himself in Notre Dame Cathedral: Napoleon I, Emperor of France. Exultant but exhausted, he said, "I'm growing old. I'm thirty-six years old. I want some peace and quiet."

There was to be no peace. Enforcing his vision and his will by force, Napoleon defeated Austria again, and the Russians, the Prussians, the Spaniards. When the pope protested, he imprisoned the pope. All Europe grovelled. Only Britain, secure on its island, eluded and defied him.

He had reached the pinnacle of power. At the age of thirty-nine, he was master of Europe. He married the daughter of the Austrian emperor and had a

son, the beginning of a new dynasty. And then the magnificent edifice began to crumble.

Guerrilla warfare, supported by Britain, festered in Spain, pinning down three hundred thousand of his best troops. Napoleon led La Grande Armée of six hundred thousand men far into Russia and occupied Moscow. Less than one hundred thousand of his men survived. Fighting, famine and winter killed the rest.

Most of Europe pounced on the weakened lord of war, defeated him in 1813 at Leipzig and banished him to the island of Elba off Italy. After dominating Europe, he was now ruler of a 222-square-kilometre (86-square-mile) poverty-plagued mini-state.

Less than a year later he snuck away from his little island for one last win-all, lose-all gamble, what the historian Robert Asprey has called "one of the boldest acts in history," the reconquest of his empire. He began with one thousand loyal men and two cannon, led them again from victory to victory until he was once more ruler of France.

He needed time to rebuild France and to rebuild his armies. He didn't get it. Terrified and vengeful, the quarrelling powers of Europe united and, led by Britain and Prussia, set out to destroy him.

Napoleon attacked. He defeated Wellington. He defeated Blücher. And then, on June 18, 1815, came Waterloo. Onslaught and slaughter, the masters, Napoleon and Wellington, pitched in the cruel game of war. The British held, the Prussians arrived and after many hours of fighting and dying, the French army broke. Sixty thousand soldiers were dead.

Napoleon escaped. Now a fugitive, he surrendered himself, to Captain Maitland of HMS *Bellerophon*, asking Britain, "the most powerful, constant and generous of my enemies," to grant him asylum or to allow him to settle in the United States.

Britain had other plans. To secure "the person...whose conduct has proved so fatal to the happiness of the World," the British government decided on banishment. "The Island of St. Helena is eminently fitted to answer that purpose."

St. Helena. The tiny island, all alone in the South Atlantic, 121 square kilometres (47 square miles) in size, 16 kilometres (10 miles) long and 9 kilometres (6 miles) wide, 1,609 kilometres (1,000 miles) south of the equator, 1,931 kilometres (1,200 miles) west of Africa, 3,218 kilometres (2,000 miles) east of South America, "rises abruptly like a huge black castle from the ocean," wrote Charles Darwin who visited it in 1836.

The island was discovered by the Portuguese navigator João da Nova Castella on May 21, 1502, the feast day of St. Helena, mother of the Roman emperor Constantine the Great. He named it and claimed it for Portugal.

Soon after, the English claimed St. Helena and then the Dutch. All wanted it because it was on the sailing route to India and the Far East, had ample fresh water, and soil suitable for growing fruits and vegetables to succour scurvy-crippled sailors. The Portuguese bowed out. The Dutch fought in St. Helena, lost and in 1652 established their victualling station near the south tip of Africa. The English government granted St. Helena to the immensely wealthy and powerful East India Company.

The company began to settle St. Helena in 1659. It built a fortress and a small town at the head of James Bay, the steep-cliffed island's only sheltered roadstead. It named its town, compressed into the bottom of a V-shaped valley, Jamestown, after James, duke of York, the man after whom New York was named, founded at about the same time as Jamestown.

Company servants arrived from England to organize and administer the town and the extensive vegetable plantations. Slaves were imported from Africa to do most of the work. Not everyone was happy. In 1678, a Mrs. Parnum was fined one shilling "for cursing the island."

The "Honourable East India Company" ruled St. Helena. Over the years, thousands of company ships stopped at the island, to refit, to heal their scurvy-stricken crews, to take on fresh water. The island, wrote the nineteenth century historian John Charles Melliss, was the company's "pet child." It ran great plantations, cut the island's magnificent forests, "punished witchcraft severely, turned Quakers away and would not suffer a lawyer to dwell" on St. Helena Island.

In 1710, the island had a population of 832 persons, half white, half black.

A century later, in 1807, measles spread from a ship to the island. So many died that there was a severe labour shortage "and the price of a good slave increased from 40 Pounds Sterling to 150 Pounds Sterling." To alleviate the situation, the company imported a few Indians and Malays and 650 Chinese from Canton.

This was St. Helena in 1815: a company fief, its governor living in Plantation House, a beautiful forty-room mansion. Jamestown was, in the words of a contemporary visitor, "a queer medley of houses," some three-storey dwellings, some modest cabins, and in the island interior "about fifty cottages, farms and villas."

A total island population, including slaves and Chinese, of nearly three thousand, to be joined, abruptly, by an emperor, his rump court, his servants and a British garrison of up to three thousand soldiers to ensure that their prize captive did not escape.

Napoleon, after a voyage of sixty-seven days from England aboard HMS *Northumberland* arrived at St. Helena on October 15, 1815. He stood at the railing, glanced up at the dark cliffs of the island and said rather mildly, "It is not an attractive place." His aide, Count Montholon, was more explicit: "The valley of Jamestown resembled an entrance to the infernal regions," he wrote later. "No matter in which direction one looked, nothing was to be seen but rows of guns, and black [rock] walls."

But Jamestown, at least, was sheltered. The British had decided Napoleon, "General Buonaparte" as they now called him, would live in Longwood, a large building that had once been a barn, right on top of the rain-soaked, wind-swept 609-metre- (2,000-foot-) high island plateau. Ship's carpenters were now busy converting the building into something reasonably fit for a deposed emperor, his court and eleven servants.

In the meantime, Napoleon lived in a small bungalow called The Briars, owned by a local merchant. By one of those odd quirks of fate a previous resident of The Briars had been Napoleon's nemesis, Arthur Wellesley, later the Duke of Wellington.

In December, Longwood was sort of finished and Napoleon and his suite moved in. It was, said Napoleon, "the most detestable spot in the Universe." His doctor, the Royal Navy surgeon Barry O'Meara, agreed. Longwood, he said, stood on "an unhealthy site with constant rains, trade-winds, rats, mud, and drinking water very scarce."

Still, at first, under the governorship of high-ranking British naval officers who were courteous and correct, life was tolerable. Napoleon rose at dawn and made short rides, for he was not allowed to go far. After breakfast, he went to the "Billiard Room," spread maps and books on the large table and, pacing back and forth, hands clasped on his back, dictated his memoirs to the Marquis de Las Cases, reliving the battles, the victories, the glory.

In the evening all assembled in the dining room, the officers in full dress uniform, the ladies in evening dresses. Meals were served by liveried servants. The food varied from mediocre to reasonably good, but it was eaten from the most exquisite dishes of Sèvres porcelain.

It was, in a way, a sad charade, a pretence to vanished glory, made even more difficult by the petty feuds and jealousies of his entourage. Napoleon's vitality and creativity, once nearly boundless, was now constricted and constrained.

It got much worse when the new governor arrived. Thin, with sparse red hair and shifty eyes, Sir Hudson Lowe was, by nearly all accounts, French as well as British, a mean-spirited, nasty martinet. "I knew him well," said the Duke of Wellington. "He was a stupid man...[and] like all men who know nothing of the world, he was suspicious and jealous."

Napoleon detested him. Lowe, he said, "is hideous, with the face of a hangman." It was hate at first sight. "That is a bad man," said Napoleon. "His eye, as he examined me, was like a hyena's caught in a trap."

Lowe, narrow in body and in mind, hated "the French general," as he usually referred to Napoleon. He was also terrified Napoleon might somehow escape (according to one rumour, by hot-air balloon to Africa) and he would then lose his fancy post and fancy pay. Longwood was now closely guarded day and night. Napoleon was only allowed to leave with an escort.

The years passed, slowly, boring, drab, and dreary. Napoleon rarely went out. He read. He spent hours immersed in very hot water in the deep copper bathtub. It eased the near-constant pain. He became paunchy, nearly flabby.

He bore his bodily and mental suffering with great fortitude and dignity. Lowe could not break him. "I am Emperor in my own circle," Napoleon told him, "and will be so as long as I live. You may make my body prisoner, but my soul is free."

His doctor suggested Longwood would be less sombre and depressing, if it had beautiful gardens and for one last time Napoleon's drive and creativity flared up.

He laid out the great gardens of Longwood with military precision and inspired a small army of willing Chinese gardeners and much less happy courtiers, counts and barons, to dig and rake, manure and plant. English admirers sent him seeds. Even Lowe, glad to see his captive

Napoleon's dining room at Longwood, his "home" on St. Helena Island. Once master of Europe, the emperor dined in this room with a small entourage of courtiers. Meals were served by liveried servants.

busy, provided tools, plants, seeds and garden furniture.

These gardens, said Napoleon proudly, were his legacy to this sad island. "When I am no longer here, the English travellers will sketch this garden, made by Napoleon. Nobody who visits will wish to leave without seeing it," he told Count Bertrand, the grand marshal of the exile court.

It was the last flickering of the flame. Napoleon was very ill, his body swollen, his feet ice-cold. He vomited often; he fainted several times. He was weak. "There is no more oil in the lamp," he remarked wryly to Count Montholon. "I have no fear of death. It would be a great joy to me if I were to die within the next two weeks."

He made his will, requesting that his body be returned to France "to repose on the banks of the Seine in the midst of the French people I have loved so much."

If this was refused, he asked to be buried in a lovely secluded valley not far from Longwood, a place he had often visited, with many flowers and a clean, burbling spring overhung by weeping willows.

Surrounded by the remaining members of his court and his servants, Napoleon lay dying. His lips moved. "France," he whispered, *"tête d'armée,"* and then he died.

It was May 15, 1821. He was fifty-one years old.

Dressed in uniform, with boots and spurs, his body was placed into four coffins: the first, made of tin and lined with satin, was soldered shut, placed into a wooden coffin, that into a leaden coffin that was sealed, and all three into a magnificent mahogany coffin.

He was buried with full military honours. Three thousand soldiers lined the route, their arms reversed. The coffins were lowered into a deep rock tomb that was sealed with a massive stone. For the next nineteen years, British soldiers guarded it day and night.

One month later, Sir Hudson Lowe and his family left St. Helena. For the islanders he had been a kind ruler. At his insistence, slavery had been abolished on St. Helena Island.

On October 15, 1840, in the presence of the Prince de Joinville, sent by the French government to bring the emperor's body to France, Napoleon's tomb was opened. In the innermost coffin, untouched by time and corrupting air, lay Napoleon, his face serene and waxen-pale, but otherwise unchanged. He was reburied at Les Invalides in Paris in a sarcophagus of red porphyry.

In 1858, by order of Queen Victoria, the Longwood estate and the "Valley of the Tomb" were given to France "as absolute owners thereof in fee simple for ever." To this, The Briars was added in 1959. All this is now part of France and looked after by a French curator and consul living on St. Helena Island.

The British Empire, once worldwide and mighty, fizzled out in the twentieth century. One remnant is St. Helena Island. Another is the RMS *St. Helena*, a Royal Mail Ship, the last of a famous fleet that once linked Britain's colonies.

When Napoleon died, most of the British garrison left St. Helena Island. But it remained important. About a thousand ships a year called at St. Helena, going to or coming from Europe and India or the Far East.

Then Napoleon's body was removed. The Suez Canal was built, no more ships came, and St. Helena lapsed into insignificance and isolation. It has no airstrip. Now the four or five yearly visits by the Royal Mail Ship are its only regular contact with the outside world.

The *St. Helena* left Cape Town on a sunny morning in January. Most of its 115 passengers were "Saints," as St. Helenians like to call themselves, returning home to their island. Many work abroad, in the United Kingdom, in South Africa, even on the Falkland Islands. There is little work on St. Helena. Its population, five thousand in 1905, was 4,200 a century later.

There was a German TV crew aboard, a retired 747 pilot and his wife who had been everywhere except St. Helena, and a happy, middle-aged group of French Napoleon worshippers on a pilgrimage. They belonged to a sort of Napoleon fan club. "We have members all over the world," they assured us. "Even in China."

Six days on an empty ocean, no other ships, a few dolphins, a few birds, occasionally a glittering of flying fish. St. Helena looked daunting, fortress-like, steep-cliffed, and dark. Three yachts lay in the roadstead and few fishing boats.

A lovely island with very little crime and lots of time, the people a mix of many races. They love their queen, are devotedly British, and extraordinarily gentle and friendly.

Jamestown, squeezed into the bottom of a V-shaped valley, seemed very much like nineteenth-century England: Dickensian without the poverty. Our flat was in the building that had once housed the town forge.

The French pilgrims visited the Napoleonic shrines and other sites with a 1929 Chevrolet eighteen-seat charabanc, the first bus to reach St. Helena, and still in excellent condition. Mileage, of course, is limited. There are 96 kilometres (60 miles) of well-paved roads, mostly up and down. We rented a car and joined the French for a tour of Plantation House, the residence of His Excellency, the island's British governor.

The chatelaine herself conducted us and tactfully did not mention once a former resident, Lieutenant General Sir Hudson Lowe, the *bête noire* of Napoleon devotees. A lovely, spacious Georgian manor house of simple elegance, wonderfully "historic" furniture, Napoleon's superb chandelier in the dining room, and a library of two thousand books in handmade rosewood cabinets.

The French left to ooh and aah elsewhere. Maud and I wandered in the lush-green manicured, tree-rimmed grounds, when we heard a familiar sound: the moaning-roaring of a sexually excited giant tortoise male trying to mate with a high-domed female, which is difficult even when she is willing. We had often heard the sound when we lived on the Seychelles Islands. Here it was impressive because the lover was Jonathan, doyen of St. Helena's giant tortoises, 172 years old, his

On May 5, 1821, Napoleon died on St. Helena and was buried in multiple, sealed coffins in a tomb in Sane Valley. His body was later returned to France. The site where he was once buried on St. Helena now belongs to France.

libido undimmed by age.

We crisscrossed this odd island: part bare and volcanic, cluttered with rust-red and sienna-brown rocks and scoria clinkers; part subtropical forest; part rural England, pastoral and pleasant, white cottages, neatly trimmed hedges, emerald-green meadows with browsing cattle, small stone churches with pebbled paths, white-painted picket fences, charmingly Pickwickian.

Gilbert Martineau, consul of France, graciously gave us permission to spend a day in Longwood, to photograph it slowly room after room.

The rooms smelled musty and moist. He opened the shuttered windows.

"Was Napoleon poisoned?" I asked Monsieur Martineau.

He smiled. "It is a question everyone asks," he said. "The answer is 'perhaps.' But I think it was probably accidental. The wallpaper then was painted with Scheele's green. That is an arsenic compound. It is always very damp at Longwood. So there may have been arsenic in the air.

"So, yes, maybe the arsenic contributed to his early death. You know, eight doctors were present at his autopsy. All agreed death was due to ulcers and stomach cancer. I also believe he died when he died, because he no longer wanted to live. Not here. Not like a prisoner.

"Please do not touch anything. If you need help, please call me." And then he left us in this house haunted by memories.

There was the billiard table on which Napoleon spread maps while reliving the glory of past victories. The simple iron camp bed with moss-green curtains on which he had slept at Marengo and at Austerlitz when he was lord of Europe. Nearby, on a taboret, lay his death mask.

We photographed the deep, narrow copper bathtub, which patient Chinese servants had filled with pails of very hot water. He lay in it for hours, dictated memoirs, had lunch, talked with his courtiers, free of pain for a while. In his bedroom stood the clock that had once belonged to Frederick the Great. And in nearly every room were pictures of an angelic-looking child, the son he never saw again.

Most poignant, perhaps, were two holes he had cut into a deep-green jalousie, one nearly a metre (3 feet) off the ground, the other more than 1.5 metres (5 feet) off the ground. Here the Emperor Napoleon had stood or sat, and watched through these peepholes the island world beyond and the men in British uniform who guarded him day and night. The eagle of France peering out of his cage.

BIBLIOGRAPHY

Chapter 1   DEVIL'S ISLAND

Blum, Léon. *Souvenirs de l'Affaire*. Paris: Gallimard, 1935.

Clair, Sylvie, et al. *Les Îles du Salut*. Cayenne (French Guiana): Ibis Rouge Editions, 2001.

Dreyfus, Alfred. *Cinq Années de ma vie (1894–1899)*. Paris: Editions La Découverte, 1994.

Epailly, Eugène. *Alfred Dreyfus, Déporté dans l'enfer du Diable*. Matoury (French Guiana): Agence Française de l'Espace, no date.

Tuchman, Barbara W. *The Proud Tower*. New York: The Macmillan Company, 1966.

Vignard, Caroline. *Devil's Island*. Matoury (French Guiana): Agence Française de l'Espace, no date.

Chapter 2   ATTU ISLAND

Bergsland, Knut. "Aleut Dialects of Atka and Attu," *Transactions of the American Philosophical Society*, new series, 49, part 3, 1959.

Fradkin, Philip L. "War on the Refuge," *Audubon Magazine*, 86, no. 6, November 1984.

Garfield, Brian. *The Thousand-Mile War*. New York: Ballantine Books, 1971.

Keating, Bern. *Alaska*. Washington, D.C.: National Geographic Society, 1969.

Mc Cracken, Harold. *Hunters Of The Stormy Sea*. London: Oldbourne Press, 1957.

Morison, Samuel Eliot. *History of United States Naval Operations in World War II*. Fifteen volumes. New York: Little, Brown and Company, 1947–1962.

Chapter 3   SKRAELING ISLAND

Bruemmer, Fred. *The Narwhal*. Toronto: Key Porter Books, 1993.

Fitzhugh, William W. ed. *Vikings*. Washington, D.C.: Smithsonian Institution Press, 2002.

Gad, Finn. *The History of Greenland*, 2 vols. Montreal and Kingston: McGill-Queen's University Press, 1971.

McCullough, Karen M. *The Ruin Islanders*. Hull, QC: Canadian Museum of Civilization, 1989.

Schledermann, Peter. "Eskimo and Viking Finds in the High Arctic," *National Geographic*. May 1981.

———. *Crossroads To Greenland*. Calgary: Arctic Institute of North America of the University of Calgary, 1990.

Chapter 4   KOMODO ISLAND

Auffenberg, Walter. *The Behavioral Ecology of the Komodo Monitor*. Gainesville, FL: University Presses of Florida, 1984.

Dalton, Bill. *Indonesia Handbook*. Chico, CA: Moon Publications, 1995.

Weiglein, Werner, et al. *Expeditionen durch Indonesien*. Frankfurt/Main: Edition Momos, 1986.

Wikramanayake, Eric. "Everyone Knows the Dragon Is Only a Mythical Beast," *Smithsonian*, April 1997.

Chapter 5   KODLUNARN ISLAND

Bruemmer, Fred. *The Arctic*. Montreal: Infocor, 1974.

Hall, Charles Francis. *Life with the Esquimaux*, 2 vols. London: Sampson Low, 1864.

McGhee, Robert. *The Arctic Voyages of Martin Frobisher*. Montreal and Kingston: McGill-Queen's University Press, 2001.

———. *The Last Imaginary Place*. Toronto: Key Porter Books, 2004.

Morison, Samuel Eliot. *The European Discovery of America: The Northern Voyages, AD 500–1600*. New York: Oxford University Press, 1993.

Ruby, Robert. *Unknown Shore*. New York: Henry Holt and Company, 2001.

Stefansson, Vilhjalmur, ed. *The Three Voyages of Martin Frobisher*. London: Argonaut Press, 1938.

Chapter 6   FALKLAND ISLANDS

Bruemmer, Fred. *Seals in the Wild*. Toronto: Key Porter Books, 1998.

Chater, Tony. *The Falklands*. St. Albans, Herts: The Penna Press, 1993.

Darwin, Charles. *The Voyage of the Beagle*. New York: Doubleday & Company, 1962.

Hodgson, Bryan. "The Falkland Islands: Life after the War," *National Geographic*, March 1988.

Strange, Ian. *The Falklands: South Atlantic Islands*. New York: Dodd, Mead & Company, 1985.

Chapter 7   SAN MIGUEL ISLAND

Bruemmer, Fred. *Seals in the Wild*. Toronto: Key Porter Books, 1998

Busch, Briton Cooper. *The War Against the Seals*. Montreal and Kingston: McGill-Queen's University Press, 1985.

King, Judith E. *Seals of the World*. London: British Museum (Natural History), 1983.

LeBeouf, Burney J. *Elephant Seals*. Pacific Grove: The Boxwood Press, 1985.

Scammon, Charles M. *The Marine Mammals of the Northwestern Coast of North America*. New York: Dover Publications, 1968.

Tennesen, Michael. "Testing the Depth of Life," *National Wildlife Magazine*, February–March 1999.

Chapter 8   SANTORINI ISLAND

Berlitz, Charles. *Mysteries From Forgotten Worlds*. New York: Doubleday & Company, 1972.

Broad, William J. "It Swallowed a Civilization," *New York Times*, October 21. 2003.

Herodotus. *The Histories*. Translated by Aubrey de Selincourt. Harmondsworth, Middlesex: Penguin Books, 1954.

Marinatos, Spyridon. "Thera—Key to the Riddle of Minos," *National Geographic*, May 1972.

Schönrock, Dirk, et al. *Santorini*. Erlangen: Michael Müller Verlag, 2001.

Warren, Peter. *The Aegean Civilization*. New York: Peter Bedrick Books, 1989.

Chapter 9   SABLE ISLAND

Berton, Pierre. *Seacoasts*. Toronto: Stoddart, 1998.

Bruemmer, Fred. "Sable Island," *Canadian Geographical Journal*, June 1968.

Christie, Barbara J. *The Horses of Sable Island*. Porter's Lake: Pottersfield Press, 1995.

De Villiers, Marq, and Sheila Hirtle. *A Dune Adrift*. Toronto: McClelland & Stewart, 2004.

Lucas, Zoe. *Wild Horses of Sable Island*. Toronto: Greey de Pencier Books, 1981.

Morison, Samuel Eliot. *The European Discovery of America*. New York: Oxford University Press, 1971.

Chapter 10   JUAN FERNANDEZ ISLANDS

Bruemmer, Fred. *Seals in the Wild*. Toronto: Key Porter Books, 1998.

Dampier, William. *A new voyage around the world*. London: James and John Knapton, 1729.

Defoe, Daniel. *Robinson Crusoe*. New York: The New American Library, 1961.

Reeves, Randall R., et al. *The Sierra Club Handbook of Seals and Sirenians*. San
    Francisco: Sierra Club Books, 1992.

Rogers, Woodes. *A Cruising Voyage Round the World*. New York: Dover Publications,
    1969.

Selcraig, Bruce. "The Real Robinson Crusoe," *Smithsonian*, July 2005.

Chapter 11   LITTLE DIOMEDE ISLAND

Bancroft, H.H. *History of Alaska*. New York: Antiquarian Press, 1959.

Bogoras, Waldemar. *The Eskimo of Siberia*. (Reprint of 1913 report.) New York: AMS
    Press, 1975.

Bruemmer, Fred. *Arctic Memories*. Toronto: Key Porter Books, 1993.

Fitzhugh, William W., and Aron Crowell. *Crossroads Of Continents*. Washington, D.C.:
    Smithsonian Institution Press, 1988.

Nelson, Edward W. "The Eskimo about Bering Strait," *Bureau of American Ethnology
    Annual Report* 18:1–518, Smithsonian Institution Press, 1899, reprinted 1983.

Stefansson, Evelyn. *Here Is Alaska*. New York: Charles Scribner's Sons, 1959.

Chapter 12   FUNK ISLAND

Birkhead, Tim. *Great Auk Islands*. London: T & A D Poyser, 1993.

Cartwright, G. *Journal of Transactions and Events, during a residence of Nearly Sixteen
    Years on the Coast of Labrador; Containing Many Interesting Particulars, both of the
    Country and Its Inhabitants not Hitherto known*. 3 vol. Newark, England: Allin and
    Ridge, 1792.

Grieve, S. *The Great Auk or Garefowl Alca impennis, its History, Archeology and Remains*.
    London: Thomas C. Jack, 1885.

Howley, James P. *The Beothucks or Red Indians*. Cambridge: Cambridge University
    Press, 1915.

Morison, Samuel Eliot. *The European Discovery of America*. New York: Oxford
    University Press, 1971.

Such, Peter. *Vanished Peoples*. Toronto: N C Press Limited, 1978.

Chapter 13   GALAPAGOS ISLANDS

Beebe, William. *Galapagos: World's End*. New York: C.P. Putnam's Sons, 1924.

Berrill, N.J. and Michael Berrill. *The Life of Sea Islands*. New York: McGraw-Hill,
    1969.

Brower, Kenneth, ed. *Galapagos: The Flow of Wildness*. New York: Ballantine Books, 1970.

Darwin, Charles. *The Voyage of the Beagle*. New York: Doubleday &Company, 1962.

MacFarland, Craig. "Goliaths of the Galapagos," *National Geographic*, November 1972.

Moore, Ruth. *Evolution*. New York: Time-Life Books, 1964.

Chapter 14 PRIBILOF ISLANDS

Busch, Briton Cooper. *The War Against the Seals*. Montreal and Kingston: McGill-Queen's University Press, 1985.

Golder, F.A. *Bering's Voyages*. 2 vols. New York: American Geographical Society, 1925.

Jordan, David S., et al. *The Fur Seals and Furseal Islands of the North Pacific Ocean; Part 3*. Washington, D.C.: Government Printing Office, 1899.

Martin, Fredericka. *Sea Bears*. Philadelphia: Chilton Company, 1960.

O'Harra, Doug. "A Puzzle in the Pribilofs," *Smithsonian*, March 2005.

Simpson, Elizabeth. *Report on Sealing in the Pribilof Islands*. Zurich, Switzerland: World Federation for the Protection of Animals, 1968.

Chapter 15 BELCHER ISLANDS

Flaherty, Robert J. "The Belcher Islands of Hudson Bay: Their Discovery and Exploration," *The Geographical Review* 5, no. 6, June 1918.

Freeman, Milton M.R. "Observations on the Kayak-Complex, Belcher Islands, N.W.T.," *National Museum of Canada Bulletin* no. 194, Anthropological Series no. 62, 1964.

Jenness, Diamond. *The People of the Twilight*. Chicago: University of Chicago Press, 1959.

Phillips, Alan. "The Tragic Case of the Man Who Played Jesus," *Maclean's*, December 8, 1956.

Sullivan, Alan. "When God Came to the Belchers," *Queen's Quarterly* 51, no. 1, 1944.

Twomey, Arthur C. *Needle to the North*. Boston: Houghton Mifflin Co., 1942.

Chapter 16 EASTER ISLAND

Diamond, Jared. *Collapse*. New York: Viking Penguin, 2005.

Ebensten, Hanns. *Trespassers on Easter Island*. Key West: The Ketch & Yawl Press, 2001.

Englert, Sebastian. *Island at the Center of the World*. New York: Charles Scribner's Sons, 1970.

Flenley, John, and Paul Bahn. *The Enigmas of Easter Island*. New York: Oxford University Press, 2003.

Heyerdahl, Thor. *Aku-Aku: The Secret of Easter Island*. London: George Allen & Unwin, 1958.

Theroux, Paul. *The Happy Isles of Oceania*. New York: Ballantine Books, 1993.

Chapter 17 AUCKLAND ISLANDS

Bruemmer, Fred. "Sea Lion Shenanigans," *Natural History Magazine*, July 1983.

Chilton, Charles, ed. *The Sub-Antarctic Islands of New Zealand*. Wellington, NZ: Philosophical Institute of Canterbury, 1909.

Marlow, B.J. "The Comparative Behaviour of the Australian Sea Lions *Neophoca cinera* and *Phocarctos hookeri (Pinnepedia; Otariidae)*," *Mammalia* 39:159–230, 1975.

McLaren, Fergus B. *The Eventful Story of the Auckland Islands*. Wellington, NZ: A.H. & A.W. Reed, 1948.

McNab, Robert. *Murihiku*. Invercargill, NZ: William Smith, Printer, 1907.

Chapter 18 HERSCHEL ISLAND

Bockstoce, John R. *Whales, Ice, & Men*. Seattle: University of Washington Press, 1986.

Bruemmer, Fred. *The Arctic*. Montreal: Infocor, 1974.

Cook, John A. *Pursuing the Whale*. Boston: Houghton Mifflin Co., 1926.

Ellis, Richard. *Men and Whales*. New York: Alfred A. Knopf, 1991.

Metayer, Maurice, ed. *I, Nuligak*. New York: Pocket Books, 1972.

Stefansson, Vilhjalmur. *The Friendly Arctic*. New York: The Macmillan Company, 1943.

Chapter 19 SOUTH GEORGIA ISLAND

Alexander, Caroline. *The Endurance*. New York: Alfred A. Knopf, 1999.

Bruemmer, Fred. *Glimpses of Paradise*. Toronto: Key Porter Books, 2002.

Ellis, Richard. *Men and Whales*. New York: Alfred A. Knopf, 1991.

Mountfield, David. *A History of Polar Expedition*. London: Hamlyn, 1974.

Robertson, R.B. *Of Whales and Men*. New York: Alfred A. Knopf, 1954.

Shackleton, Ernest. *South: The Last Antarctic Expedition of Shackleton and the Endurance*. New York: Lyons Press, 1998.

Chapter 20 THE DRY TORTUGAS

Bishop, Jim. *The Day Lincoln Was Shot*. New York: Harper, 1955.

Gannon, Michael. *New History of Florida*. Gainesville: University Presses of Florida, 1996.

Miller, Mark. *The National Geographic Traveler: Miami and the Keys*. Washington, D.C.: National Geographic Society, 1999.

Sherril, Chris, and Roger Aiello. *Key West: The Last Resort*. Key West, FL: Key West Book & Card Company, 1978.

Smith, Gene. *American Gothic: The Story of America's Legendary Theatrical Family, Junius, Edwin, and John Wilkes Booth*. New York: Simon & Schuster, 1992.

Williams, Joy. *The Florida Keys: A History and a Guide*. New York: Random House, 1988.

Chapter 21 LEMBATA ISLAND

Barnes, R.H. "Report on Marine Mammal Harvests at Lamalera, Lembata (Lomblen), Nusa Tenggara Timur, Indonesia in Recent Years." Oxford: University of Oxford, Institute of Social Anthropology, 1986.

——. *Cetaceans and Cetacean Hunting: Lamalera, Indonesia*. Gland, Switzerland: World Wildlife Fund Project No. 1428, 1980.

Carey-Johanson, Lenora. "Lembata's Sea Hunters," *Ligabue Magazine*, no. 9, 1986.

Ellis, Richard. *Men And Whales*. New York: Alfred A. Knopf, 1991.

Melville, Herman. *Moby Dick*. London: Collins, 1953.

Chapter 22 LORD HOWE ISLAND

Doubilet, David. "Lord Howe Island," *National Geographic*, October 1991.

Hutton, Ian. *Lord Howe Island*. Australian Capital Territory: Conservation Press, 1986.

Nicholas, Max. *A History of Lord Howe Island*. Moonah, Tasmania: Mercury-Walch, 1975.

Quammen, David. *The Song Of The Dodo*. New York: Scribner, 1996.

Slater, Peter, et al. *A Slater Field Guide to Australian Birds*. Sidney: Weldon Publishing, 1992.

Chapter 23 ZANZIBAR

Else, David and Heather Tyrrell. *Zanzibar: The Bradt Travel Guide*. Chalfont St. Peter, England: Bradt Travel Guides., 2003.

Gray, J. *History of Zanzibar from the Middle Ages to 1856*. London: Oxford University Press, 1962.

Miller, Charles. *The Lunatic Express*. Nairobi, Kenya: Westlands Sundries, 1987.

Moorehead, Alan. *The White Nile*. New York: Dell Publishing, 1962.

Ommanney, F.D. *Isle of Cloves*. London: Longmans, 1957.

Rice, Edward. *Captain Sir Richard Burton*. New York: Harper Collins Publishers, 1991.

Rugoff, Milton, ed. *The Travels of Marco Polo.* New York: The New American Library, 1961.

Chapter 24 ROBBEN ISLAND

De Villiers, Simon A. *Robben Island.* Cape Town: Struik Publishers, 1971.

Maharaj, Mac, ed. *Reflections in Prison.* Cape Town: Zebra and the Robben Island Museum, 2001.

Mandela, Nelson. *Long Walk to Freedom.* New York: Little, Brown and Company, 1995.

Markovitz, Irving L. *Power and Class in Africa.* Englewood Cliffs, NJ: Prentice-Hall, 1977.

Simpson, George Gaylord. *Penguins.* New Haven: Yale University Press, 1976.

Smith, Charlene. *Robben Island.* Cape Town: Struik Publishers, 1997.

Chapter 25 ST. HELENA ISLAND

Asprey, Robert B. *The Reign of Napoleon Bonaparte.* New York: Basic Books, 2001.

Field, Margaret. *The History of Plantation House.* Penzance, Cornwall: The Patten Press, 1998.

Korngold, Ralph. *The Last Years of Napoleon—His Captivity on St. Helena.* New York: Harcourt Brace, 1959.

Martineau, Gilbert. *Napoleon's St. Helena.* New York: Rand McNally, 1966.

Martineau, Michel. *The Napoleonic Sites on St. Helena.* Privately printed, 2002.

Steiner, Sue. *St. Helena.* Chalfont St. Peter, England: Bradt Travel Guides, 2002.